DEVIANCE IN THE WORKPLACE

Volume 8 • 1999

RESEARCH IN
THE SOCIOLOGY
OF WORK

DEVIANCE IN THE WORKPLACE

Guest Editors: IDA HARPER SIMPSON
Department of Sociology
Duke University

RICHARD L. SIMPSON
Department of Sociology
University of North Carolina at Chapel Hill

RESEARCH IN
THE SOCIOLOGY
OF WORK

Editor: RANDY HODSON
Department of Sociology
The Ohio State University

VOLUME 8 • 1999

Emerald

United Kingdom – North America – Japan
India – Malaysia – China

Emerald Group Publishing Limited
Howard House, Wagon Lane, Bingley BD16 1WA, UK

British Library Cataloguing in Publication Data
A catalogue record for this book is available from the British Library

ISBN: 978-0-76-230608-4
ISSN: 0277-2833 (Series)

Printed and bound by CPI Group (UK) Ltd, Croydon, CR0 4YY

CONTENTS

LIST OF CONTRIBUTORS vii

INTRODUCTION
Ida Harper Simpson and Richard L. Simpson ix

WORKER DEVIANCE AS SOCIAL CONTROL
James Tucker 1

DEFINING DEVIANCE UPWARD: THE SHRIMPERS' CONFLICT OVER TEDS REGULATIONS
A.V. Margavio and Shirley Laska 17

DEVIANCE AND CONFORMITY IN THE WORK OF COMPANY DOCTORS
Elaine Draper 39

DEEP IN THE HEART OF TEXAS AND CALIFORNIA: SAVINGS AND LOAN FRAUD IN TWO STATES
Kitty Calavita 73

A MULTI-LAYERED SOCIETY IN CONTEMPORARY RUSSIA: CRIMINALS AND OLIGARCHIES AS ITS MAJOR ACTORS
Vladimir Shlapentokh 93

STRUCTURE AND CONTROL: "DEVIANCE" IN POLICE ORGANIZATIONS
Peter K. Manning 117

EXTERNALIZATION AND INTERNALIZATION AS FRAMES FOR UNDERSTANDING WORKPLACE DEVIANCE: THE MANAGEMENT OF ALCOHOL AND DRUG ABUSE
Paul M. Roman and Terry C. Blum 139

MEASURING EVERYTHING THAT MOVES: THE NEW SURVEILLANCE AT WORK
Gary T. Marx 165

CONTROLLING WORKPLACE DEVIANCE: STATE REGULATION OF OCCUPATIONAL HEALTH AND SAFETY
Bridget M. Hutter 191

DISCLOSING MISCONDUCT IN WORK ORGANIZATIONS: AN EMPIRICAL ANALYSIS OF THE SITUATIONAL FACTORS THAT FOSTER WHISTLEBLOWING
Joyce Rothschild and Terance D. Miethe 211

LIST OF CONTRIBUTORS

Terry C. Blum	College of Management Georgia Institute of Technology
Kitty Calavita	Department of Criminology, Law and Society University of California, Irvine
Elaine Draper	Institute for the Study of Social Change University of California, Berkeley
Bridget M. Hutter	Department of Sociology London School of Economics and Political Science
Shirley Laska	Department of Sociology University of New Orleans
Peter K. Manning	School of Criminal Justice and Department of Sociology Michigan State University
A.V. Margavio	Department of Sociology University of New Orleans
Gary T. Marx	Professor Emeritus MIT
Terance D. Miethe	Department of Criminal Justice University of Nevada, Las Vegas
Paul M. Roman	Department of Sociology University of Georgia
Joyce Rothschild	Department of Sociology Virginia Polytechnic Institute and State University

Vladimir Shlapentokh Department of Sociology
Michigan State University

James Tucker Department of Sociology
University of New Hampshire

INTRODUCTION

This volume is about deviance in the workplace. It defines deviance as departures from laws or organizational rules by workers, managers, or an organization as an entity. Parallel to the industrialization of our economy in the nineteenth and early twentieth centuries and its subsequent transformation to a service economy have come new forms of corruption, fraud, unfair competition, exploitation, and other illegal activities. Even though antitrust legislation, regulatory acts, and other laws were enacted from the late nineteenth through the twentieth centuries, sociologists were slow in considering the workplace a criminal scene. In his 1939 American Sociological Society presidential address, Edwin Sutherland (1940) called attention to unlawful behavior in business, and later in *White Collar Crime* (1949), he documented crimes of the 70 largest corporations and the 15 largest public utilities. Despite this crime in the workplace, sociologists of work were largely inattentive to it, and criminologists were not as interested in it as they were in the more visible crime on the street and in the home (Braithwaite 1985). There were notable exceptions. Marshall Clinard, in *The Black Market* (1952), examined price control violations, and Donald Cressey, in *Other People's Money* (1953), identified social psychological processes involved in embezzlement. Following these works, research essentially ceased until the 1980s, when the subject was revisited (see, for example, Clinard and Yeager 1980; Jesilow, Pontell, and Geis 1993; Braithwaite 1984).

Sociologists of organizations, work, and occupations have also intermittently studied deviance and other questionable behavior in the workplace, chiefly by lower-level workers, but have rarely conceived it as unlawful or even undesirable conduct. Rather, it has been studied as organizational and behavioral outcomes arising from the social processes of management (e.g., Dalton, *Men Who Manage* 1959; Jackall, *Moral Mazes* 1988); or from workers' reactions to managerial actions (e.g., Gouldner, *Wildcat Strike* 1954; Roy on restriction of production 1952). Studies such as these are seldom considered by scholars of deviance and crime, just as work on white collar crime and corporate malfeasance is seldom examined in the study of work.

This volume brings together contributions by scholars in the sociology of work and of crime and deviance, and identifies workplace deviance as a subject shared by the two. The contributions center around two main topics: deviance-making processes, and the social control of deviance through workplace regulation to detect and correct deviant behavior. Deviance-making processes arise from loose coupling of work roles and other structural gaps in work organizations. Six papers examine these processes. Three of the six show how deviance is fostered by contradictions or conflict between officially defined and workers' perceptions of work roles. Tucker examines workplace behaviors that defy official norms, including violence, destruction and theft of property, work slowdown and stoppages, and other types of insubordination, which he sees as reactions to extreme subordination. While superiors, and even the state, condemn such actions as illegitimate and often unlawful, subordinate workers, acting under a self-protective set of interests and norms, reject the rights of superiors to control them and rebel. Unionization and other efforts to expand workers' rights grew out of workers' reactions to harsh managerial practices. (See for example, Montgomery 1974; Milkman 1997).

Margavio and Laska's study of shrimpers' resistance to enforcement of the Endangered Species Act illustrates Tucker's thesis, and it also touches upon ways in which the demands of regulatory agencies are implemented, a topic addressed more fully by Hutter. The shrimpers ignored and sabotaged TEDS, the officially prescribed "turtle excluder devices" inserted in shrimping nets to allow sea turtles to escape the trawls. Shrimpers had no interest in catching turtles, but they resisted using the TEDS because devices big enough for turtles to escape also allowed some shrimp to escape. From the shrimpers' point of view, the TEDS were a federal imposition that reduced their harvest and threatened their livelihood. Shrimpers rebelled against using the TEDS, but found little sympathy for their situation as the environmental movement gained increasing state support.

The other study that shows how competing sets of work norms produce deviance is Draper's study of company physicians. Unlike the shrimpers who resisted federal laws, company physicians set aside professional norms that collided with their companies' interests. They shed their white coats to be company team players. Working apart from other doctors and other health caregivers, physicians are directly exposed almost exclusively to company pressures. Contrary professional pressures are more distant from their work.

Common to the three cases is the geographic isolation of the work situation. The shrimpers in a shrimp boat, like the company physician in a factory, were separated from bearers of competing official norms, federal inspectors and other physicians and professional associations respectively. The effect is to intensify the relevance of workaday norms that are close at hand, at the expense of contrary norms from more distant, less intrusive sources. These workers' isolation shielded their violation of opposing official norms and reinforced their feelings that their behavior was justified.

The other three papers on deviance-making situate the processes in the dilution of formal controls and the ascendancy of loose informal ties. Calavita shows how the deregulation of state-chartered savings and loan associations together with federally insured deposits allowed, even encouraged, innovative deviant entrepreneurial practices such as land flips, loan swapping, and junk bonds, which were implemented through "good old boy" networks and protected by the thrift executives' "connections" with state and federal legislators. The fraudulent practices that collapsed the thrifts arose in the "gray" areas of financial dealings that were shielded from state intervention. The impact of the weakness of the state on the criminalization of a society is analyzed by Shlapentokh in his study of contemporary Russia as a multi-layered society of authoritarians (state bureaucrats), oligarchs (the financial elite), criminals, and liberals (Parliament, commercial bankers, media). Each segment operates relatively autonomously from the others with its own "economy," though the liberal sector is weak and ineffectual. These economies are propelled by corrupt and criminal practices, unchecked by the liberal institutions. Thugs are the ascendant actors in the workplace, who get things done as "ordered" by their bosses. The opposite situation is described by Manning in his study of deviance in police organizations. In the United States, police have a near monopoly over maintaining law and order; they interpret the law and simultaneously enforce it, and must do so with split-second action. This dual work responsibility without time for reflection can lead to overly zealous enforcement of the law, without any censure from within the squad or superiors. Like Margavio and Laska's shrimpers, the police have their own definitions of "catches" evolved from shared work experiences and work in relatively autonomous situations. But unlike the shrimpers, the police as instruments of the state have the authority to interpret the legality of their work. Thus, too little or too much authority can give rise to work deviance.

The social control of deviance in the workplace is the other general topic. Four papers address it. These papers examine different strategies organizations use to control deviance: two company initiatives, regulation by state agencies, and individual workers' reporting. Workplaces tend to be tightly controlled, with access regulated and workers closely monitored. Since labor is a major cost, companies seek ways to control workers' behavior to weed out potentially costly deviants or to rehabilitate their deviant behavior. Roman and Blum discuss companies' use of these two approaches, which they term externalizing the deviance, such as firings and refusals to hire unpredictable persons, and internalizing it through programs to help workers change their undesirable behavior. Which form is adopted varies with the misconduct and its location within the organization. Also, fads and fashions in the larger society's approaches to deviance spill over into company policies or may be commanded by the state. For example, Roman and Blum comment on how the medicalizaion of deviance influenced companies to institute Employee Assistance Programs to deal with substance abuse, in part because these programs are outside the functional division of labor and can be easily accommodated to the organization without threatening the workplace.

Deviance that occurs outside the work organization and is brought into the workplace by numbers of workers poses problems that are qualitatively different from deviance that arises from the demands of the job. In the latter case, management can control the work situation by ousting the nonconforming worker. But when the deviance originates externally, management is limited to refusals to hire, discharges, ignoring the troublesome behavior, or trying to correct it. In the case of substance abuse, the substance is seen to cause the misbehavior. From this it follows that elimination of the abuse corrects the behavior. When significant numbers of workers abuse substances, firing is a less practical option than treating the worker to expunge the substance use. Moreover, participation in internalized programs, such as the Employee Assistance Programs, is an investment in workers that may well repay the company in added commitment to the job. In contrast to EPA is drug testing as a screening device for employment. Workers who test positive are dropped from consideration, and may feel discriminated against. Unlike workers who have suffered degradation on the job or some other injustice, they cannot join together for collective defense because of the anonymity of drug testing.

Marx describes and comments on the increase in employers' use of modern surveillance technology as a control strategy. Companies have always kept records on workers' productivity and workplace behavior. But the technological innovations in imaging, recording, and storing information have created means of surveillance far beyond what the unaided eye can see. Since the surveillance is technical, it ignores the employment relations that compose the work process. It focuses on precise details of work performance and on-job behavior without attention to context, much more thoroughly than in the dreams of Frederick Winslow Taylor. Given the efficiency of the technology, unrecorded deviant activities on the workfloor should be exceptionally rare. Marx, however, thinks this may not be the case because the managers for whom the mass of information is reported cannot possibly digest or react to all of it, and also because the reported information is not contextualized within work relations important to judging and evaluating the supposed deviance. Marx worries about the consequences of unchecked high-tech surveillance for workers and for the society.

The growth of our market economy gave rise to new profit-making opportunities that were centered in the workplace and uncovered by laws and traditional norms of work. Regulatory acts were passed to protect workers, the public, the environment, and valued goods and animals. While these acts are protective in purpose, their implementation can create deviance as Margolis and Laska show, just as lifting the regulatory constraints invites graft and fraud as Calivata shows. Enforcement and implementation of regulatory laws is the subject of Hutter's article. She studies how regulatory officials charged with implementing occupational health and safety regulations in Britain approach their work, and also how those whose work is regulated react to the regulations and their enforcement. The regulations cover the factory, industrial air pollution, and railways. Inspectors seek cooperation with companies and use persuasion, negotiations, and education to get compliance. The preferred regulatory model is a compliant company that is committed to the well-being of its workers and takes steps to create a safe and healthy workplace. Companies are expected to implement health and safety standards. Managers and workers are expected to observe the standards. Companies vary in their compliance, with large firms more informed about the laws and inspectors' expectations and policies. Small firms have less knowledge of the regulations but are also less mindful of enforcing the standards they are aware of. Within companies, the knowledge and interest in implementing workplace health and safety standards declines with movement down the chain of command, from a majority of managers to a minority of workers. But in cases of violations, managers attribute failures in enforcement of health and safety standards to a lack of information on them and to workers' derelictions. While the workers evade regulations in the interest of "getting their work done" and because of the discomfort of safety clothing, management allows workers to be inattentive to health and safety standards. Companies whose top management is committed to health and safety have the best records, and inspectors feel that the most effective requisite for gaining compliance is management commitment to health and safety. The examination of enforcement from the perspectives of the enforcers and the subjects of the regulations captures the dynamics of deviance control. Hutter, like Margolis and Laska, shows that enforcement may have deleterious consequences for companies and workers; yet on the other hand, the lifting of regulations may have even greater consequences, as Calavita finds in the collapse of the savings and loan industry in the 1980s. Regulatory agencies have significantly reduced deviance in the workplace, though what is defined as deviant may be disputed, as in the case of the sea turtles.

Individual actions to report or control deviance are sporadic and situational. They are often unwelcome to management, which may prefer to be, or pretend to be, unaware of the facts. While management wants to know what workers do, it is not always so open with respect to its own actions. Management considers its own behavior private, and will take extraordinary steps to keep what it considers prejudicial to its interests under tight control, even when its actions may have serious consequences for workers, the public, and the common good. Workers may come to know about managerial misdeeds. If management institutes secure and effective upward communication channels, and workers use these channels to report deviance, the wrongs can be righted or efforts made to do so. But when the channels are blocked, the blockage implicitly tells workers that divulging a deviant situation may be dangerous, perhaps even leading to termination of employment. Closed channels direct workers to the outside; they see that there is no safe and effective conduit inside the company to remedy a problem, hence, the whistleblower, the subject of Rothschild and Miethe's article. Rothschild and Miethe define whistleblowing as the reporting of misconduct in the workplace, and compare the efficacy of work roles and organizational conditions to personality and demographic attributes in explaining the willingness of workers to report misconduct. While whistleblowing is a heroic act involving risk-taking and requiring much moral fortitude, it is organizationally based. Rothschild and Miethe look inside organizations and identify positional and situational conditions that support it. Whistleblowers do not differ significantly from non-whistleblowers in personality or sociodemographic characteristics, but they do differ in the size of their employing company, work roles, and views of their employers. They work for small companies more than non-whistleblowers. They observe misconduct more frequently, in part because their work positions enable them to see a wider variety of the jobs, especially in a small business; because they tend to be in professions with written codes of ethics, and because they tend to believe their employers are immoral; beliefs that undoubtedly encourage an observant, and even suspicious, attitude at work. Organizational conditions affect the route the whistleblower takes. Bypassing the organization to report the deviance to outsiders is more characteristic of whistleblowers from small companies than from large ones. This finding on small company employees, together with Hutter's finding that small companies were more lax in enforcing proper conduct, suggests that small companies take more dangerous risks and that they lack internal organizational shields to make wrongful acts invisible to their work forces.

Ida Harper Simpson
Richard L. Simpson
Guest Editors

REFERENCES

Braithwaite, J. 1984. *Corporate Crime in the Pharmaceutical Industry*. London: Routledge & Kegan Paul.

Braithwaite, J. 1985. "White Collar Crime." *Annual Review of Sociology* 11: 1–25.

Clinard, M. 1952. *The Black Market: A Study of White Collar Crime*. New York: Holt, Rinehart.

Clinard, M., and P.C. Yeager. 1980. *Corporate Crime*. New Yo rk: Free Press.

Cressey, D. 1953. *Other People's Money: The Social Psychology of Embezzlement*. New York: Free Press.
Dalton, M. 1959. *Men Who Manage*. New York: Wiley.
Gouldner, A. 1954. *Wildcat Strike: A Study in Worker-Management Relations*. New York: Harper.
Jackall, R. 1988. *Moral Mazes: The World of Corporate Managers*. New York: Oxford University Press.
Jesilow, P., H.N. Pontell, and G. Geis. 1993. *Prescription for Profit: How Doctors Defraud Medicaid*. Berkeley, CA: University of California.
Milkman, R. 1997. *Farewell to the Factory: Auto Workers in the Late Twentieth Century*. Berkeley and Los Angeles, CA: University of California Press.
Montgomery, D. 1974. "The 'New Unionism' and the Transformation of Workers' Consciousness in America, 1909–1922." *Journal of Social History* 7: 509–529.
Roy, D. 1952. "Quota Restriction and Goldbricking in a Machine Shop." *American Journal of Sociology* 57: 427–442.
Sutherland, E.H. 1940. "The White Collar Criminal." *American Sociological Review* 5: 1–12.
Sutherland, E.H. 1949. *White Collar Crime*. New York: Dryden.

WORKER DEVIANCE AS SOCIAL CONTROL

James Tucker

ABSTRACT

This paper examines several workplace behaviors—violence, sabotage, theft, and withdrawal from work activities—that are usually considered deviant, but under many circumstances may be just the opposite: social control. Donald Black's (1976, 1984, 1990, 1993, 1998) general theory of social control provides a framework that allows us to explain these types of deviance—what M.P. Baumgartner (1984) calls "social control from below"—with the structure of social relations in the workplace. I present evidence from a variety of work settings past and present indicating that, as Blackian theory predicts, the severity of upward social control varies directly with the amount of inequality and social distance between superiors and subordinates (Black 1990, pp. 47–49; 1993, p. 154). Physical attacks on supervisors, destruction and appropriation of property, and withholding labor are most likely in work settings where superiors and subordinates are separated by large distances in social space such as slave plantations, serf estates, migrant farm enterprises, and early factories. In the modern workplace, subordinates are socially closer to superiors and social control from below is accordingly less aggressive than in the past.

Research in the Sociology of Work, Volume 8, pages 1-16.

ISBN: 0-7623-0608-4

Deviance is conduct that is subject to social control. Yet it may be social control itself. In other words, deviance can be a reaction to deviance. Donald Black (1983) demonstrates, for example, that much crime involves the pursuit of justice: People who engage in murder, assault, vandalism, and other conduct defined as criminal are frequently punishing the wrongdoings of their victims. Likewise, deviance in the workplace—criminal and noncriminal—is often moralistic. It is mostly what M.P. Baumgartner (1984) calls "social control from below," a means by which subordinates express grievances against superiors.

This paper examines several worker behaviors that are usually considered deviant, but under many conditions may be more appropriately classified as upward social control. These behaviors include violence, sabotage, theft, and withdrawal from work activities. Donald Black's (1976, 1984, 1990, 1993, 1998) general theory of social control allows us to explain these types of deviance—or social control from below—with the structure of social relations in the workplace. Over the last quarter century, Black has developed a theoretical framework that addresses the universe of social control, a universe that contains "phenomena as diverse as litigation, violence, mediation, gossip, ostracism, psychotherapy, sorcery, sabotage, and suicide" (Black 1993, p. xiii). The framework, which Black also applies to forms of social life beyond social control, is based on an explanatory strategy he calls "pure sociology" (Black 1979, 1995). Social life, including social control, is explained not by people's motivations or interests, but by the "social structure" in which it occurs. The social structure of any form of social life is defined by the social characteristics of all of the participants and the relations among them. The important predictors of social control include the degree of inequality and social distance: How stratified are the parties? Are they intimates or strangers? How similar or different are they culturally?

Below I present evidence from a variety of work settings past and present indicating that, as Blackian theory predicts, the severity of upward social control varies directly with the amount of inequality and social distance between superiors and subordinates (Black 1990, pp. 47–49, 1993, p. 154). Physical attacks on supervisors, destruction and appropriation of property, and withholding labor are most likely in work settings where inequality and social distance are extreme such as slave plantations, serf estates, migrant farm enterprises, and early factories. Subordinates in the modern workplace are more equal and closer to superiors, and social control from below is less destructive than in the past. But like subordinates everywhere, when contemporary workers exert social control upward, it is often "defined and processed as itself an offense by the superiors against whom it is directed, and often by the larger public that accepts their version of events" (Baumgartner 1984, pp. 338–339).

This paper does not provide a comprehensive review of workplace deviance. After all, not all deviance in the workplace is social control. Organizational elites, for example, engage in criminal behavior of various kinds, including fraud, commercial bribery, tax evasion, safety violations, and collusion (Sutherland 1949;

Coleman 1985). These crimes do not punish the enterprise, but instead help it financially. Some workplace deviance thus has more in common with behavior such as robbery and burglary, and is best understood with a theory of criminal predation rather than a theory of social control.

SOCIAL CONTROL FROM BELOW

Social control is most forceful when initiated by superiors and directed downwardly. In the workplace, for instance, managers verbally reprimand, demote, fine, fire, and even (in the past) beat workers who act out of line. Parents, teachers, and superiors of other kinds also use punitive measures to deal with misbehaving children, students, and other underlings. Subordinates, on the other hand, have no formal authority to sanction upward. In fact, efforts to subject superiors to social control are usually prohibited and sometimes illegal (Baumgartner 1984, p. 304). This does not mean, however, that subordinates ignore the misdeeds of their superiors. Under some circumstances, those in positions of authority find themselves punished by subordinates for violating informal prohibitions.

As Baumgartner (1984, pp. 305–308) demonstrates, open violence is the most visible and potentially the most destructive form of upward social control. Throughout history, aggrieved slaves, servants, soldiers, seamen, and prisoners have occasionally knifed, shot, poisoned, burned, and tortured their superiors. Yet violent attacks can entail risks, including capital punishment from above, and subordinates often resort to other means. They may, for example, covertly appropriate or destroy the property of their superiors (Baumgartner 1984, pp. 308–312). Subordinates can also refuse to fully cooperate with superiors. This may include working at a slower pace than normal, being absent from duty, and disobeying orders (Baumgartner 1984, pp. 312–316). Those at the bottom of hierarchies are also known to pursue upward grievances by mobilizing others to help fight their causes, fleeing from their superiors, and injuring or otherwise incapacitating themselves (Baumgartner 1984, pp. 316–331).

Because upward social control is often covert, it can be difficult to observe. In fact, subordinates frequently take great care to express their grievances in ways that escape detection. Studying social control from below therefore presents certain methodological challenges. For example, how do we know whether an action such as theft is social control and not something else? We can try to identify an incident—grievance—that may have sparked an act of social control. But this can also be difficult to detect, especially if the incident (or incidents) that triggered social control occurred sometime in the distant past. It is sometimes possible to rely on the words of those initiating social control, although this strategy has its own limitations. We can never be sure that people describe their behavior honestly. Fortunately, sociologists, historians, and others have gathered a sizeable empirical literature on worker behavior that, despite its methodological constraints, allows us to draw some tentative conclusions about the behavior of social control from below.

Under what conditions do subordinates engage in the most aggressive forms of upward social control? When do they physically attack superiors, destroy and steal their property, and deprive them of labor and other services? Black (1993, pp. 144–157) shows that authoritative social control (violent and otherwise) thrives in social structures where parties are separated by great distances in vertical, relational, and cultural space. Other social scientists applying the Blackian framework have also found that as people become more distant they become more forceful and punitive in their application of social control (Baumgartner 1988, 1992; Borg 1992; Cooney 1988; Horwitz 1990; Morrill 1989, 1992, 1995; Mullis 1995; Senechal de la Roche 1996, 1997; Tucker 1999; Tucker and Ross 2000). This applies to both superiors and subordinates (Black 1990, pp. 47–49, 1993, p. 154). So when subordinates are subject to the most punishment from above, as they are when socially inferior and remote, they exert the most punishment upward (Baumgartner 1984, p. 336). The difference is that upward punishment is often covert. In the pages that follow, we see that this pattern holds in the workplace: *Violence, sabotage, theft, and withdrawal from work activities occur most frequently in rigidly hierarchical and socially segregated work settings.*

VIOLENCE

Although it is uncommon in the modern workplace, violence is a regular feature in work settings of the past. Subordinates attack superiors for various offenses, including the nonpayment of wages, poor working conditions, and physical harassment. As Blackian theory predicts, violence is most likely and most severe in work settings with large amounts of inequality and social distance. Laboring under the most extreme conditions of subordination and segregation, slaves are particularly likely to seek violent revenge against superiors. On Brazilian slave plantations in the nineteenth century, for example, owners were constantly concerned about violent ambushes by aggrieved slaves. Aware of the dangers surrounding them, plantation owners kept large dogs by their sides and many hired armed guards to protect themselves. Planters were particularly worried about slaves joining together and initiating direct attacks. To circumvent this possibility, rest periods were staggered so that slaves would not all be idle at the same time. Noting the drastic measures that owners took to thwart slave reprisals, some observers described them as suffering from "planter's paranoia" (Dean 1976, p. 85).

Migrant workers, who labor much like slaves under conditions of great inequality and social distance, also use violence to express grievances. Early in the twentieth century, for instance, migrant agricultural workers in Eastern Europe sometimes rebelled violently against their superiors. Consider the events in the

Prussian province of Saxony. In 1908, several workers walked off an agricultural work site and threatened to kill the foreman. Armed with hoes, spades, and stones, they clashed with the police before surrendering (Müller 1991, p. 87). In 1911, striking workers "smashed the windows at the flat of their foreman in protest against discriminatory work and living conditions." (Müller 1991, p. 87). During the same period of history in another part of the world, supervisors working for British planting companies in the Solomon Islands constantly faced the threat of violence by native laborers:

> [R]esistance in the form of physical violence was probably at its apex in 1917.... Laborers fought back against maltreatment of kinfolk, the violation of socio-religious beliefs, being verbally abused, being forced to work overtime, short rations, and excessive tasks.... [L]aborers had little redress except self-help (Bennett 1993, p. 167).

Violent social control from below also occurs in factory settings with steep hierarchies and large social gaps between superiors and subordinates. For example, peasants working in the factories of precommunist Russia at the end of the nineteenth century engaged in a series of strikes, ranging "from isolated spontaneous outbursts of rage against low wages, fines, living conditions, illegal firings, and other abuses, to longer and more organized protests demanding substantive changes in industrial relations" (Glickman 1984, p. 20). Some of these actions were violent. In one case, several hundred mostly women weavers, upset with verbal insults and sexual intimidation, banded together and invaded a factory office, where they destroyed furniture, record books, and other company property: "They then moved on to the company store, which they looted and destroyed. They invaded the weaving department and wrecked the looms. Finally, they went in search of the factory director and, not finding him on the premises, went to his house with the intention of killing him" (Glickman 1984, p. 166). The director escaped physical harm, but the strike lasted more than a week.

Family, friends, and others may assist workers in their violent protests against superiors. With lots of potential allies available, upward social control can be especially violent (on partisanship, see Black 1993, pp. 125–143; on collective violence, see Senechal de la Roche 1996, 1997). For example, individuals employed in the transport industry of early twentieth-century northern China, who worked under the strict authority of guild bosses, had strong kinship ties that could easily be summoned. Grievances against bosses were often expressed violently, usually with the assistance of family members:

> The 1935 case of transport worker Su Zhenbao is typical of a worker-boss conflict. Laid off by a foreman named Yu for a trivial offense, Su went to Yu's house with a wooden club and assaulted him. Two of Yu's nephews, as well as Su's brother, jumped into the fray, and Su bit a large chunk out of Yu's hand. Yu was luckier than Yang Derun, one of Tianjin's most famous transport guild bosses. One of Yang's workers, angry at being cheated out of his fair share of pay, got into an argument with Yang and stabbed him six times in the head and once in the

chest.... Another boss, who made what his employees regarded as excessive deductions from their pay, was assaulted by a group of them and beaten (Hershatter 1986, p. 135).

Violence in modern work settings is largely confined to those that emulate the past such as multinational corporations located in non-Western societies. Where members of indigenous populations work at low wage factory jobs, the cultural distance between managers and workers is especially great. The local workforce may also have strong ties to the larger community, further enhancing the probability of violent protest. Consider foreign-owned manufacturing plants in Malaysia, where local young men sympathetic to the plight of young female workers would sometimes attack misbehaving foremen:

In 1976, an Indian foreman was set upon, "beaten and badly hurt on the face and stomach by an unknown gang" according to [company] records. A Malay assistant foreman coming to his aid was also beaten up. According to an informal questioning of workers, the foreman deserved punishment because he refused workers their 15 minute breaks, insulted them about personal matters, followed women into the locker room, and threatened to terminate their employment whenever he felt necessary. He became blacklisted among village youths (Ong 1987, p. 211).

A Chinese foreman was beaten by locals for dating an operator, a practice that violated a warning by the community that sexual encounters with young Malay workers were forbidden (Ong 1987, p. 213). Moreover, "[t]here had been at least two other incidents of nocturnal attacks on male workers—none of local origin—outside the [company] gates" (Ong 1987, p. 212).

In modern America, violence against superiors is a relatively uncommon occurrence. The exception is the rare (although often highly publicized) case of a dismissed worker returning to his workplace and attacking a former boss and others who happen to get in the way.

SABOTAGE

Because direct attacks on superiors can be dangerous, subordinates often protest by engaging in what Baumgartner calls "covert retaliation" (1984, pp. 308–312). One way to retaliate covertly is to destroy the property of the enterprise. Like physical violence, this strategy is most likely in work settings with large amounts of inequality and social distance. On slave plantations in America and elsewhere during the eighteenth and nineteenth centuries, for example, arson was a regular method of protest (Baumgartner 1984, p. 313). In the mines of southern Rhodesia earlier this century, where black workers labored in slave-like conditions by white owners, attacks on mine property, including the maiming of cattle and burning of thatch roof huts, were used to strike back at owners for long hours of work and oppressive working conditions (van Onselen 1976, p. 242).

Those working under colonial regimes also engage in sabotage with some regularity (see Scott 1985). In the late nineteenth century, for instance, Melanesian workers on the sugar plantations of Queensland would "[hide] rocks in the cane going to the mills, with disastrous effects on the machinery" (Moore 1993, p. 86). Moreover, "[a]cres of cane mysteriously caught fire and mill sheds also went up in smoke" (Moore 1993, p. 86). For peasant laborers at the turn of the twentieth century in the cornfields on the Yucatecan Estates, "[a]rson...became a formidable mode of resistance...looming as a constant threat to production." (Wells and Joseph 1993, p. 272).

Sabotage also appeared in early American factory regimes. It was especially common in the automobile industry, where workers were mostly recent immigrants earning low wages. At the Lincoln Motor Company, for instance:

> [m]ishaps—whether caused by sabotage or carelessness—occurred constantly. Machines would be thrown out of adjustment overnight so that the operation next morning might go on for hours turning out scrap before inspection could catch it. Screws were loosened, bolts were removed which could allow parts to fall and be damaged. Loose nuts were found in crankcases of engines, feed pipes were plugged. On one occasion, cans full of powder were found in the coal supply, and fire extinguishers were plugged with cotton. (Leland 1966, p. 187; quoted in Gartman 1986, p. 171).

At a large engine manufacturing plant, workers committed sabotage in response to management attempts to increase the speed of the assembly line:

> Motors were defectively assembled or damaged in route—gaskets were left out, wrong sized spark plugs put in, bolts left loose, plug wires assembled in the wrong firing order. Inspectors rejected three out of every four or five motors, and they did their own share of sabotage (Gartman 1986, p. 160).

Workers in modern America also engage in sabotage. As Blackian theory predicts, the most likely participants are those at the bottom of organizational hierarchies and most socially distant from superiors. The conditions for sabotage are found, for example, among the growing population of temporary and part-time employees. Consider a small construction site where workers, many of whom were students employed for the summer, expressed their frustration for not receiving a promised pay increase:

> We would abuse our tools so they would break.... We believed that by increasing the cost and decreasing the profit on jobs, the president would get the message loud and clear (quoted in Tucker 1993, p. 36)

Some sabotage is more symbolic than destructive. This was the case when a low ranking hourly employee at a small electronics corporation in the southern United States attempted to "get back" at his overbearing boss by periodically urinating on the floor of the men's bathroom (Tucker 1999, pp. 105–106). Such behavior is mild compared to the similar yet considerably more direct method of protest used by Indian plantation laborers in the 1800s on the Fiji Islands:

> [A] European overseer quit his job after being overpowered by a group of Indian women laborers, who held him down while each took her turns urinating upon him (Munro 1993, p. 24).

On another occasion, a misbehaving European overseer was forced into a sewer pit by a group of female workers: "The women then threw shit at him" (Munro 1993, p. 24).

Employees may attempt to indirectly inflict harm on employers. Retail employees, for example, may "badmouth" their companies to friends and other potential customers. Under some circumstances, such behavior can damage an enterprise more than the destruction of its property (Tucker 1993, p. 36). This conduct, like destroying property, is considered deviant by employers and may violate the law. Badmouthing a company, for example, can be libelous.

THEFT

Besides destroying and defacing property, aggrieved workers may steal it and use it for their own purposes (see Baumgartner 1984, pp. 309–310; Tucker 1989). As Black (1993, p. 51) notes, theft in the workplace and elsewhere is often "compensatory self-help by people taking what they rightfully regard as theirs." Like other types of upward social control, theft appears most frequently when superiors and subordinates are separated by great distances in social space. Thus, in southern Rhodesia (now Zimbabwe) at the beginning of the twentieth century, theft was commonly used by black laborers to punish white mine owners and managers:

> Daily, hundreds of crimes were committed on the mining properties with the specific goal of rectifying the balance between employees and their employers. African workers constantly pilfered small items of mine stores—such as candles—or helped themselves to substantial quantities of detonators and dynamite which they used for fishing. Wage rates were altered on documents, and hundreds of work and "skoff" tickets [indicating the number of hours worked] were forged by miners who sought to gain compensation for what they had been denied through the system (van Onselen 1976, p. 240).

Theft was also a regular feature of life on Samoan plantations in the late 1800s, where laborers stole coconuts from the trees owned by their German employers (Munro and Firth 1993, p. 116), and in rural Guatemalan coffee fields at the turn of the century, where aggrieved plantation workers would occasionally steal coffee beans (McCreery 1993, p. 228). In fact, theft appears to be widespread in peasant communities everywhere (Hoch 1986, p. 170).

Theft occurs in industrial settings as well. Again, it is most likely when employees work under rigid hierarchies and are socially distant from superiors. Laborers in nineteenth century English cotton mills regularly confiscated company property as a form of protest (Tobias 1972, p. 165; cited in Henry 1978, p. 10) as did manufacturing workers in Nazi occupied Poland in the middle of the twentieth century (Gross 1979, p. 414; cited in Baumgartner 1984, 310). Likewise, theft is prevalent among low ranking dock workers in contemporary Great Britain, where it is considered "a morally justified addition to wages [and] an entitlement due from exploiting employers" (Mars 1982, p. 244).

In modern America, employee theft is common, and is frequently a type of upward social control. A large-scale national study found that more than one-third of employees in the retailing, hospital, and manufacturing industries had engaged in workplace theft at least once while on their current job (Hollinger and Clark (1983). The researchers concluded that "when employees felt exploited by the company or by their superiors...we were not surprised to find these workers more involved in acts against the organization [including theft] as a mechanism to correct perceptions of insecurity or injustice" (Hollinger and Clark 1983, p. 142).

Ethnographic reports of American corporate life also indicate that employees may steal as a way of seeking justice. Consider the comments of an accountant convicted of embezzlement:

> The individual who is the head of the company where I worked was extremely repulsive. He is an arrogant, filthy rich, old-school type of master and servant and everything that went with it. The rebelliousness in me just cropped (up) and asserted itself without any prompting of any kind. (quoted in Cressey 1953, p. 58).

These comments mirror those of another man imprisoned for embezzling funds. This individual became upset after being blamed for a shortage he claimed was not his fault:

> The manager was very nasty about it and said that I had to "pay or else." I thought it was a pretty tough deal. I'd been with the company ten years and everything. So I thought, "If he is going to toss one at me I'll toss one at him." So I did (quoted in Cressey 1953, p. 58; also quoted in Baumgartner 1984, p. 310).

Similarly, a clerical assistant employed with an engineering firm started stealing office equipment after several unsuccessful attempts to get her boss to raise her hourly wage to the same level as others in her position: "I occasionally swiped some computer disks and small office supplies for personal use, but I felt, and still feel, I deserved them" (quoted in Tucker 1993, p. 36).

As Blackian theory predicts, those at the bottom of the corporate ladder and those with weak ties to the enterprise are most likely to use theft as revenge (Tucker 1989). It is therefore common among individuals in low status temporary occupations, including waiters (Mars 1973; Hawkins 1984), department store employees (Robin 1969), and "fast food" workers (Terris and Jones 1982). Also supporting the theory is research indicating that employee theft is inversely correlated to length of tenure on the job (Robin 1969, p. 20; Hollinger and Clark 1983, p. 66).

WITHDRAWAL

Another option for aggrieved subordinates is to withdraw from work activities. This may involve actively refusing to cooperate with the demands of superiors (on "noncooperation," see Baumgartner 1984, pp. 312–316). Scott (1986, p. 6), for example, discovered that peasants use "everyday forms of resistance" such as "footdragging, dissimulation, false-compliance, [and] feigned ignorance" to protest the actions of their superiors. Such practices were employed by Melanesian laborers in Queensland at the turn of the twentieth century:

> Malingering and working slowly were...covert means by which Melanesians resisted their work environment. Once out in the fields, if they could escape the beady eye of the overseer, they could take a dip in a nearby creek or have quick naps among the cane rows (Moore 1993, p. 86).

Similar behaviors—including organized work slowdowns—were popular modes of protest in American automobile factories at mid-century (Gartman 1986). Likewise, early ethnographic studies of the workplace showed that goldbricking (shirking work responsibilities) and soldiering (making a pretense of working) were characteristic of hierarchical settings such as machine shops (Roy 1952) and restaurants (Whyte 1948).

Employees in modern American corporations use comparable means of retaliation. For example, people in "dead end" jobs sometimes express their frustrations with employers by creating "counter-systems," which stress solidarity among peers and rejection of corporate goals:

> Their rebelliousness is more likely to take the form of passive resistance.... Or it could be gossip, joking, or ridicule at the expense of the advantaged. The ring leader of such a group is likely to be a good resister or a "comic" or a person with a sassy tongue well placed in a gossip network (Kanter 1977, p. 150).

Aggrieved employees often have areas where they come together to socialize and complain about their treatment by managers. The company restroom may serve this purpose. At a contemporary British manufacturing plant, for example, workers express their grievances in the "loo" (bathroom):

> The widespread shopfloor view of the toilet as a collusive retreat was discernible on its walls that were covered in a "graffiti of resistance"; a typical comment was "Evans (the superintendent) is a cunt" (Collinson 1992, p. 137).

Workers in a large American factory also retreat to the bathroom to get away from the rigors of the overbearing foremen. Besides a venue to complain about managers, the toilet provides a safe place to read the newspaper and violate the unpopular no smoking policy:

> [I]n the men's bathroom, there are times during the day when you are in big trouble if you need a stall. You have to wait, listening to the rustling of paper, and watching smoke roll over the closed stall door (Balzer 1976, p. 86).

Withdrawal from work activities need not be an organized event. Individual workers who are upset for one reason or another may simply "slack off" on the job. Consider the experiences of two young employees working part-time in retail establishments on the east coast of the United States. Both were upset for not receiving promised pay raises. The first, a male stockroom clerk, thought about resigning, but decided to stay and put in a less than complete effort:

> I didn't really want to quit so I goofed off a lot. I didn't do anything unless I was specifically asked to. [When working] at night I would listen to music for hours and do nothing.... If I was goofing off and saw the manager, I would act as if I was really doing something (quoted in Tucker 1993, p. 37).

A second employee, a female sales clerk, first tolerated her manager's misconduct before eventually taking action:

> At first I did nothing.... As time went by, my work started to slack off. I did less and less every day. And I really did not feel guilty, because I thought the company should give me more for my work.... I began to care less and less about my work. I would come in late on Fridays, call in sick when I did not feel like coming in. I would take longer lunch breaks when my manager was not there, and I would socialize with other employees on company time (quoted in Tucker 1993, p. 37).

Those in professional positions also withdraw from their jobs as way to protest their employment situation. In one large American firm, discontented employees refuse to participate in the social life of the workplace beyond what their job requires and are sarcastically referred to by colleagues as "zombies" and "mummies" (Kanter 1977, p. 146).

Not showing up for work, which is a kind of withdrawal or temporary avoidance (see Baumgartner 1988, pp. 24–26), can also express a grievance. In fact, absenteeism is popular form of upward social control in a range of settings. For example, at times during the early American automobile industry workers stayed away from their jobs to protest their mistreatment by employers:

> Indirect and individualistic forms of worker resistance were most important in the early auto shops that were undergoing the rudimentary transformations of the labor process. Instead of directly and collectively confronting their bosses over changes in work that stripped them of control, auto workers indirectly registered their discontent by individually quitting or being absent from their newly degraded jobs (Gartman 1986, p. 151).

Absenteeism in the modern workplace is also, as we would expect, highest among low level employees who have complaints against their companies (Adams 1965; Green 1980).

It may be appropriate to consider alcohol and illegal drug use—often considered to be "deviant" workplace behaviors—as means by which employees withdraw from unpleasant jobs (on the use and regulation of alcohol and illegal drugs in the workplace, see Roman 1980; Weiss 1986). On the other hand, the consumption of mind-altering substances is not always prohibited by employers, nor is it always seen as an impediment to production. In some work settings, for example, alcohol is a part of the workplace culture, valued for its ability to improve social interaction between workers and employers (see below).

THE DECLINE OF WORKER DEVIANCE

If violence, sabotage, theft, and withdrawal are byproducts of inequality and social distance, then these behaviors should become less frequent when subordinates and superiors become equal and socially close. And they do. In settings such as worker collectives and employee-owned companies, for instance, grievances are handled more peacefully, often through negotiation, mediation, and counseling (Tucker 1999). But even in hierarchical enterprises, social control from below may become less destructive if mangers are able to reduce the distance between themselves and workers. For example, on the northwestern coast of America, foremen actively close the gaps with longshoremen under their supervision, and are able to limit aggressive protest:

> Few of the foremen ever attempt to assume any role other than that of "one of the boys," and those who maintain themselves as part of the longshore in-group enjoy a good deal of popularity among the men and maintain good production records, because the longshoremen will usually give a break to a foreman who maintains his status as one of the men (Pilcher 1972, p. 99).

Drinking alcohol can play an important role in weakening hierarchy and social distance (even if only temporarily) and in turn the likelihood of peaceful grievance expression: "The raising of the first glass, bottle, aluminum can, or paper cup is a sign that participants may take to mean a relaxation of ordinary work rules" (Van Maanen 1992, p. 39). The contemporary "office party" is a setting where workers and managers socialize and share grievances. In London's Metropolitan Police Department, for example:

> the office party allows for some often blunt discourse across...ranks. With alcohol obvious and everyone drunk, an officer is not responsible for what he says and does. Higher officials can criticize lower ones, and, more important, lower ones can "come on about their complaints" with the higher ranks (Van Maanen 1992, p. 49).

Other events where drinking is commonplace, including "pub crawls," are also valued by police officers for their "tension relieving" effects. Similarly, in Japanese corporations, "office parties with dinner and drinks permit the subordinates to adopt the guise of mild inebriation" and openly voice their complaints to managers (Ouchi 1981, p. 45). An anthropologist documenting life at a large Japanese bank noted that "[t]he gesture of filling another's glass is a convenient bridge across strained relationships" (Rohlen 1974, p. 109). Golf outings also provide Japanese employees an opportunity to break down social barriers: "At these times subordinates can feel free to ask questions and raise objections suppressed in the office and expect the boss to respond sympathetically" (Ouchi 1981, p. 45).

Work settings today are overall less hierarchical and socially segregated than in the past. According to Blackian theory, this change should foster a general decline in the more potent forms of worker protest such as violence and sabotage. Indeed, employees are less likely to attack their superiors and destroy their property. With less inequality and social distance, upward social control, when it does occur, is milder and more of an individual affair. Less aggressive forms of protest, including theft and withdrawal, are more common (see Edwards 1979, pp. 152–157; Tucker 1989).

We might also expect worker deviance—aggressive measures of social control from below—to decline when employees have access to legitimate means of grievance expression (on the inverse relationship between self-help and law, see Black 1983). Labor unions provide such means as does the state under some circumstances. While union membership is on a steady decline, a growing number of companies have developed internal judicial systems that allow workers to formally protest the actions of superiors and others (Westin and Feliu 1988; Ewing 1989). Evidence suggests that these quasi-legal systems are most common in large firms with close ties to the public sector (Edelman 1990). Violence, sabotage, theft, and withdrawal should therefore be uncommon in these settings because employees have legitimate avenues to pursue justice.

CONCLUSION

Much of what is called workplace deviance is just the opposite. It is upward social control, a reaction to employer deviance. Like other forms of social control, it is attracted to a particular social structure. The previous pages have shown that punitive forms of upward social control—violence, sabotage, theft, and withdrawal—are most frequent when the social structure of the work setting contains large amounts of inequality and social distance. As social space shrinks, upward social control weakens and worker deviance declines.

ACKNOWLEDGMENTS

Donald Black, Mark Cooney, and Roberta Senechal de la Roche made helpful comments on a previous draft.

REFERENCES

Adams, J.S. 1965. "Inequity in Social Exchange." *Advances in Experimental Social Psychology* 2: 267–299.

Balzer, R. 1976. *Clockwork: Life in and Outside an American Factory*. Garden City, N: Doubleday and Company.

Baumgartner, M.P. 1984. "Social Control from Below." Pp. 303–345 in *Toward a General Theory of Social Control*, Volume 1: *Fundamentals*, edited by D. Black. Orlando, FL: Academic Press.

Baumgartner, M.P. 1988. *The Moral Order of a Suburb*. New York: Oxford University Press.

Baumgartner, M.P. 1992. "War and Peace in Early Childhood." Pp. 1–38 in *Virginia Review of Sociology*, Volume 1: *Law and Conflict Management*, edited by J. Tucker. Greenwich, CT: JAI Press Inc.

Bennett, J.A. 1993. "'We Do Not Come Here To Be Beaten': Resistance and the Plantation System in the Solomon Islands to World War II." Pp. 129–185 in *Plantation Workers: Resistance and Accommodation*, edited by B.V. Lal, D. Munro, and E.D. Beechert. Honolulu: University of Hawaii Press.

Black, D. 1976. *The Behavior of Law*. New York: Academic Press.

Black, D. 1979. "A Strategy of Pure Sociology." Pp. 149–168 in *Theoretical Perspectives in Sociology*, edited by S.G. McNall. New York: St. Martin's Press.

Black, D. 1983. "Crime as Social Control." *American Sociological Review* 48: 34–45.

Black, D. 1984. "Social Control as a Dependent Variable." Pp. 1–35 in *Toward a General Theory of Social Control*, Volume 1: *Fundamentals*, edited by D. Black. Orlando, FL: Academic Press.

Black, D. 1990. "The Elementary Forms of Conflict Management." Pp. 43–69 in *New Directions in the Study of Justice, Law, and Social Control*, prepared by the School of Justice Studies, Arizona State University. New York: Plenum Press.

Black, D. 1993. *The Social Structure of Right and Wrong*. San Diego, CA: Academic Press.

Black, D. 1995. "The Epistemology of Pure Sociology." *Law and Social Inquiry* 20: 829–870.

Black, D. 1998. "Prologue to the Revised Edition." Pp. xiii–xxii in *The Social Structure of Right and Wrong*. San Diego, CA: Academic Press (Revised Edition).

Borg, M.J. 1992. "Conflict Management in the World System." *Sociological Forum* 7: 261–282.

Coleman, J.W. 1985. *The Criminal Elite: The Sociology of White Collar Crime*. New York: St. Martin's Press.

Collinson, D.L. 1992. *Managing the Shopfloor: Subjectivity, Masculinity, and Workplace Culture*. Berlin: Walter de Gruyter.

Cooney, M. 1988. "The Social Control of Homicide: A Cross-Cultural Study." Unpublished Doctoral Dissertation, Harvard Law School.

Cressey, D.R. 1953. *Other People's Money: A Study in the Social Psychology of Embezzlement*. Glencoe, IL: The Free Press.

Dean, W. 1976. *Rio Carlo: A Brazilian Plantation System, 1820–1920*. Stanford, CA: Stanford University Press.

Edelman, L.B. 1990. "Legal Environments and Organizational Governance: The Expansion of Due Process in the American Workplace." *American Journal of Sociology* 95: 1401–1440.

Edwards, R. 1979. *Contested Terrain: The Transformation of the Workplace in the Twentieth Century*. New York: Basic Books.

Ewing, D. 1989. *Justice on the Job: Resolving Grievances in the Nonunion Workplace*. Boston: Harvard Business School Press.

Gartman, D. 1986. *Auto Slavery: The Labor Process in the American Automobile Industry, 1857–1950*. New Brunswick, NJ: Rutgers University Press.

Gersuny, C. 1973. *Punishment and Redress in a Modern Factory*. Lexington: Lexington Books.

Glickman, R.L. 1984. *Russian Factory Women: Workplace and Society, 1880–1914*. Berkeley, CA: University of California Press.

Green, J.R. 1980 *The World of Worker: Labor in Twentieth-Century America*. New York: Hill and Wong.

Gross, J.T. 1979. *Polish Society Under German Occupation: The General Government, 1939–1944*. Princeton, NJ: Princeton University Press.

Hawkins, R. 1984. "Employee Theft in the Restaurant Trade: Forms of Ripping off Waiters at Work." *Deviant Behavior* 5: 47–69.

Henry, S. 1978. *The Hidden Economy: The Context and Control of Borderline Crime*. Oxford: Martin Robertson.

Hershatter, Gail. 1986. *The Workers of Tianjin, 1900–1949*. Stanford, CA: Stanford University Press.

Hoch, S.L. 1986. *Serfdom and Social Control in Russia: Petrovskoe, a Village in Tambov*. Chicago: University of Chicago Press.

Hollinger, R.C., and J.P. Clark. 1983. *Theft by Employees*. Lexington, MA: D.C. Heath and Company.

Horwitz, A.V. 1990. *The Logic of Social Control*. New York: Plenum Press.

Kanter, R.M. 1977. *Men and Women of the Corporation*. New York: Basic Books.

Leland, Mrs. W.C. 1966. *Master of Precision: Henry M. Leland*. Detroit: Wayne State University Press.

Mars, G. 1973. "Chance, Punters, and the Fiddle: Institutionalized Pilferage in a Hotel Dining Room." Pp. 200–210 in *The Sociology of the Workplace*, edited by Malcolm Warner. New York: Haldsted Press.

Mars, G. 1982. *Cheats at Work: An Anthropology of Workplace Crime*. London: George Allen and Unwin.

McCreery, D. 1993. "Hegemony and Repression in Rural Guatemala, 1871–1940." Pp. 217–239 in *Plantation Workers: Resistance and Accommodation*, edited by B.V. Lal, D. Munro, and E.D. Beechert. Honolulu: University of Hawaii Press.

Moore, C. 1993. "The Counterculture of Survival: Melanesians in the Mackay District of Queensland, 1865–1906." Pp. 69–99 in *Plantation Workers: Resistance and Accommodation* edited by B.V. Lal, D. Munro, and E.D. Beechert.

Morrill, C. 1989. "The Management of Managers: Disputing in an Executive Hierarchy." *Sociological Forum* 4: 387–407.

Morrill, C. 1992. "Vengeance Among Executives." Pp. 51–76 in *Virginia Review of Sociology*, Volume 1: *Law and Conflict Management*, edited by J. Tucker. Greenwich, CT: JAI Press Inc.

Morrill, C. 1995. *The Executive Way: Conflict Management in Corporations*. Chicago: University of Chicago Press.

Müller, H.-H. 1991. "Migrant Workers from East-Elbe and Eastern Europe in the Prussian 'Sugerbeet' Province of Saxony, 1830–1914." Pp. 77–91 in *Migrants in Agricultural Development: A Study of Intrarural Migration*, edited J.A. Mollet. New York: New York University Press.

Mullis, J. 1995. "Medical Malpractice, Social Structure, and Social Control." *Sociological Forum* 10: 135–163.

Munro, D. 1993. "Patterns of Resistance and Accommodation." Pp. 1–43 in *Plantation Workers: Resistance and Accommodation*, edited by B.V. Lal, D. Munro, and E.D. Beechert. Honolulu: University of Hawaii Press.

Munro, D., and S. Firth. 1993. "Samoan Plantations: The Gilbertese Laborers' Experience, 1867–1896." Pp. 101–127 in *Plantation Workers: Resistance and Accommodation*, edited by B.V. Lal, D. Munro, and E.D. Beechert. Honolulu: University of Hawaii Press.

Ong, A. 1987. *Spirits of Resistance and Capitalist Decline: Factory Women in Malaysia*. Albany, NY: State University of New York Press.

Ouchi, W. 1981. *Theory Z: How American Business Can Meet the Japanese Challenge*. New York: Addison-Wesley.

Pilcher, W.W. 1972. *The Portland Longshoremen: A Dispersed Community*. New York: Holt, Rinehart, and Winston.

Robin, G.D. 1969. "Employees as Offenders." *Journal of Research of Crime and Delinquency* 6: 17–33.

Rohlen, T.P. 1974. *For Harmony and Strength: Japanese White-Collar Organization in Anthropological Perspective*. Berkeley: University of California Press.

Roman, P. 1980. "Medicalization and Social Control in the Workplace: Prospects for the 1980s." *Journal of Applied Behavioral Science* 16: 407–423.

Roy, D. 1952. "Quota Restriction and Goldbricking in a Machine Shop." *American Journal of Sociology* 57: 427–442.

Scott, J.C. 1985. *Weapons of the Weak: Everyday Forms of Peasant Resistance*. New Haven, CT: Yale University Press.

Scott, J.C. 1986. "Everyday Forms of Peasant Resistance." *Journal of Peasant Studies* 13: 6.

Senechal de la Roche, R. 1996. "Collective Violence as Social Control." *Sociological Forum* 11: 971–928.

Senechal de la Roche, R. 1997. "The Sociogenesis of Lynching." Pp. 48–76 in *Under Sentence of Death: Lynching in the South*, edited by W.F. Brundage. Chapel Hill, NC: University of North Carolina Press.

Sutherland, E.H. 1949. *White Collar Crime*. New York: Dryden Press.

Terris, W., and J. Jones. 1982. "Psychological Factors Related to Employees' Theft in the Convenience Store Industry." *Psychological Reports* 51: 1219–1238.

Tobias, J.J. 1972. *Crime in Industrial Society in the Nineteenth Century*. Harmondsworth, U.K.: Penguin.

Tucker, J. 1989. "Employee Theft as Social Control." *Deviant Behavior* 10: 319–334.

Tucker, J. 1993. "Everyday Forms of Employee Resistance." *Sociological Forum* 8: 25–45.

Tucker, J. 1999. *The Therapeutic Corporation*. New York: Oxford University Press.

Tucker, J., and S. Ross. 2000. "Corporal Punishment and Black's Theory of Social Control." Forthcoming in *Corporal Punishment in Theoretical Perspective*, edited by M.J. Donnelly and M.A. Straus. New Haven, CT: Yale University Press.

Van Maanen, J. 1992. "Drinking our Troubles Away: Managing Conflict in a British Police Agency." Pp. 32–62 in *Hidden Conflict in Organizations: Uncovering Behind-the-Scenes Disputes*, edited by D.M. Kolb and J.M. Bartunek. Newbury Park, CA: Sage.

van Onselen, C. 1976. *Chibaro: African Mine Labour in Southern Rhodesia, 1900–1933*. Johannesburg: Raven Press.

Weiss, R.M. 1986. *Managerial Ideology and the Social Control of Deviance in Organizations*. New York: Praeger Publishers.

Wells, A., and G.M. Joseph. 1993. "Structure and Domination and Forms of Resistance on Yucatecan Estates During the Late Pofiriato, ca. 1880–1915." Pp. 241–296 in *Plantation Workers: Resistance and Accommodation*, edited by B.V. Lal, D. Munro, and E.D. Beechert. Honolulu: University of Hawaii Press.

Westin, A.F., and A.G. Feliu. 1988. *Resolving Employment Disputes without Litigation*. Washington, DC: Bureau of National Affairs.

Whyte, W.F. 1948. *Human Relations in the Restaurant Industry*. New York: McGraw-Hill.

DEFINING DEVIANCE UPWARD

THE SHRIMPERS' CONFLICT OVER TEDS REGULATIONS

A.V. Margavio and Shirley Laska

ABSTRACT

In 1989, shrimpers from Texas to North Carolina staged the largest protest of fishery regulations in U.S. history. Believing that the regulations mandating the use of turtle excluder devices threatened their livelihood, shrimpers initiated a resistance movement but were unsuccessful in altering their public image. Social construction theory is used to examine the way segments of the conservation and environmental movements orchestrated public opinion, redefined traditional marine harvesting, influenced government agencies to regulate shrimpers, and used science to legitimize their claims that shrimping threatened sea turtles and other marine stock. We explore the interests of the challenging groups and the failure of shrimpers to counter their own demonization.

In the summer of 1989, shrimpers blockaded strategic waterways in the Gulf of Mexico. They brought to a halt not only the nation's largest oil artery, the Houston

Research in the Sociology of Work, Volume 8, pages 17-37.

ISBN: 0-7623-0608-4

ship channel, but other waterways as well. They relented only after the government promised to lift the turtle excluder device (TEDs) regulations.[1] The largest protest of fishing regulations in U.S. history bought some time for the shrimpers, but by the summer of 1990 shrimpers found themselves facing criminal charges for violation of TEDs regulations.

Most readers will find it difficult to understand how a government regulation could have the effect that the TEDs regulation had on shrimpers. At first, we also found it difficult to fathom. What we have learned is that shrimpers actually believe that TEDs are a threat to their way of life. They are both afraid of and have contempt for TEDs. At the occasion of a government-sponsored demonstration of TEDs, one observer reported that shrimpers encircled it, stared at it, touched it and quickly withdrew as if it were a snake (personal interview, 1990). On another occasion, shrimpers torched the TED while a government official was demonstrating its proper use, which engendered no small amount of fear in the demonstrator. We ultimately came to the realization that shrimpers see TEDs as a symbol of everything wrong in the fishery.

The TEDs conflict, that is, the conflict over the incidental taking of sea turtles in shrimp trawls, began in the early 1970s when naturalists first raised concern over the plight of sea turtles and it continues up to the present. Since then, shrimpers and shrimping have been redefined. Virtue has become vice and a traditional occupation has taken on deviant overtones. By the late 1980s, the vision of shrimpers as marine harvesters and one of the last strongholds of traditional America, whether real or imagined, had given way to an image, in the eyes of many, of "greedy outlaws" on the high seas. In the process, shrimpers have had to redefine themselves.

How can we account for this transformation? One could argue that the case of shrimpers violating TEDs regulations is the product of conflict between urban middle class values and rural values (Sellin 1938). With the increasing complexity of society, there is a high probability that legislation will be enacted which reclassifies previously non-criminal behavior as crime (Rossi 1961, p. 236; Forsyth and Marckese 1993, pp. 20–21). Our focus is on the processes of redefinition. We view the problem from a social constructionist perspective to underscore how social movements redefine "reality" (Berger and Luckmann 1967; Lopata 1984; Smith 1997). We will argue that by the 1970s, two powerful interest groups of the upper middle class emerged to challenge commercial harvesters' historical claims over the "commons," America's marine resources. Recreational interests and a segment of the environmental movement composed of environmental lawyers with corporate ties applied legal and public opinion pressure on the government at all levels to curtail traditional harvesting practices. Numerous state and federal agencies, some willing some unwilling, became a part of the redefinition process. How and why this transformation took place and what effect it had on the public's conception of shrimpers, as well as their self definition, is the subject of our present effort.[2] A brief sketch of the conflict follows.

OVERVIEW OF THE TEDS CONFLICT

By the 1970s, offshore shrimpers took advantage of the new international agreement that created an economic zone out to 200 nautical miles from each nation's coastline. U.S. fishers harvested the marine resources in the "exclusive economic zone" free from the competition from the large Japanese, Russian, and other foreign trawlers. In addition, Congress passed the Magnuson Act in 1976 which directed the Department of Commerce to develop marine resources. Among other things, this entailed calling upon existing federal agencies to assist the fishing industry with technical and other forms of assistance. The Magnuson Act also created eight regional fisheries management councils to manage fisheries in a way consistent with scientific and conservation principles. The regional councils[3] were specifically mandated to take into account social and economic factors in managing fisheries. The peculiar political structure of the councils and the way that its members were selected almost insured that there would be conflict between user groups and particularly between recreational and commercial fishers (Durrenberger 1987). While the councils were never officially embroiled in the TEDs conflict, most parties to the conflict were influenced by the established procedures the councils used.

The councils recommend management plans to the Secretary of the Department of Commerce. The councils are mandated to use the best available biological, economic, and social data in making recommendations. When the needed data are non-existent, they request data from the National Marine Fisheries Service (NMFS). This agency's scientists gather the data the councils request and/or fund outside scientists directly or indirectly through government and industry foundations. Our general impression is that the scientists who advise the councils on the kind and quality of data that are necessary to inform the councils are frustrated by the lack of information and the quality of information made available. While adequate data is generally lacking, economic and social data are particularly inadequate or non-existent. Because the councils are mandated to take social and economic impacts into account in making recommendations to the Secretary of the Department of Commerce, the data deficiencies, particularly in social and economic factors, make the soundness of the councils' recommendations problematic. As a matter of course, the councils generate data wars among user groups. Frequently, the quality and objectivity of the work of scientists are in dispute; NMFS in-house scientists have been particularly singled out for criticism by user groups.

Theoretically, none of this should have impacted the TEDs issue, but in a practical sense, it is easy to see how the players in the TEDs conflict found it difficult to divorce themselves from the fisheries management thinking in which they were immersed. The TEDs conflict, while it arose out of a very different law (Endangered Species Act), followed a Magnuson Act fisheries management protocol.

The Endangered Species Act (ESA) (1973) provides the legal protection of endangered or threatened species. The teeth of the law is the provision that citizens can sue the federal government agency that endangers or permits others to endanger protected species. While the law does allow some Native American groups to take endangered species or compensates them for not harvesting them, the law otherwise strictly forbids the taking of endangered or threatened species. Beginning with the Kemps ridley, the most endangered sea turtle, five species of endangered or threatened sea turtles were listed for protection. The two primary agencies of the federal government that are responsible for listing, protecting, and recovering endangered species are Wildlife and Fisheries of the Department of the Interior and the National Marine Fisheries Service (NMFS) of the Department of Commerce. Through an in-house division of labor, the job of protecting sea turtles is the responsibility of NMFS (Reed and Drabelle 1984). Under the Magnuson Act, NMFS is also mandated to manage and regulate fisheries for the economic and social benefits of user groups.

From the beginning of the TEDs conflict, a certain level of confusion and misdirection exacerbated the conflict. To a certain extent, NMFS responded to the claims of environmentalists that shrimping endangered sea turtles according to a pattern followed in the tuna/dolphin dispute. The Marine Mammal Protection Act mandated protection of dolphins incidentally caught by tuna trawlers. The original response was to permit a certain number of takings. The analogy between the two cases is not perfect. Dolphins are attracted to the tuna nets and become hopelessly entangled; struggling to free themselves they eventually suffocate. By contrast, sea turtles are caught in shrimp trawls infrequently. How infrequently is part of the conflict. It is generally thought that the location, time of year, and depth to which the trawl is submerged are related to the probability that a trawl will encounter a turtle. The other question in dispute revolves around the issue of turtle strandings. The fact that large numbers of turtles wash ashore when shrimping effort is at its highest (spring) has resulted in attributing these kills to shrimp trawls. The fact that strandings do occur at other times of the year when there is very little shrimping effort has caused some observers to question that attribution. It is interesting to note that attributions of turtle mortality discussed in NMFS reports in the 1970s usually listed incidental kills in shrimp trawls at the bottom of a fairly long list that included beach development, rig removal, pollution, and the like. By the 1980s, reports generally listed shrimp trawls at the top.

In the early stages of the TEDs conflict, NMFS essentially asked the shrimping industry to cooperate in reducing the number of turtles incidentally caught in trawls. NMFS also published guidelines on how to resuscitate drowning turtles, because many turtles are alive when they are caught but are stressed and drowning. Despite these efforts and the curtailment of intentionally taking turtles for their meat, a common practice prior to protection, turtle strandings did not decrease. Furthermore, a number of environmental organizations were focusing on the effort or lack of effort by NMFS to protect sea turtles. Chief among them was the Center for Marine Conservation. This Washington-based environmental group accused NMFS of dragging its feet and threatened to use the citizen's suit provided for under ESA if NMFS failed to protect turtles.

Continuing its perceived responsibilities to provide "service to user groups" NMFS desperately wanted to solve the problem in a way that minimized economic harm to the shrimp fishery. It spearheaded gear research in the hopes that it could satisfy the increasing demands by environmentalists for NMFS to protect turtles, as well as head off the economic fallout on the shrimp industry.

After investing a considerable amount of money in TEDs development (NMFS claims it came to about two million dollars), NMFS settled on a technical solution based on a device shrimpers have used for a long time. At times shrimpers encounter shrimp concentrated in sea grass or large concentrations of unusable fish (bycatch). Under these circumstances, shrimpers used homemade devices that allowed grass or excessive bycatch to pass through an opening, while the shrimp are funneled into the bag. Of, course, numerous shrimp exited the trawl along with the unwanted portion of the catch. In other words, shrimpers know from experience that devices that eliminate unwanted portions of a catch lose shrimp. It would be fair to say that when NMFS developed its hard frame NMFS-TED, shrimpers were skeptical. Gear experts outside of NMFS who had tested the original device thought that the device was heavy and awkward and only worked under certain conditions. NMFS scientists responded by developing a smaller and lighter TED.[4] The gear experts we spoke with said that the "improved" NMFS-TED performed no better than the original NMFS-TED. NMFS was hoping that shrimpers would voluntarily adopt the use of TEDs and thereby ward off the impending collision between shrimpers and environmentalists.

Prior to this point, the TEDs conflict was essentially over the question of whether or not turtles are endangered by shrimping and what should be done if turtles are. Originally, the conflict involved shrimpers, environmentalists, and the federal agency that regulated shrimping, NMFS. It soon expanded, however, to include other issues and other groups. As soon as NMFS settled on their technical fix with which shrimpers were unimpressed, the efficacy of TEDs became part of the conflict. Since NMFS called on its sister agency, Sea Grant Extension, to educate shrimpers on how to use TEDs properly, that agency was pulled into the widening circle of contention.

Sea Grant Extension is analogous to the Extension Service run by the Department of Agriculture. Marine agents are like county agents in that they live in the communities in which they work and have teaching roles. They cannot express a strong pro-government stance and still have the confidence of their clients. NMFS was asking marine agents to "push" TEDs, as Sea Grant people saw it. Marine agents for the most part were not sold on TEDs. Some marine agents actually criticized the devices publicly. A rift between the two agencies became part of the expanding TEDs conflict.

During the period of the Voluntary Program, NMFS's people were so unpopular among shrimpers that while traveling, agents used unmarked cars. Fortunately, it was Sea Grant's marine agents and gear experts and not NMFS people who were to conduct workshops for the purpose of encouraging adoption of TEDs. The Program was a bitter disappointment. Shrimpers were not inclined to adopt the "new" technology that NMFS hoped would save them and themselves from the legal and political battle that environmentalists were waging. As the shrimpers saw it, TEDs are dangerous, they lose shrimp, and they don't work (White 1989). NMFS efforts only served to further widen the conflict.

A rift between two key agencies in fishery management was added to the conflict as well as a number of new issues. Do TEDs lose shrimp? How much? Which TEDs are best? NMFS was forced to defend its technical fix for shrimpers' woes. To be sure, there were glimmers of hope for a peaceful compromise. NMFS's parent organization, the National Oceanic and Atmospheric Administration (NOAA) managed to get both industry leaders and environmentalists to agree to negotiation sessions after the Texas Shrimp Association requested mediation. The grassroots shrimper organization, Concerned Shrimpers of America, through its president, Tee John Mialjevich, was also represented at these mediation meetings.

Four mediation meetings were held in 1986 to stem off the mandatory imposition of TEDs. In New Orleans, Jekyll Island Georgia, Houston, and Washington, DC, mediation between representatives of environmental groups and industry leaders tried to map out a compromise (Conner 1987). Hopes were running high that an agreement could be reached. The shrimpers were hoping for what they believed was a reasonable solution. They were arguing for linking TED use to turtle concentration. While turtle migrations are still poorly understood, it is commonly accepted that turtles are more frequently encountered at certain times, places, and depths. Therefore, the shrimpers were hoping that an agreement could be reached that would require only a limited use of TEDs.

BACKGROUND AND THE ROAD TO DEVIANCE

In order to understand the predicament that shrimpers faced during the conflict, we must describe shrimpers and shrimping prior to World War II. The traditional harvester fished the shallow bays and coastal waters from North Carolina to Texas, but only near their own home port. In largely wooden vessels, they pursued white shrimp (Penaeus setiferous). They remained away from their home port typically only a few days on any one trip. While strategies of harvesting differed from one place to another, their occupation was always seasonal and rarely caused major disruptions in family life. Particularly in Louisiana, shrimping was wedded to the local culture. Shrimping is what most coastal residents did. Young boys accompanied their fathers or uncles on shrimping trips in the summer months when school was out of session. As the apprentice grew in stature and skill, the desire to shrimp prompted the majority to quit school and adopt the life of their fathers. Consequently, the majority of full-time shrimpers have not much more than a grade-school education. While this pattern was common all across the South Atlantic and Gulf, it was particularly characteristic of Cajun Louisiana where shrimping had become preeminently a way of life. What may be most unique about Cajun shrimpers is that their shrimping effort is almost always with family members. By contrast, Maril (1983, p. 41) describes the Texas shrimper as almost incapable of shrimping with relatives.

The pace of harvesting changed after WW II (Klima 1989). Larger, steel-hulled vessels were introduced. Marine radios and gear modifications including rigging that allowed the use of two and even four trawls were eventually introduced. In pursuit of not only the white shrimp that can be taken near the coasts, shrimpers ventured farther to harvest the pink shrimp (Penaeus duorarum) off the south of Florida and more importantly, the brown shrimp (Penaeous aztecus) in the southern Gulf. Equipped with refrigeration and electronic navigational gear, the offshore shrimper, regardless of their home port, make the run from the Tortugas of South Florida to harvest the pinks and pursue the browns in the deeper waters off Louisiana, Texas, and Mexico.

Offshore oil development after WW II also had impacts on the shrimping effort of Louisiana and Texas shrimpers. Oil work supplied some of the capital that made the move to larger vessels possible. Offshore oil jobs were easy to get and the pay was good. Workers could quit their jobs during the shrimp season and find another at season's end. A kind of symbiotic relationship developed between oil work and shrimping (Margavio and Forsyth 1996, pp. 23–27). But offshore oil work also brought changes to the coasts of Texas and Louisiana.

Particularly in Louisiana and parts of the Texas coast, the historically small communities grew rapidly from the influx of capital and outsiders. With the increase in wealth and population, traditional values began to change. As one lifelong resident of Isle de Jean Charles remarked, "before they built this road, my wife would shop once or twice a year. Now, she has to go to town once or twice a week." Like so many of Louisiana's coastal communities, Isle de Jean Charles was once accessible by water only. The growth and progress occasioned by oil exploration not only increased the number of waterways and roads, it altered traditional values. The story of how progress changes traditions is too well known to recount it here. We will, however, underscore a few important points.

With progress, traditional work is retained as a pastime. Oil field workers who bought new unheard-of luxuries "on time," could always return to the open sea as a pastime or recreational activity or to pay off what was owed on a large purchase. This is important for two reasons. First, skills once learned were not lost, and if the oil worker needed to, he could always return to harvesting. Second, the view that harvesting is a pastime played well to an increasing number of urbanites descending on the coasts to hunt and fish.

Considering the first point, our research showed that in the 1980s during the oil bust, unemployed oil workers returned to shrimping. Furthermore, a very large number of part-time shrimpers entered the fishery, chiefly from urban areas. The "weekend warriors," as they are known by full-time commercial fishers, presented a difficult obstacle for commercial harvesters intent on solving the problem of over harvesting. Commercial harvesters were unwilling to support initiatives that would exclude people who had entered the fishery as subsistence harvesters and relatives and friends who were augmenting their incomes.

In the 1980s, full-time commercial harvesters were facing stiff competition at home and even stiffer competition from abroad. Imported shrimp, largely farm-raised, had steadily increased throughout this period and represented more than 70 percent of U.S. consumption at the end of the decade. As commercial harvesters tried to deal with their economic woes by redoubling their effort, they were being challenged on the local and regional front by a recreational fishing lobby.

It is useful to draw a distinction between interests and interest groups. There are numerous interests in redefining marine resources. Land developers are keen on waterfront properties, hotels, and motels near water amenities. Marinas and other leisure-based enterprises blossom in developments near water. For these developments to succeed, people must be attracted to the coasts by the water amenities. Louisiana and Texas do not have the attractive blue water and white sand of Florida, but what they do have is an abundance of wildlife and fish. Understandably, the push for a leisure/tourist use of the coasts of Louisiana and Texas was spearheaded by recreational fishing interests.

The effort of the sportfishing lobby on behalf of recreational and development interests is part of the larger picture that links development with fishery regulations. Sinclair (1988) has described the impact of Canadian policy as having a negative impact on sustaining fishing communities in Newfoundland. Similarly, Orbach and Johnson (1988) have argued that the State of Florida's development policy has routed commercial harvesters in some coastal communities. Bailey (1988) has described how Indonesia's policy to develop an aquaculture industry has undermined the way of life of traditional fishers.

The general pattern that local development takes has been described by Logan and Molotch (1987) as the "growth machine." In their examination of urban growth, the structural components of the "growth machine" rest on a working arrangement among speculators, local elites, and politicians. The partnership among all three is essential for "growth" to be hawked to the public. While personal economic and political fortunes are the underlying reasons for the push for "growth," the public is persuaded to back the plan for the common good.

The Gulf Coast Conservation Association (GCS) was initiated by several wealthy Texans who met in a Houston sporting goods store in 1977 (Margavio and Forsyth 1996, pp. 80–81). In addition to their abiding interests in conservation, they shared interests in land development, resorts, marinas, and yacht sales. One of the organizers of the GCCA is Walter Fondren Jr., whose father founded

Humble Oil. Fondren also initiated "Ducks Unlimited" and served as Chairman of the Gulf of Mexico Fisheries and Management Council. Perry Bass of the Texas banking family was also one of the original organizers of GCCA.

In the 1980s, GCCA was challenging commercial harvesters in two ways. First, GCCA was attempting to get red drum and speckled trout, two important commercially harvested finfish, classified as game (recreational) fish. The reclassification of these species was not successful. However, a commercial moratorium on red drum in 1988 did impact those shrimpers with small to medium-sized vessels who depended on harvesting red drum to supplement their shrimping. More importantly, GCCA continued to press the bycatch issue. Working through the councils and state legislatures, the GCCA and similar local groups of recreational fishers pressed the issue. Trawls, from their point of view, are wasteful in that they catch other marine organisms (bycatch) besides the targeted species. One fish that is frequently caught in shrimp trawls is the red snapper, a highly prized species by commercial and recreational harvesters. Since the stock of red snapper had declined, GCCA could argue that shrimp trawls were to blame. Trawls should be, in their view at least, modified to exclude finfish as well as turtles.[2] In reality, the TEDs conflict included not only the obvious challenge from environmental groups, but the background conflict between commercial harvesters and a sportfishing lobby. Rather than address these separately, we choose to underscore their similarities in the redefinition process.

VIRTUE AND VICE: MAKING THE NORM ABNORMAL

Following the formula that Logan and Molotch (1987) used to examine urban growth, the chief components of the effort used by the sportfishing lobby and environmental groups that challenged shrimping are: disguising interests, creating a partnership with elites, capturing politicians and government agencies, endowing the "new" use with virtue and selling it to the public, and legitimizing these actions by employing the magic of science.

It was obvious to the people we interviewed why the sportfishing lobby both from an economic standpoint (investments in the leisure industry) and lifestyle interests challenged commercial harvesters. We, of course, are not saying that the sportfishing lobby's professed commitment to conservation is inauthentic. What we are saying is that the virtue of being a conservationist partially conceals actions based on self interests. We are suggesting no more than an unmasking which is the work of sociology. But if the sportfishing lobby can use the high moral ground of conservation to conceal other motives, what can be said for "saving the turtle"? What are the interests behind the crusade the environmentalists launched? Most shrimpers simply could not fathom the middle-class propensity to fight for a "holy cause."

Some leaders of shrimping associations truly believed that a sinister motive was behind the "turtle problem." Essentially, their theory was that Washington, DC-based environmental groups are tied to corporate polluters who are interested in dumping in the Gulf, and that commercial harvesters, who successfully fought them in the past, are in their way (Bailey and Faupel 1989). As the theory goes, corporations are funding the challenge from environmentalists, who knowingly or unknowingly are making it easy for corporate polluters to dump in the Gulf. We found very little evidence that the rank and file shrimpers knew about, much less believed, this scenario. A consideration of this issue is beyond the scope of our present effort, but we have dealt with it elsewhere (Margavio and Forsyth 1996).

Protecting turtles was a well thought out strategy by the Center for Marine Conservation. Apart from the obvious—a genuine concern for the fate of sea turtles—why champion the cause? What interests are being served? The Weber-Michels thesis suggests that the answer is organizational maintenance (Zald and Ash 1966). The personal and collective empowerment is a sufficient cause under the mask of a noble cause. But, the corporations that fund and support such marketable crusades must have an interest, too, beyond making a contribution to a laudable goal. It is a tenable hypothesis that the corporations who have funded and hold directorships on environmental groups like the Center for Marine Conservation do so for public relations purposes. One could say that the dirtier the image, the greater the need to cleanse.

CONNECTING WITH ELITES

In our research we encountered elites largely indirectly. We had neither the time nor the resources to interview the most prominent representatives of the sportfishing lobby and turtle protection crusade. When we attempted to do so, we generally got refusals. Our impressions, therefore, derive from encounters with what could be called the "untouchable" attitude. They are expressed as background assumptions that "things are what we say they are." The state of mind we encountered is best described as a supreme confidence that things will progress as planned coupled with a bit of peevishness when the hoi polloi or politicians resist. Perhaps an example or two would clarify our point. When we were notified that we had received funding from NOAA to do a study of the TEDs conflict, we were introduced to this attitude. One of the prominent members in the sportfishing lobby in Louisiana expressed amazement and anger that he was not informed by NOAA. Apparently, because of the potential for violence surrounding the TEDs conflict and a sense of urgency, routine routing of our grant application was streamlined. Another example will further clarify our meaning.

Our book publisher called one morning to discuss how she might respond to a telephone call from one of the lead scientists working for the Center of Marine Conservation. The biologist who called expressed no small amount of irritation because she had learned belatedly that Texas A&M Press was publishing a book on endangered species and the Center was not informed. After correcting her perceptions about the nature of the book, the good doctor from the Center complained that no one had discussed this with the Center. It was only after our publisher corresponded and informed the anxious scientist that the authors had conducted several interviews with their lead environmentalists at the time were the scientist's fears assuaged. Connected with elites, the sportfishing lobby and the turtle protection cause set aim on the apparatus of the state.

CAPTURING THE STATE AND STATE AGENCIES

State transformation theory suggests, among other things, that a dialectical relationship exists between the state and societal factors (Quadagno 1992). What is of particular relevance to our study is the link that Quadagno makes between state agencies' autonomy from the goals of social movements and their permeability to social movements' demands (Quadagno 1992, pp. 630–632). In Quadagno's analysis of the contrasting responses of the Department of Justice and the Department of Labor to the demands of the Civil Rights movement, we see a parallel in the TEDs case.

At the federal level, NMFS was fairly insulated from the goals of the environmental movement when the TEDs issue emerged in the late 1970s. For the most part, NMFS had established a comfortable working relationship with the industry it regulated, not unlike the working relationship between the Department of Labor and craft unions. In contrast, Wildlife and Fisheries historically "served" recreational and conservation groups. Its history reveals a somewhat more aggressive attitude toward protecting species. It had no long-standing relationship with commercial harvesting groups. However, a transformation of NMFS took place, slowly at first. Apart from the obvious—that the agency, in responding to outside criticism as in the TEDs case and also criticism from within, particularly from its parent agency—began to allocate more of its resources to the species protection functions. Its regulatory functions were strengthened to some extent by diminishing its service functions. Increasing conflict among commercial user groups and a realignment of missions between Extension Service and NMFS contributed to interagency conflict (Helfrich and Griswold 1991; Becker 1973).

After the acute phase of the TEDs conflict, the lead spokesman for the Center for Marine Conservation occupied a position at the national office of NMFS. Even though he served for a short period of time, his appointment betokens a real transformation of NMFS. As state transformation theory argues, social movements are not just co-opted by the state, they can evoke real change (Quadagno 1992, p. 630).

Prior to the TEDs conflict, a sportfishing lobby was contributing to changes in the way fisheries management was conducted by influencing state agencies. The regional management councils are in effect a political balancing act between recreational and commercial users. Typically with equal numbers of commercial and recreational user groups represented on the councils, recommendations are highly charged compromises. Because state interests are represented in the membership formula used, the councils can be shifted to either a recreational or commercial lean depending on the stances of the individuals serving on behalf of the states. The penetration of the sportfishing movement into state agencies has been quick and dramatic. One of the most "commercial harvesters-friendly" state agencies, Louisiana's Wildlife and Fisheries, has experienced a refocus from one protective of commercial harvesters to one that is responsive to the recreational lobby. This process of change took place largely after Louisiana had elected the reform governor "Buddy" Roemer. Old line appointees under previous Governor Edwin Edwards were replaced with outsiders. Some of the appointees in the most important agencies dealing with the environment were not native Louisianians. Even after former Governor Edwards returned to office and returned some of the personnel who were more sympathetic to commercial harvesters, the penetration into the State Legislature by the sportfishing lobby had progressed past the point of no return. Our impression is that the political hegemony of the sportfishing lobby took place a bit earlier in the other Gulf and South Atlantic states affected by the TEDs ruling. Most likely this was caused by the earlier identification in those states of sportfishing and coastal development as an important niche of their economy. In any event, capturing government agencies is required in winning the public relations war against commercial harvesters.

PUBLIC RELATIONS AND REDEFINITION

As one marine agent we interviewed reported, "these people (sportfishing lobby) have money and leisure to pursue their objectives" (Louisiana marine agent 1990). The same is true for the environmental groups that pushed turtle protection. It is necessary to unmask the euphemism, public relations. Whether we call it spin or public relations does not change the fundamental reality that it is, after all, propaganda. In effect, all propaganda is distortion, whether it simply involves putting one's best face on or resorting to blatant lies. If images count more than substance in our contemporary democracy than the worst fears of DeTocqueville have been realized. "Shrimpers are turtle killers" and "trawling is a selfish act of wastefulness." To repeat the charges often enough has the same effect as a TV commercial repeated until it becomes a habit of memory. It's no accident that so many viewers overlook brand X.

The movements that challenged the status quo over marine resources were able to use their allies and sympathizers in the mass media. The advantage of speaking and, therefore, being quoted while using polished prose or having the services of those who can, is a necessary resource of social movement organizations. To be able to link one's objectives to the public good is a craft at which commercial harvesters are not adept. When confronted with these attacks, shrimpers more often than not simply got mad and cursed their accusers. All of which simply confirmed in the minds of the public the image the shrimpers' accusers desired.

If a picture is worth a thousand words, one only need to have TV cameras focused on thousands of dead fish (bycatch) in a trawl. Such a scene was staged for the media by the Audubon Society in its contribution to the "truth" about shrimping. One can only imagine what public reaction is evoked by scores of stranded sea turtles on a beach. But in all the staged media events of sight and sound, none approaches a coloring book aimed at future supporters of the turtle cause. A grisly Cajun alligator aboard a shrimping vessel heartlessly killing baby turtles sends an unambiguous message to a youthful public. Using these ploys and others like it, the phrase "redefinition of shrimping" seems less than adequate to capture the reality. Demonization and criminalization are perhaps more appropriate.

LEGITIMIZING THROUGH THE MAGIC OF SCIENCE

The shrimpers believed that science would vindicate their claims that (1) trawling did not endanger sea turtles and (2) that TEDs did lose shrimp. The data that NMFS compiled to estimate turtle mortality from trawling required the cooperation of shrimpers. Shrimpers voluntarily allowed observers on board during trawling so that turtle identification and counts could be estimated for the Gulf and South Atlantic. For their part, shrimpers were willing to do so because they believed that the data would show that the actual number of turtles incidentally killed by trawls was very low except for the Cape Canaveral area off the central east coast of Florida, where seasonally large concentrations of turtles can be found. It was a surprise to shrimpers when NMFS compiled the samples multiplied by estimates of shrimping effort and extrapolated the total to be more than 40,000 each year (Henwood and Stuntz 1987). Immediately shrimpers challenged the findings and their allies in Congress got the necessary support and funding to have the National Academy of Sciences study the dispute and hopefully settle it.

The Academy's findings were published in 1990 after the regulations requiring TEDs were a fait accompli. The Academy's conclusions were that even a greater number of turtles than NMFS's projections are killed each year in trawls (National Academy of Science 1990). Another study shrimpers were successful in getting conducted, the National Observer Program, did find significant levels of shrimp lost in trawls equipped with TEDs (Renaud et al. 1990).

It is doubtful, at this point in the conflict, that any of the combatants were able to find the "truth." Shrimpers wanted vindication for their point of view. NMFS had managed to link its credibility to the efficacy of TEDs.

Environmentalists were unprepared to concede restricting TEDs to turtle-rich waters (personal interviews, 1990 and 1994). Furthermore, the fact that many environmental challenges are based more on faith than science has been amply documented (Fumento 1993). In short, none of the parties to the conflict were in a position to accept the tentativeness of science. What they wanted was certainty. What they got was something closer to magic than science. By magic we mean that a social judgment was rendered that constructed reality.

To be certain, there is nothing magical about elites being well connected in government circles. The Center for Marine Conservation worked very hard on the turtle cause including cultivating close ties with the Academy on its study of turtle mortality. And there is nothing magical about discrediting scientists whose opinions or findings are inconsistent with the "team." One "non-team" player, Professor Frank Schwartz, a turtle expert at the University of North Carolina, Chapel Hill, was asked by NMFS to review the Academy's report. In nine pages of comment he tore it to pieces. "I find the report lacking, full of assumptions, lacking substantiating data, firmly prejudiced that shrimp trawling is the causal agent for sea turtle mortality, and that TEDs are the solution." Of course, if one wants consensus, one should never include participants like Professor Schwartz. It is sufficient to cordially ask for impute to demonstrate one's catholicity and then summarily ignore the cacophonous opinion. There is nothing magical about the processes of power and influence, but what is like magic is that once committees of scientists boldly proclaim the "truth," the proclamation becomes reality.

It is a familiar enough process wherein a gathering of scientists are asked to make a scientific statement about phenomena that is intended to settle a dispute. The resultant consensus rests on social judgments. The social and political influences that form the bases for their judgment are not always easy to discern. Nonetheless, the outcome is a declaration of "truth." What was uncertain is now certain. What was unknown is now known. This magic is particularly apparent whenever scientists are asked to evaluate existing studies and render a collective decision as in the case of the Academy's report on turtle mortality. Examples abound of similar constructions of reality. The American Psychiatric Association declares a previously accepted mental disorder (homosexuality) to be normal. Similarly, children who in the past were merely more active than most children are presently declared to be mentally disordered and are medicated (Cockerham 1996). Likewise, a social judgment is rendered when a committee of scientists declare drug X is safe. In all cases, science is confused with policy and social judgments become as important as scientific facts in coming to a decision. Reality is magically transformed. Thus, the old reality of what shrimpers and shrimping was gave way to the new definitions, but not without a fight.

THE SHRIMPERS RESPONSE AND SEARCH FOR REDEMPTION

During the challenges from the sportfishing lobby and the turtle protection push, shrimpers responded in ways that surprised and angered many. The highly emotional language shrimpers used to express their anger played into the hands of their challengers. But, despite the rhetoric of individual shrimpers, the collective response to the challenges was to work through industry leaders with NMFS to forge a compromise. What began as a rather typical industry response to new government regulations at the beginning of 1980s grew into an unprecedented challenge of fishing regulations by the end of the decade.

WORKING WITH INDUSTRY LEADERS AND GOVERNMENT AGENCIES

While every little bay and coastal hamlet has an association of commercial harvesters, The Texas Shrimp Association (TSA) came to be synonymous with the shrimp industry in the minds of government officials. Despite the fact that it represented processors, wholesalers, and other segments of the industry besides offshore shrimpers, NMFS had no choice but to work with TSA as the only legitimate representative of shrimpers. This, in time, would prove to be disastrous, but for the moment, NMFS and TSA worked on possible solutions to the incidental taking. A variety of solutions grew out of the cooperation between TSA and NMFS. For example, reducing the time the trawl is towed increases the survival chances of turtles caught in trawls. However, this solution did not meet the protection levels environmentalists demanded. With continuing evidence of turtle strandings, environmentalists demanded speedy action and accused NMFS of dragging its feet. Shrimpers continued to argue that trawling does not endanger turtles. Under the threat of lawsuits, NMFS hastened its gear research. The TED was the fruit of that research. Convinced of the efficacy of TEDs, NMFS's challenge was to convince shrimpers that it was in their best interest to adopt the device. However, shrimpers remained unconvinced of the necessity of using TEDs. While individual shrimpers were angrily resisting TEDs, Concerned Shrimpers of America was mounting political and legal counter-challenges to TEDs.

Using their political allies at the state and national levels, shrimpers were successful in getting favorable changes in the Magnuson Act, where stronger language was written requiring that social and economic costs be considered before regulations could be mandated. Similarly, politicians from shrimping states were able to hold up reauthorization of the Endangered Species Act also. The political allies of shrimpers tried to get shrimpers some relief from the competition from imported shrimp by requiring importers to demonstrate that the imported shrimp were harvested with TED-equipped trawls. One of the most impressive political maneuvers was to mobilize the Louisiana government to resist TEDs.

It made good sense for Louisiana to back its shrimpers during the TEDs conflict. Along with oil, shrimping is a major resource in coastal Louisiana. A very large number of families are connected directly and indirectly to shrimping. Furthermore, the TEDs conflict came at the time Louisiana's oil patch was shrinking. Prompted, understandably, by the potential economic and political fallout from TEDs, Louisiana passed an anti-TEDs law forbidding the use of TEDs in State waters. Louisiana's Attorney General filed suit to block TEDs use in federal waters. The Fifth Circuit Court of Appeals, however, ruled against the shrimpers and Louisiana. The political astuteness that shrimpers exhibited through these actions annoyed some of the leaders for the turtle cause as well as some of the elites in the sportfishing lobby.

Apart from the deviant actions of individual shrimpers, as a group, shrimpers primarily used the institutional avenues available to them. But, with the exhaustion of all the institutional forms of redress, shrimpers faced mandatory TEDs. Their situation, as they saw it, was desperate.

FROM INDIVIDUAL TO COLLECTIVE ACTS OF DEVIANCE

As the day of reckoning approached in 1989, shrimpers were successful in getting several postponements of mandatory TEDs, but they could not prevent the inevitable. In a curious mixture of spontaneity and choreographics, hundreds of large shrimping vessels pulled in their trawls and steamed toward the coast. At Aransas, Texas three passes were blockaded. Above Galveston leading to the Houston ship channel an excited Coast Guard radar operator, seeing more than 400 vessels converging on the ship channel, yelled, "What the hell is going on?" For 36 hours, shrimp vessels tied up the most important oil depot in the United States. Three or four vessels deep, they anchored side by side. Hundreds of smaller vessels that were unable to participate in the blockade came to add their moral support. Against water cannons from the Coast Guard and tidal changes, the shrimpers held their formation. Some guardsmen cut anchor lines, and vessels were set adrift dangerously in the stiff current. The untethered vessels resumed their positions in the formation. What started out as a plan to show solidarity by parading vessels along some busy navigational channels turned into an illegal blockade.

Because the Coast Guard was prosecuting participants, we were never sure we could get candid responses from the shrimpers about their participation. The plan we describe here is based partly on eyewitnesses and partly on our inferences. We found it hard to believe that the shrimpers had planned merely a parade of vessels. They did, however, acquire the necessary permits to do so. We think it more likely that their idea of a fleet parade was an enormous bottleneck of vessels intended to give the government a hard time. In any event, the general plan was that when the signal was given, shrimpers were to pull up their trawls and head for the nearest pass. Some shrimpers were assigned land positions near the affected passes to coordinate participation. Several were near the Houston ship channel. Others were to coordinate the "show" at Aransas. One shrimper coordinated the blockade at Grande Isle, Louisiana and dealt with the press. Originally, he was to coordinate things at Galveston, but the Texas shrimpers jumped the gun and there was some concern that the Louisiana shrimpers would not be ready (personal interview, 1990).

While the collective effort of shrimpers to protest on such a massive scale was impressive, the press they received was negative. Not surprisingly, they subsequently picketed the main office of the *Times Picayune* newspaper in New Orleans to protest the coverage.

The organization that was given credit or discredit, depending on one's point of view, for pulling off an unprecedented protest of fishery regulations was the Concerned Shrimpers of America (CSA). CSA was the organized expression of the collective determination of shrimpers to resist TEDs. It was formed by an extraordinary man in an extraordinary way. During the period when NMFS was encouraging shrimpers to adopt TEDs with the help of Extension Service, numerous workshops were held in coastal communities from North Carolina to Texas. Tee John Mialjevich, a Louisiana shrimper and the son of a Louisiana shrimper whose roots stretch to the Dalmatian coast, took advantage of the workshops to initiate CSA. In what was a tour de force, Tee John asked permission to speak to the shrimpers at the end of each workshop. After government officials completed their session on TEDs, Tee John would take the floor and tell the shrimpers why they should join with him to resist TEDs. All the logistical problems facing a movement with a base spread across hundreds of coastal villages was solved by taking advantage of the largesse of the United States government. Quickly, the movement spread and so did the reputation of Tee John. He was called the "Jesus of the shrimpers." Some government officials complained, "We had the shrimpers ready to accept TEDs until Tee John and his Louisiana gang stirred them up." One environmentalist mused about the demagoguery of Tee John and how Louisiana shrimpers are so eager to follow the Huey Long types.

Concerned shrimpers created local chapters in fishing villages from North Carolina to Texas. Tee John did not, however, attempt to supplant the existing shrimping associations. The old organizations were not challenged, they were utilized in building a CSA base. Shortly after he launched the CSA, Tee John had the assistance from some of the most capable officeholders from the older organizations. To understand how Tee John managed to recruit so many diverse individuals into a new organization of "people who shrimp for a living," one has to see him.

He is a big man, rather rotund, with a baby face reminiscent of Jackie Gleason. His dark eyeglasses are held safely to his face by a black eyeglass guard. He is good-natured and quick to laugh and even quicker to speak. His voice seems a bit too high-pitched for a man of his size. But he is a powerful speaker, hard-hitting and tough, but can sprout a sentiment that is both genuine and touching.

At one CSA meeting at which Tee John had scheduled speakers as he served as MC, he revealed the breadth of his ability to speak and to lead. In one breath, he confessed his personal limitations and in the next breath, he moved the audience to ear-breaking applause. He talked down a score of angry shrimpers who began to heckle a NMFS official. In the next moment he led the shrimpers in solemn prayer.

Tee John outlined seven goals of CSA at the public meeting held March 24, 1990 in Thibodeaux, Louisiana. He said, we must: "end TEDs, do something about the bycatch issue, stop the practice of foreign shrimp being sold as domestic shrimp, launch a grassroots ladies' auxiliary to coordinate pressure on Congress, find a way to finance CSA and add to its membership, launch a Concerned Shrimpers' magazine, and use nonviolent action similar to the civil rights movement to protest unjust laws and regulations."

In his parting words, he spelled out the strategy that the shrimpers were to follow. The blockades of 1989 didn't prevent mandatory TEDs and Tee John made it clear the shrimpers were not even going to try to change the TEDs regulations. He cautioned the shrimpers about how best to use nonviolent disobedience. "Don't turn a civil offense into a criminal offense. Be nice." He quickly added, "Do what you got to do to make a living. This is America. Be nice to the Coast Guard and take the ticket." Tee John told the gathering that an administrative judge said that shrimpers could simply refuse to pay the fine for not using TEDs ($8,000). He ended his instructions by saying, "They cannot take your boat over a civil fine. Put your foot down."

Despite the Coast Guard's claim in the spring of 1990 that compliance was over 90 percent, shrimpers at least in the central Gulf region had followed Tee John's lead. They simply refused to use TEDs. In an unprecedented move in fishery regulation history, NMFS "went criminal." In July 1990, criminal charges were levied at violators and the Coast Guard and NMFS enforcement units could confiscate gear, shrimp catch, and the vessel. Shortly thereafter, shrimpers were evading the regulations by using TEDs with the turtle escape opening sewn shut. In the ensuing seasons, despite high compliance levels, large turtle strandings prompted tougher measures. NMFs officials argued that improper rigging of TEDs was the cause. The agency threatened to shut down the industry if turtle mortality could not be reduced. It was clear to most shrimpers that the end game had commenced and that they faced a difficult and uncertain future.

In 1992, CSA disbanded, and even though Tee John tried to remain optimistic and talked about organizing shrimpers internationally, he was, at least for a while, a beaten man. He has quit shrimping and makes his living onshore. For a while his closest friends feared he would not recover from defeat. Just as Tee John was forced to come to grips with the new "reality," the shrimpers who had participated in the resistance effort had to re-evaluate themselves.

Although the majority of shrimpers we interviewed thought the protest helped their overall cause, there was a good deal of ambiguity in the way they felt about themselves after the protest. To be sure, there were those who from the beginning distanced themselves from the "lawbreakers." Some would say that the "hot heads" took over. But the majority felt that "something had to be done." In an attempt to justify their actions to themselves, shrimpers spoke of the protest as a hated thing that they would rather not have done. The act of blockading genuinely bothered them because the act did not square with their self image. They had not developed the ideology necessary to justify civil disobedience. They could not, as a group, sustain the civil rights movement type ideology. Perhaps, it is too much to expect from traditional harvesters who find in harvesting freedom and independence.

In half of a decade, the sportfishing lobby and the cause to protect turtles had redefined commercial harvesting and harvesters. Working through government agencies at all levels, they successfully demonized and criminalized shrimpers. While mounting an impressive counter-challenge, shrimpers were unable to escape government regulations or turn the tide of public opinion against them. In the process, a whole industry has been pushed closer to the margins of the American economy. While once harvesting the sea was seen as a virtuous way of life, it is now deemed to be in need of redemption.

ACKNOWLEDGMENT

This research was supported by the University of New Orleans Environmental Social Science Research Institute and the National Oceanic and Atmospheric Administration Office of Sea Grant, Department of Commerce, under grant No.NA85AA-D-SG141. The University of New Orleans Sea Grant activities are a part of the Louisiana Sea Grant Program which is administered by Louisiana State University.

NOTES

1. Essentially a TED is a device that is attached to a shrimp trawl that allows turtles to escape. Depending on the kind of TED, it is a rigid metal frame or soft webbing; the escape opening may be at the top or at the bottom (Watson, Mitchell, and Shah 1986). The principle is to incorporate a barrier to prevent turtles from entering the bag at the base of the trawl where shrimp are collected when trawling and provide an opening for turtles to escape. The fact that the devices would lose some shrimp, particularly when trash or grass would prevent the escape opening from closing was well known to shrimpers. We choose to call the device a turtle excluder. Some government officials argue that TED stands for trawl efficiency device. The original NMFS TED was designed to exclude fish and the name first proposed was FED. The government officials we spoke to believed that the name FED would have made it difficult for NMFS to put a good spin on the device. Fish excluder devices are now being

imposed on shrimpers in federal waters (three miles off the coast); however, government officials insist on calling them bycatch reduction devices, BRDS, pronounced "birds."

2. We have used a variety of methodological strategies. We developed an interview schedule which included background information, employment history, as well as attitudes about fishing regulations in general and TEDs in particular. We randomly sampled Louisiana shrimpers and augmented this sample with a non-random sample of shrimpers from Texas, Florida, Georgia, and the Carolinas. In all, 67 shrimpers were interviewed. In addition, we interviewed scores of other shrimpers on selected aspects of the TEDs conflict, such as details about the blockade and encounters with law enforcement officials. Since we wanted to study the "big picture," we sought out a variety of informants including government agency officials (state agencies as well as NOAA, NMFS, Sea Grant at regional and national levels), elected officials at all levels, environmentalists, conservationists, shrimpers in leadership positions, shrimp wholesalers and processes, and scientists. Our intentions were to talk to all categories of participants involved in the TEDs conflict, both partisans and those that defined themselves as "neutrals." Finally, we examined a variety of documents, including scientific reports, laws, court proceedings, newletters, newspaper articles, and personal letters. We attended a variety of public hearings and meetings, and we were priveleged to be invited to some executive meetings of the CSA and to serve on a committee of the Gulf of Mexico Fisheries and Managment Council.

3. Our remarks on the functioning of the regional councils are based on conversations with individuals who presently serve or have served on the Gulf of Mexico Fisheries and Management Council and our own experiences serving on advisory panels to the Council.

4. Interestingly, NMFS did design their TED to exclude finfish as well as turtles. The hope was that this would be a selling point for the device. If one reduces the overall unwanted catch, the weight of a trawl (drag) is reduced and a gas savings is realized.

REFERENCES

Bailey, C. 1988. "The Political Economy of Fisheries Development in the Third World." *Agriculture & Human Values* 5: 35–48.

Bailey, C., and C.E. Faupel. 1989. "Out of Sight is Not Out of Mind: Public Opposition to Ocean Incineration." *Coastal Management* 17: 89–102.

Becker, H.S. 1973. *Outsiders: Studies in the Sociology of Deviance*. New York: Free Press.

Berger, P.L., and T. Luckmann. 1967. *The Social Construction of Reality*. Garden City, NY: Doubleday, Anchor Books.

Cockerham, W.C. 1996. *Sociology of Mental Disorder*. Upper Saddle River, NJ: Prentice-Hall.

Conner, D.K. 1987. "Turtles, Trawlers, and TEDs: What Happens When the Endangered Species Act Conflicts with Fishermen's Interests." *Water Log: A Legal Reporter of the Mississippi-Alabama Sea Grant Consortium* 7: 3–35.

Durrenberger, E.P. 1987. "Shrimpers and Turtles on the Gulf Coast: The Formation of Fisheries Policy in the United States." *MAST* 1: 196–214.

Endangered Species Act. 1993. USCS 16: 1539.

Forsyth, C.J. and T.A. Marckese. 1993. "Folk Outlaws: Vocabularies of Motives." *International Review of Modern Sociology* 23: 17–31.

Fumento, M. 1993. *Science Under Siege*. New York: Quill.

Helfrich, L.A., and B.L. Griswold. 1991. "Public Education in Fisheries: A Review of the Role of Extension." *Reviews in Aquatic Sciences* 4: 317–337.

Henwood, T.A., and W.E. Stuntz. 1987. "Analysis of Sea Turtle Captures and Mortalities during Commercial Shrimp Trawling." *Fisheries Bulletin* 85: 813–817.

Klima, E.F. 1989. "Approaches to Research and Management of U.S. Fisheries for Penaeid Shrimp in the Gulf of Mexico." In *Offprints from Marine Invertebrate Fisheries: Their Assessment and Management*, edited by J.F. Caddy. New York: John Wiley and Sons, Inc.

Logan, J.R., and H.L. Molotch. 1987. *Urban Fortunes: The Political Economy of Place*. Berkeley, CA: University of California Press.

Lopata, H.Z. 1984. "Social Construction of Social Problems over Time." *Social Problems* 3: 249–272.

Margavio, A.V., and C. Forsyth, with S. Laska and J. Mason. 1996. *Caught in the Net*. College Station, TX: Texas A&M University Press.

Maril, R.L. 1983. *Texas Shrimpers: Community, Capitalism, and the Sea*. College Station, TX: Texas A&M University Press.

National Academy of Science. 1990. *Decline of the Sea Turtles: Causes and Prevention*. Washington, DC: National Academy Press.

Orbach, M.K., and J.C. Johnson. 1988. "The Transformation of Fishing Communities: A Public Policy Perspective." Paper presented at Marine Resource Utilization: A Conference on Social Science Issues. Mobile, AL: University of South Alabama College of Arts and Sciences Publication and the Mississippi-Alabama Sea Grant Consortium 1: 65–70.

Quadagno, J. 1992. "Social Movements and State Transformation: Labor and Racial Conflict in the War on Poverty." *American Sociological Review* 57: 616–634.

Reed, N.P., and D. Drabelle. 1984. *The United States Fish and Wildlife Service*. Boulder, CO: Westview Press.

Renaud, M., G. Gitschlas, E. Klima, A. Shah, J. Nance, C. Caillouet, Z. Zein-Eldin, D. Koi, and F. Patella. 1990. "Evaluations of the Impacts of Turtle Excluder Devices (TEDs) on Shrimp Catch Rates in the Gulf of Mexico and South Atlantic, March 1988 through July 1989." National Oceanic and Atmospheric Administration Technical Memorandum NMFSSEFC-254.

Rossi, H.L. 1961. "Traffic Law Violation." *Social Problems* 8: 231–241.

Schwartz, F. 1990. Personal correspondence (letter) to Nancy Foster, NMFS National Office, July 23.

Sellin, T. 1938. *Culture Conflict and Crime*. New York: Social Science Research Council.

Sinclair, P.R. 1988. "Fisheries and Regional Development: Contradictions of Canadian Policy in the Newfoundland Context." Proceedings of Marine Resource Utilization: A Conference on Social Science Issues. Mobile, AL: University of South Alabama Publication Service.

Smith, B.E. 1997. "Black Lung: The Social Production of Disease." Pp. 62–75 in *The Sociology of Health and Illness: Critical Perspectives*, edited by P. Conrad. New York: St. Martin's Press.

Watson, J.W., J.F. Mitchell, and A.K. Shah. 1986. "Trawling Efficiency Device: A New Concept for Selective Shrimp Trawling Gear." *Marine Fisheries Review* 48: 19.

White, D.R.M. 1989. "Sea Turtles and Resistance to TEDs among Shrimp Fishermen of the U.S. Gulf Coast." *MAST* 2: 69–79.

Zald, M.N., and R. Ash. 1966. "Social Movement Organizations." *Social Forces* 44: 327–341.

DEVIANCE AND CONFORMITY IN THE WORK OF COMPANY DOCTORS

Elaine Draper

ABSTRACT

Professionals increasingly work in corporations, subject to the decisions of company managers, and a growing percentage of the corporate work force is made up of workers who think of themselves as professionals—persons whose education and specialized knowledge distinguish them from other workers. Drawing on interviews with 100 company physicians, scientists, and government and labor officials across the United States, as well as trade association data and field research, this article examines how company physicians' conception of themselves as team players affects their work in defining deviance and conformity. Company doctors help managers remove workers who are considered troublesome, such as labor activists and whistleblowers, and workers whose biological predisposition or personal lifestyle could make them appear to be high-risk. When physicians screen these workers, they routinely turn the information over to management; in dramatic contrast, however, they zealously protect managers at risk, creating what could be called V.I.P. health care in the workplace. After analyzing deviance and conformity in company doctors' work, the paper considers some policy implications of this research, specifically: taking effective preventive health measures to reduce long-term and social

Research in the Sociology of Work, Volume 8, pages 39-72.

ISBN: 0-7623-0608-4

costs, creating social policy protections and organizational incentives that could foster individual accountability and social responsibility, and separating health screening from employer control. The paper concludes with some implications for a sociological understanding of corporate professional work.

Professionals increasingly work in corporations, subject to the decisions of company managers, and a growing percentage of the corporate work force is made up of workers who think of themselves as professionals—persons whose education and specialized knowledge distinguish them from other workers. Their swelling ranks now include not only doctors, lawyers, and engineers, but also newer professionals such as computer programmers and health technologists.

In medicine, solo practitioners have declined steadily in the past several decades, so that employment has become the typical case for physicians. Company doctors—who receive a salary from corporations to provide medical services to employees—share neither the independence nor the high status of many other physicians. They help employers respond to regulation and the threat of lawsuits, burnish their public image, and set corporate policy regarding employment and chemical hazards.

It is a company doctor's job to conduct medical tests, diagnose illness, manage disability cases, implement government regulations, and develop wellness programs. Some also treat workers and try to control workers' compensation costs. They disproportionately are found in large manufacturing and service corporations, making important decisions about health hazards in society, as is clear from the role of physicians in Manville Corporation and firms that use large amounts of asbestos. While many work for one company, others divide their time among multiple corporate employers. To some extent, company doctors perceive themselves to be under siege, as employers are contracting out many jobs that in-house physicians held and as contracting doctors are experiencing heightened competition from other physicians. The work of company physicians is intrinsically conflicted, particularly for those in profit-oriented corporations that are not in the business of providing professional services.

In the mid-1950s, William H. Whyte's *The Organization Man* (1957) analyzed the changing values that accompanied expanding bureaucratization, and Mills's *White Collar* and Bendix's *Work and Authority in Industry* (both 1956) examined changing orientations to work among middle-level corporate employees. "The organization man" was an apt description of corporate professional employment for its time, but times have changed. Although professionals are still expected to do what their organization demands, they also read professional journals, belong to professional organizations, and have certain professional standards and concerns. Moreover, they no longer expect lifetime employment in exchange for loyal service to a corporation. For the 1990s, "the company doctor" is a more appropriate metaphor for understanding professional and managerial work in large corporations, for it suggests the conflicting demands and values that corporate professionals experience in the globalizing corporate economy.

The erosion of professional autonomy that affects many professionals within the corporate world is particularly stark in the case of company physicians.[1] Many processes that transform corporate professional work generally—such as corporate restructuring, changing labor–management relations, the ascendence of legal departments, and management by nonprofessionals—profoundly affect company physicians. They have been under pressure to be corporate functionaries when their professional values conflict with company demands. They are supervised by non-physician managers, who are increasingly attuned to the legal and financial dimensions of physicians' decisions. Conflicts erupt over resources, and professional discretion in diagnosis and treatment declines. Managers now intervene in treatment decisions, job placement, employee testing, and information conveyed to employees. The formal corporate structure and the informal cultural dimensions of work lead company doctors to help construct definitions of deviance and conformity that serve managerial goals. Doctors label employees as deviant by medicalizing their conduct or by de-medicalizing their medical complaints.

This paper draws on interviews with 100 company physicians, scientists, and government and labor officials across the United States, as well as trade association data and field research, as part of a larger study of corporate physicians. Here, with the main focus on the interview data, we will examine how company physicians' conception of themselves as team players affects their work in defining deviance and conformity. We will then consider the ways in which company doctors help managers remove workers who are considered troublesome, as well as those whose biological predisposition or personal lifestyle could make them appear to be high-risk. We will next explore how, in dramatic contrast, company physicians zealously protect managers at risk. Finally, we will consider some implications of this research for policy and for a sociological understanding of corporate professional work.

TEAM PLAYERS VERSUS WHITE COATS

Company doctors describe the ideal professional as a "team player," but this does not simply mean someone who works well with other people in a complex organization. The corporate model of loyalty and service to the employer is in tension with the medical profession's model of loyalty and service to the patient. In the corporate culture, it is understood that team players get resources and power whereas "white coats"—with perspectives typical of the solo private practitioner—are ignored, held in contempt, or terminated. A textile company doctor said:

> Being a good occupational physician in a corporation requires a person who has the ability to be patient, to shift with the paradigms within the business, and to sense what the people you

work for value and try to see if you can bring your values into alignment and get them incorporated into their values.

Professionals are often considered outsiders who are not businesspeople and must earn their spurs through years of trying to be a team member. Those who cannot either leave or remain at a low level. But team players and professionals are "ideal types"; most people—and most careers—are a blend. Team players appear to be loyal, in that they follow corporate directives and pursue their employers' goals. But their preferred view is not solely to serve the company. Rather, they are team players who bring professional and career interests to their corporate roles. *Being a team player is the new kind of professionalism.* Professionals define it in terms of individual career, self protection, and survival in corporate employment. When professionals operate as team players, they usually are not sacrificing for the good of the society or even for the good of the corporation. Their seeming loyal to the corporation is often out of fear of losing their employment or concern for their career opportunities as individuals.

Doctors constantly have to cast their medical judgments in profit terms and show the business value of medicine, which they sometimes cannot do when services are simply good for the employees' health. The doctor's opinion and medical priorities more often prevail in a clinical setting, whereas implementing an idea or policy within a corporation requires building consensus among people with diverse perspectives on an issue and recognizing that health is only one need of the corporation. A physician for an oil company said,

A key criterion in working in a corporation is being able to work with an organization whose main focus is not its employees' health and welfare. You need to be aware of the priorities of the large organization that surrounds you to find successful ways of getting your programs to move forward while at the same time supporting the business objectives.

Doctors in corporations who favor the "white-coat" approach tend actually to wear a white coat or have one hanging prominently in their office, whereas those who favor the team player approach often actually wear a white shirt with a tie at work. White coats are more likely than team players immediately to mention professional competence and board certification in occupational medicine as important for company doctors. The very characteristics that team players say are so detrimental for company doctors are ones from private practice that white coats advocate, as this banking industry doctor did:

The best corporate physician is one who makes the best private physician, caring for people and not letting anything from the business interfere with the relationship of taking care of people. What's good for the person is usually good for the corporation and what's good for the corporation is good for the person. Good medicine is good medicine.

Someone who puts on a white coat and says, "I'm a doctor. Leave me alone" is often the person who fails in the business managers' terms because of pressures within the corporation to show that the operation is profitable and to defend medical goals within a business that is not medical as its primary interest. An oil company physician said,

> Occupational physicians must be opportunistic, must be able to survive in the corporate arena. The standard medical education does not equip doctors to be relevant to what a corporation needs out of doctors, and old-style doctors sooner or later will be goners if they think their white coat and stethoscope and reputation and aura of respect alone will be sufficient in the corporate world and that's all they have to contribute.

Team players are more likely than white coats to have backgrounds as military physicians, whereas white coats are more likely to be drawn to occupational medicine because of a public health interest. A military background shapes their expectations about what a corporate doctor should do and makes screening employees more palatable. Unlike medical training, military experience also prepares doctors for simply carrying out orders, such as performing whatever tests management asks for.

Doctors who seek to thrive as company physicians must be able to adapt to the corporate culture, which doctors describe as in sharp contrast with hospital or medical school culture. Engineers tend to dominate in industrial corporations, as an oil company physician described:

> You have to find out what their receptors are, basically what they want to hear, how they want to hear it. Company physicians are among engineers basically trying to render medical decisions comprehensible to people who think in right angles. Our corporate culture is dominated by an engineering mentality and it's implicit in how day-to-day business is run, which is quantitative, precise, black and white, with minimum appreciation for probability, judgment, intuition, creativity. A lot of it is totally foreign to doctors by nature and by training.

The perspective of the CEO certainly affects the way doctors treat workers' health. A CEO's sense of noblesse oblige and long-standing support of employee programs boosts company medicine. Although the overall corporate culture affects whether the occupational medical program is beneficial or not, medical may not benefit from a favorable corporate culture without the CEO's support. It does not matter who the medical director is, or even if they have one, if senior leadership is not already persuaded that in-house medicine is good for employees or the business. Corporate medical directors have spent years building up a program, then the CEO changes and dismantles the whole department because the CEO says, "We're in the business of producing oil, not health care." The entire medical department then may be eliminated abruptly.

One main way in which doctors become team players is by, as they say, learning to "*pick your battles.*" Doctors sound the theme again and again that they must do this to avoid becoming isolated in the corporation. Physicians who have provided medical services to many companies said,

> You have to choose your battles very carefully. You have to say to management, "Okay, I won't go to the mat over these fifty-fifty things, where it's not real clear. Management could be right, the worker could be right—who knows? I won't alienate the legal department or my co-employees over it. I want to go to the cafeteria and have somebody sit with me.

> Being a part of a corporation, making team decisions, a physician wears velvet handcuffs. You're quiet about it even if you don't like what's going on.

Physicians face loyalty dilemmas that are invisible to them because they take the form of pragmatic self-censorship. They do not always try to persuade managers every time they see something would be good for health, because they know it will not succeed. Physicians sometimes envy the ability to initiate and act on ideas without the many constraints of being a team player. But they speak of a balance, maturity, and the need to pick their battles carefully and martial evidence to go to bat for a few things. One chemical company physician said:

> Picking your battles is part of being a good politician. You can't fight or win them all, because you're perceived as constantly tilting at windmills as soon as you try to do that.

Doctors feel threats to their security, even though most could go out into private practice and survive. A publishing and broadcasting company physician said,

> I don't want to go into private practice because it's hard out there with managed care, and doctors in private practice are hurting. It's not the time. You always pick your time and your place when you want to make some pointed remarks. There's no sense rocking the boat at this stage of the game.

Company professionals have constraints on publishing and speaking, conducting studies of suspected exposure hazards, and drawing attention to problematic working conditions. Company managers and lawyers set up screening procedures out of concern with professional staff members using the company's name. Doctors may collect information on what seems to be a disease pattern among employees that they want to publish, give a paper on, alert employees about, or publicize, but few collect information that could demonstrate a health hazard, partly because of how employers have defined company doctors' jobs. Many companies have public personas that they protect avidly, while other companies assume that nothing they do in health matters much. The filter may work even more fervently in companies with a strong, more polished reputation. A physician with a major computer company said:

> Publishing is a problem, no question about it. There's a tremendous filter, levels of approval; the image of the corporation is their life. And people have the job to jealously protect that image. Executives are assigned whose sole job is to promote and protect that name.

Company doctors become more powerful within corporations and successful in the eyes of other corporate physicians as benefits managers and cost-containment experts who help manage their corporations' enormous health costs, including group-health insurance and disability. Companies generally spend more on health benefits than on workers' compensation and other occupational illness costs. This role of the company doctor as benefits manager extends far beyond the traditional model of taking care of the sick and injured, and thus has little to do with the typical education and training of clinical physicians.

Other company doctors become successful in corporations that perceive a need for them to attend to potentially costly occupational and environmental health hazards. These corporations are more likely to hire doctors and provide resources that can make the physicians more influential. Company doctors also become important to corporations through helping employers interpret hazardous substance regulation and respond to it, where risk management within a company is a significant issue. Despite these routes to success, powerful physicians in companies remain atypical.

Physicians have tried to get management to recognize health problems and take action to solve them. Some managers take the position that they want to be the first to know about a problem when it first comes to light; they reward doctors for doing so or punish physicians for not bringing it to management's attention. However, physicians are often punished for bringing bad news to management when managers assume the stance that knowing about hazards creates problems for them and so they do not really want to know about them. Company doctors seek to protect themselves by not telling managers what they do not want to hear, but feel obligated from time to time to do just that. Management may consider the message from company doctors especially odious if they believe it really comes from resented government regulation. An oil company physician said:

> Because you often do things that the government tells corporations they have to do, you can be tarred with the same brush. It makes us look like we're just one of those regulators every time the government passes another law that you have to comply with. We're a necessary evil: "If we had our choice, we wouldn't have you. But no, the government makes us do these things, so I guess we have to have you around."

A doctor for a major oil company knew about a physician colleague who was terminated because he brought bad news to the company executives in the interest of protecting the company. He said that at the annual meeting, the CEO said "We don't shoot the messenger," as he heard many other people in the company say. The physician said,

> They do say that in this company they don't shoot the messenger. *Normally* they don't.

Some companies have established internal mechanisms—such as quality circles or ombudspersons—whereby individuals may be freer to express their views.

However, corporate professionals recognize that for their own self-preservation, providing risk information to the government, unions, or internal committees is risky because it typically would be clear where the information comes from by its nature. Thus, it is difficult for professionals to protest company policies, even where the employer has procedures for employees to report errors, illegal activity, and unethical conduct.

Whistleblowers frequently are not disgruntled marginal employees, but rather people in quality control, health and safety, and other parts of companies who are supposed to identify problems and act. They blow the whistle when they find the organization responding inadequately to problems that they think the employer has a responsibility to solve (see Rothschild and Miethe 1994 and Miethe and Rothschild 1994). But most corporate professionals do not blow the whistle when they find major problems in corporations. This is often because they know whistleblowers have suffered retribution in the past or because managers keep them out of the informational loop after they conclude the professionals are not reliable team players in the sense of solving business problems as managers define them. Even some who have high-level positions in large corporations are not consulted on important company matters and do not get the ear of the top executives or gain access to information about the production of new products. Whether management consults them generally depends on employers' relationship with their own professionals and their experience handling previous problems.

Although corporate professionals are not generally encouraged to bring costly problems to management's attention, when they do and are rebuffed, they can make an entity outside the employment relationship—such as their professional organization or state regulatory agencies—aware of the problem. For example, if their employer refuses to take remedial measures, company physicians can report exposure hazards to their professional organization, ACOEM—an organization whose professional ethical code itself proclaims that a physician's loyalty is to his or her patients. The organization's professional journal (*Journal of Occupational Medicine*) includes in its monthly journal reminders to company doctors that their responsibility is only to their patients and that general medical ethics principles of informed consent and confidentiality apply in corporations. Despite these pronouncements and the fact that the professional organization's members may confidentially counsel individual physicians, company doctors have had little recourse in professional organizations. The organization's ethics board has not sanctioned physicians for following their employer's directives or formally censured them for ethics violations, even when serious injury or breaches of confidentiality have been involved.[2] Millman (1981) analyzes a similar pattern with medical mortality review boards, describing the functioning of these boards as "a cordial affair" that shields fellow professionals from repercussions for their actions and infrequently sanctions them. Company doctors rarely punish deviance among their own. Corporate physicians, like other professional groups, argue that they can best police themselves.

REMOVING THE THORN IN MANAGEMENT'S SIDE

Managers will sometimes send people they view as troublemakers to the medical department for evaluation, in the hope that doctors can discover some medical, drug, or psychological problem. They refer whistleblowers and union activists, people who attempt to uncover health hazards, and people they simply do not like to company physicians for their review. They tell doctors they suspect a problem and want it diagnosed, sometimes with the implied request to recommend removal of the employee from the workplace. (Managers who have a role in determining the physician's pay raises and promotion can exert particularly heavy pressure of this sort.) A physician from a large metals corporation said:

> Everybody will go out of his or her way to accommodate an employee who's well-liked who has an impairment; but plant managers look for an expeditious way to get rid of an individual who is a thorn in management's side. A time-honored way to do that is for the individual to be considered disabled and unable to return to work, and of course the physician is the mechanism by which that happens. That's probably the most common source of pressure from management for a plant physician. Management sends the person in for a consultation and an opinion from the physician as to whether that person is fit for work, with or without work restrictions. It's very evident that the person is a thorn in management's side by their reluctance to accommodate him.

Employers use the doctor's evaluation to determine—or to justify—whether employees should be prevented from returning to their normal duties. Permitting employees to remain at work with certain restrictions does not solve the supervisor's or employer's problem. If the medical department identifies a drug or psychological problem or disease, they may recommend that the person be sent out on disability. Their recommendations also may result in the worker's being fired.

Employees are sometimes sent to a psychiatrist or psychologist because managers claim that they have problems with authority or with getting along with fellow employees—conditions that leave considerable room for interpretation. Assessing an employee's alleged psychological problem presents a particularly difficult case for a physician when people who have an interest in getting rid of the person present the evidence. As a physician with a major chemical corporation commented:

> People who management doesn't like, whether they are troublemakers or have performance problems, are sometimes sent over to us to evaluate. That's called Russian psychiatry: you're sick if you're a troublemaker. That's the way psychiatry is used in some cultures: you're sick if you're a dissident or if you disagree with the party line.[3]

Some company physicians conduct or supervise psychological testing designed to reduce theft, pilfering, absenteeism, and safety hazards. Employers often direct these tests at particular groups, such as security officers and employees with access to restricted areas. They also test those they consider "problem employees." A union health official said:

> One mine instituted a very sophisticated policy of screening applicants in an area of the country where the union historically is very strong. They screened people out using psychological testing and they brought in families for interviews. They wanted to make certain that people were not going to be voting for the union. It has been very successful. They have kept the union out.

Management also uses doctors to try to find a psychological explanation for physical or behavioral symptoms that workplace chemical exposure may cause. These psychological analyses deflect attention from workplace exposure hazards. As a doctor who performs psychological assessments of many such workers from the chemical industry and other industries said:

> We see cases of people who fall under the rubric of multiple chemical sensitivities. They have seen many other doctors, and some doctors say, "This is an immunologic disorder." Others say, "This seems hysterical." Invariably they get to a psychiatrist to try to piece out what might be going on unconsciously to cause them to have these various sensitivities.

An example of the de-medicalizing of health hazards is the dismissal of workers' complaints of medical symptoms from chemical exposures as merely "psychogenic illness."[4] Here is how an airline physician psychologized workers' medical complaints:

> Many times the employee and company disagree on whether the worker can go to work because of an issue that is not even related to their job that they are unable or unwilling to deal with. It may be a very significant personal thing in their lives or in their past history that may never have surfaced before. We're trying to make a better person. Then they will automatically become a better employee because they become more productive and dependable, whereas in the past they may have hidden behind a lot of medical disorders.

Employers also call in psychiatrists to evaluate whether a person's claim of repetitive-motion injury is psychological or malingering. A psychiatrist who evaluates many workers for employers defended his identifying employees who claim physical injuries from work as malingerers, which supported employers' interests:

> We see claims of repetitive-motion injuries involving some question about whether this person is exaggerating their symptoms or trying to get out of a work situation for some other reason. The supervisor or the person's shift changed so that a working mother who comfortably arranged child care is now put on swing shift where she can't get a babysitter, and within a week ends up developing symptoms that allow her to leave that work setting for a time.

Sometimes managers reprimand workers who go outside the company for medical care or advice about symptoms that may be work-related. By viewing such action as insubordination rather than as a legitimate physical complaint, management *de-medicalizes* legitimate medical concerns.

Employees can go to the medical department voluntarily, but supervisors have the right to order employees to go there, to determine if a medical issue has contributed to performance problems. Physicians know that when an employee arrives by supervisory referral, he or she is considered a "thorn in the side" of management. As a physician for a chemical company said,

> Some corporate managers and supervisors unfortunately like to use the medical department as the way to get people out of the company instead of dealing with performance. So they send troublemakers to the medical department to see if they are psychiatrically or physically sick. They like it that way, because they don't want to fire somebody as a troublemaker, but they can get somebody out who has an illness.

Of course, employers do not need to go through doctors in order to fire an employee. As a textile union official said:

> They have plenty of other ways to finger people and blacklist them, get rid of them, harass them. Employers don't have to question supervisors' loyalty, whereas with doctors they do.

Nevertheless, managers often ask company doctors to examine employees for behavior problems that may in fact reflect managerial inadequacy. A major chemical company physician said:

> It's not always crystal clear whether the manager or the subordinate is the problem. There might be a psycho-emotional component, but it's unusual to have a prominent medical component—the guy doesn't need pills or anything like that. Managers refer people to medical after their failure to confront and deal with a bad practice that gets totally out of control. It's a management issue and it happens all the time. It's like attendance, which is a management issue and not a health issue.

Company doctors routinely help employers remove employees whose union activities prove troublesome. A union official who assisted with one case said:

> The company wanted to get rid of [the employee] because he was head of the health and safety committee and caused the company a problem as a union activist. Somebody who's entirely healthy could also suddenly get sent to the company doctor, who pulls something out of thin air. That's clearly unethical and a reach, but some companies might go that far with doctors willing to put their basic practice on the line by playing that game. The usual scenario is that the company just decides the worker's condition is serious enough that he shouldn't go back to work at all, whereas other people with similar injuries are doing the job quite well. It happens more often in unorganized workplaces than in organized workplaces, but it's not rare.

A smelter worker and labor official explained:

> I worked as a smelter worker on staff with the union and I had open-heart surgery while I was on leave of absence from the plant. That company would have poisoned me with arsenic if they could have. The company canceled my leave of absence and said that the only way they could sustain my medical benefits was if I retired immediately. They decided that I had to see their company physician, who just signed the forms without examining me, without even asking what the blood values were, without asking *anything*; and they officially retired me from that company. They just didn't want me back on their property for any reason. Their getting rid of me entirely had to do with my political activities and had nothing to do with my health.

Employees have better protection in unionized workplaces, especially when the company tries to get rid of a worker through a psychological determination. An official with the United Steelworkers said,

> The removal of somebody based on a psychological evaluation as opposed to their behavior is a pretty easy grievance to win. If somebody hits somebody in the workplace or goes after somebody with a club or takes off all their clothes and pretends they want to do a high dive into a ladle of hot metal, then that's behavior. But if there's nothing like that in the background and no infraction of the rules, and somebody is just sent for an evaluation and the doctor says the person is schizophrenic or delusional or paranoid, then we won't lose that case.

THE TREATMENT OF DISABILITY, STRESS CLAIMS, AND DRUG USE

Employers now collect extensive medical information on a wide array of risk factors in an attempt to prevent on-the-job health damage to especially vulnerable individuals. The prospect of higher costs for insurance, workers' compensation, lawsuits, and further regulation associated with worker disease makes any means of identifying those with threatening medical conditions or personal habits appear especially attractive to employers. Doctors and managers use screening information from questionnaires, co-worker reports, insurance records, or their own tests to determine workers' employability and to hold workers responsible for problems that corporate officials themselves create, such as stressful and dangerous jobs (see Hanson 1993; Draper 1991; and Nelkin and Tancredi 1989).

The public-health focus on eliminating workplace environmental hazards such as asbestos has now largely given way to a search for workers with an inappropriate biological predisposition or lifestyle, such as one involving drug use. During the past 10 years, corporations that could focus on preventing illnesses and monitoring the exposure hazards that all workers confront have instead reduced or completely abandoned their health and environmental staffs. Looking for the possible predispositions of individuals is a way of shifting the focus away from hazardous working conditions. Major examples of the screening approach are companies' treatment of disability, stress claims, and drug use. In each case, company physicians identify workers they perceive to be deviant or otherwise high-risk; they refer to themselves and other company doctors as "rub-out artists" who help managers get rid of employees by showing that their health problems are not caused by the workplace.

Disability Cops

Employers expect company physicians to testify, advise them, and submit evidence on the causes of occupational illnesses in order to determine the health care and benefits that sick or injured workers are entitled to receive under workers' compensation. Company physicians' decisions about assigning risk help determine who must pay the costs of occupational disease, including medical bills, lost work time, unemployment, and custodial care. Physicians frequently testify about whether an employee's illness is due to work or to non-work-related causes. Those who testify for the employer on workers' compensation claims generally know that their job is to try to find a non-occupational cause for the worker's ailment and to provide a judgment that would serve the company's interest. Although it can be difficult to determine medically what exactly caused an employee's disease, employers in many cases rely on physicians to defend their corporation by testifying that the workplace could not possibly have caused a disease. Corporate physicians rarely take the plaintiff's side or argue that specific chemicals are so hazardous that they require stricter regulation. In the absence of firm evidence, pressure from employers and company attorneys inclines them to downplay the effect of occupational exposure in causing disease. Many in-house physicians who testify in workers' compensation cases say they feel strong pressure from their employer to prove that the illnesses of workers are not work-related. Some physicians said that their predecessors in the company job were fired or had left because they did not adapt well to that pressure.

Managers expect company physicians to police illness and disability claims and to try to bring individuals back to work. Employers expect them to identify which workers are "gaming the system," manipulating disability claims in order to stay off work. Company doctors claim to use objective criteria in deciding whether to send people back to work. They often say that reassigning injured workers to lighter duties rather than sending them home is in the best interest of both the employee and the company. But the fact remains that doctors ultimately depend on their employers for their salary, and this limits their ability to diagnose people and advise on disability claims objectively.

Filing a claim against a company can be expensive for a worker, who may also risk being blackballed from employment elsewhere. Two physicians, with a chemical and a utility company respectively, described how they try to persuade employees not to file workers' compensation claims:

> I tell people, "There are better ways to go through life than lining yourselves up with lawyers and having negative opinions about the company that you work for. Get on with your life and do something positive." I see these people who are completely consumed by getting back at the

> company, and they are miserable. I feel sorry for anybody who gets mired in this whole workers' compensation mess. The lawyers end up getting most of the money anyway. And they are not giant sums of money, especially considering the amount of energy it takes to go after it.
>
> I try to talk patients out of filing workers' compensation cases, because I know the dynamic, what the payoff and time commitment will be and what it will do to them. They may have trouble getting another job. I try to make it clear to them that workers' compensation is the last-ditch desperation protection. There are a lot of other answers. I say, "I don't think you want to do this. Let's see if we can work somehow within the bureaucracy." I still have to sign off on a lot of them. It's not a good system.

Company doctors complain about workers taking advantage of time off and disability benefits. Here are three representative comments from airline, aerospace, and telecommunications company doctors, respectively:

> Employees tend to take advantage of the system as much as they possibly can. Sending someone home rather than keeping them at the work site is definitely in the interest of the patient, but it may not be in the interest of the company. We sometimes find ourselves between a rock and a hard place. Our hope and goal is that whatever is in the employee's best interest is also in the company's best interest. We do everything we can in our power to minimize the number of lost work days.
>
> You don't have the same degree of satisfying patient-doctor relationship as in private practice. It tends to be an inherent adversarial relationship, and you have to constantly be on the alert for people just trying to get out of work or establishing phony claims.
>
> I don't like trying to be a policeman; that's not why I got into medicine. People have very generous sick time and workers' comp time in our company. Some people are legitimately sick for a long time, but some stay out for as long as they can get away with it.

Company physicians either initiate or go along with their employer's policy of getting rid of or refusing to hire workers who have already filed claims. That hurts employees' ability to work and leads to long-term disability. An occupational physician who works with company doctors on evaluating employees' disabilities said,

> An injured worker who gets involved in a workers' compensation battle is labeled a troublemaker and the company would rather get rid of that person than find him a new job. Instead, the employer puts him on disability and then terminates him after the disability benefits run out. Even if I clear him medically to return to some form of work, management makes no attempt to find another job for him.

Employers sometimes have doctors outside the company serve much the same function as in-house doctors: evaluating the person's fitness-for-duty, reviewing qualifications for long-term disability benefits or workers' compensation benefits, and assessing drug abuse or behavioral problems. Companies can choose who to rely on for opinions about health effects, especially when the evidence is ambiguous. Their economic interest is to avoid using a doctor with the reputation for giving high estimates of occupational health hazards. The need for physician testimony has spurred the growth of an entire industry of medical-legal physicians. In litigated disability cases, the plaintiff and the defendant company typically line up medical experts to testify before workers' compensation judges. These experts are usually pitted against each other in testifying about return-to-work issues, vocational rehabilitation benefits, need for modified duty, or whether the disease is related to work. Physicians in this field generally develop a reputation for being either pro-plaintiff or pro-defendant. An auto company doctor said:

> It's generally known within the industry which doctor is known as a rub-out artist. It's someone who is hired to kill the case and get the claim denied. They will say that this person's ailment is the result of something other than the workplace, or say there are no physical findings for it.

A railroad physician who gives about 25 depositions a year said:

> In most of our cases that go to court, the men could work if they were motivated to work, and I'll testify to that fact: "Based on the medical information I have, this man could do this job if he wanted to. I will let him come back to work if his doctor releases him." So I put it back on his doctor. If his doctor releases him with restrictions, I'll have a work-capacity evaluation done on him and still let him come back to work with specific restrictions. Every city we operate in has doctors and attorneys for the plaintiff who will say and do anything. When I get a report from particular doctors, I don't believe a word they say because they just say what the lawyer wants him to say.

Company physicians testify at Congressional and regulatory hearings as well as in lawsuits regarding corporate medical liability. They have testified on exposure standards for benzene, vinyl chloride, sulfur dioxide, cotton dust, and on basic OSHA risk evaluations. With few exceptions, they defend their corporations or advocate government standards that require personal protective devices instead of more costly engineering controls. The Labor Department hearing transcripts are filled with examples of doctors testifying for companies at public evidentiary hearings concerning setting standards. A national OSHA official said:

> Doctors argue the case of whoever employed them. Companies that employ physicians employ them to say that a substance is not as dangerous as OSHA thinks it is. A lot of physicians who testify for companies think that the rules and regulations that we promulgate are totally unnecessary. I think the doctors believe what they say, but sometimes companies pay them very well to do that.

Company physicians frequently say that private physicians have an economic bias to do whatever the patient wants, or whatever will make the doctors the most money, such as treating a continuing disability. Private physicians therefore are willing to exaggerate workplace hazards to accommodate their patients' desire for disability leave or other company benefits. Company doctors challenge private doctors who support workers' claims and say they misread test results and facilitate employees' illegitimate absences from work. While criticizing private physicians, however, company doctors tend to minimize the effect of economic motivation on their own judgment and decisions and they also tend to de-medicalize employees' medical complaints. A doctor with a large metals and mining company that uses 1,500 local doctors around the country to evaluate employees said:

> How do you deal with chronic absenteeism and a fellow who keeps coming in with excuse slips from local doctors? We periodically run across physicians who have become an excuse-slip factory. We simply approach them professionally, which works for a little bit, and then they are back into the same thing again.

An electronics company physician said:

> We have doctors in the community who are a real black eye to medicine. I call them "medical prostitutes." They are very biased in how they approach the patient and always blame the employer and make it look like the employer has purposefully done something negative to the patient. They may perceive us as just the hired gun of the company, but it's not true. I always make the best decision for the patient and I don't consider expense. They think they do the patients a favor by giving them a month off for a hangnail. Time and time again they just give people an inordinately long time off that costs society a lot of money and costs patients a lot too, because most don't get their full salary during that nonproductive time, and eventually the employees get a reputation for needlessly missing a lot of time and it hurts their career.

Workplace Stress Claims

Rather than consider the workplace as a source of problems that affect health and productivity, management generally looks for problems that employees supposedly *bring* to the workplace, such as drug or alcohol abuse, depression, marital troubles, and financial difficulties. Although stress and wellness programs have become major concerns in occupational medicine, company programs tend to ignore workplace factors, such as occupational stress, that contribute to employees' behavioral problems and illness. They treat work stress as a controversial area that is best avoided because it places too much responsibility for worker problems on employers. Yet substance abuse may be a way that workers cope with a stressful work environment that management has imposed; it may in this sense be management-driven, rather than a problem that workers bring to the workplace. While not all stress is related to work, the work environment can contribute to spousal abuse and other problems at home. Job satisfaction and control over work processes are critical factors, because people who are dissatisfied and have less control over their work suffer greater psychological strain, chronic disease, and substance abuse.[5] Work-related stress can come from a supervisor yelling at employees, work overload, poor air quality, repetitive motion at computers, and macro issues such as anxiety over job insecurity and economic restructuring.

Another reason company physicians and employers avoid the work-stress issue is their desire to minimize workers' compensation claims. Stress claims in many companies are hotly contested, as employers assert that they are illegitimate on their own merits. Work stress has become a major cost concern, particularly in California, with many people filing stress claims and suing corporations. Companies that draw workers' attention to problems of work stress could thereby encourage claims against themselves.

Stress management programs in corporations often suggest that stress is highly subjective, and that individuals respond to stressful stimuli very differently. A company's focus on worker health promotion can to some extent "blame the victim" insofar as it tells people that they alone have full responsibility for their own health (see Ryan 1971). Their behavioral problems and illnesses are seen to stem from entirely personal limitations, which they can remove with guidance from counselors and therapy programs.

Employers who do recognize worker stress generally argue that it greatly overshadows workplace environmental problems. They maintain that personal and emotional problems are far more threatening to employees' health than work exposures, as did this physician with a major chemical company:

> Stress is the most important epidemic that we have in occupational medicine today. From the standpoint of the sheer numbers of people that it's affecting and the impact on numbers of workers, stress has a far greater impact than any other issue, including the chemicals in my own company. The stress issue makes the toxic-chemical issue look like Bambi.

Company Employee Assistance Programs began dealing with drug dependency and alcoholism in the 1970s, then broadened to encompass other factors affecting worker health and productivity, such as depression and family problems. Many companies offered incentive plans for wellness, such as additional benefits for employees who would stop smoking or lower their cholesterol levels. Other companies established fitness facilities and no-smoking policies. The shift has been toward screening and wellness programs and away from routine care of the sick and injured.[6]

Since turnover and the training of new employees are also expensive, some employers are willing to have treatment programs to retain workers with problems. But such programs also cost money, and companies in financial trouble are therefore likely to abandon them. Moreover, not all employers give employees an opportunity to rehabilitate themselves before being terminated. An aerospace company physician said:

> When you had a robust economy, it made both economic and medical sense to put forth a significant amount of effort to get people with drug problems and alcohol back on the job; when you have good people without alcohol and drug problems also being put out on the street, it sometimes becomes very difficult to rationalize why you would continue to put out that effort for those individuals.

Even well-intentioned employee-assistance programs still serve the function of screening employees in the employer's interest. An occupational health specialist who screens workers as part of a large medical surveillance program said:

> Employees have some concern that we are the people with the big bat who can take away their jobs. My emphasis is more on this wonderful thing we're doing for them, and how we will make them healthy. But a lot of employees look at this from the standpoint of, "If I go there, they'll find out I don't see as well as I used to, so now I can't drive a forklift anymore." You can't get around that because that *is* one problem with medical surveillance. Employees are mandated to come to the clinic; they're not like sick people who come on their own volition.

Drug Use

Drug testing is a principal way in which physicians define and justify themselves as useful to management because it is a common device used to blame workers for their own injuries and illnesses, thus escaping corporate liability. A physician who conducts drug testing and participates in workers' compensation cases explained:

> Sometimes a claimant's urine or blood will be tested; and if they are definitely intoxicated at the time of the injury, we can get out from under the responsibility of paying for it because intoxication is a defense. So if you are intoxicated on the job and you get hurt, the employer is no longer liable for it.

Doctors who once complained about the burden of drug testing now say they are grateful that it helps them justify their time and their medical staff, especially when their medical departments are embattled or shrinking. Without drug testing defined as a medical function, they expect they would lose the infrastructure now devoted to it or even have their programs eliminated. In addition, drug testing helps medical units within large corporations demonstrate that they serve their company's customers because it is popular and has customer appeal. Thus drug testing is of special benefit to company doctors seeking to defend their turf and resources.

Companies that have a policy of drug testing every time an injury occurs may selectively choose which employees to test: for example, shop floor workers but not managers. A physician who supervises employee drug testing said:

> Except for safety-sensitive positions, we don't do drug testing, unless there is some indication, like a history of use. That can be pretty arbitrary and minor, but it isn't done routinely.

Drug testing has come to pervade workplaces. Large companies generally test job applicants, workers in safety-sensitive jobs, and people whose accident or functional deficit creates the suspicion that drugs were involved. The American Management Association (1996, p. 1) found in 1996 that 81.1 percent of its member companies in the U.S. conducted drug testing.[7] However, drug testing is a problematic screening approach. Physicians use tests that they acknowledge are not effective in detecting many problems; for example, corporations that routinely test job applicants and do for-cause testing typically get a positive rate of only one to five percent (American Management Association 1996; Durbin and Grant

1996). Employers say that although the policing function is not particularly effective in catching drug users, drug screening nonetheless deters drug users from applying to work for them and keeps some casual drug-user employees away from drugs (see Normand, Lempert, and O'Brien 1994; and Wolkinson and Block 1996). This creates a *lemming effect*, a rush to corporate conformity: When one company adopts drug testing other companies quickly follow it, even without strong evidence that the tests are scientifically defensible. This phenomenon is similar to the "bandwagon" effect seen among research organizations that rush to develop medical technologies that are not necessarily the most promising scientifically.[8] Drug testing is a short-sighted approach that conveniently replaces any concern that repetitive or dangerous jobs may be contributing to drug use.

As with drug testing, company doctors have carried out fetal exclusion policies, in which women have been barred from particular jobs because of possible fetal damage, following concern over reproductive effects, lawsuits, and adverse publicity. In the 1991 *Johnson Controls* case, the Supreme Court ruled that banning all fertile women from particular jobs because of possible fetal damage is unlawful discrimination.[9] However, the *Johnson Controls* decision failed to deal with companies' vulnerability to third-party suits and thus left many companies who formerly had fetal protection policies in a quandary as to what they should do instead. Company physicians have used waivers with individuals considered high-risk and then given them the choice of taking on hazardous work; or employers have required them to get private doctors to sign agreements permitting their exposure to environmental hazards. Yet health screening information is inappropriately applied in the case of fetal exclusion. Although individuals in a particular group—in this case, fertile women—may be considered high risk, many others may also be at risk. For example, employers often excluded women from jobs that entailed exposure to lead, but the men who held these jobs, as well as the children they might father, remained vulnerable to damage from lead.[10]

A parallel here with drug testing and fetal exclusion is company doctors' use of information about the employees' possible genetic predisposition. Companies have initiated programs even when valid scientific evidence does not justify them (see Office of Technology Assessment 1990), out of concern with protecting the safety of employees, saving the money that high-risk employees could cost, and shielding employers against legal liability for disease caused by the work environment that management has imposed.[11] Under the law, employers are not supposed to screen out disabled individuals except for a job-related disability that cannot be accommodated.[12] However, physicians can still screen for drugs, collect genetic information, and give virtually any test they want after employers have made applicants a conditional employment offer, even if the information is not job-related. Employers also can modify their health insurance coverage to exclude individuals with special risks from medical coverage.[13]

In short, physicians and employers have advocated ineffective screening policies that impose heavy social costs in order to accomplish various non-health-related goals. As an increasing number of individuals are labeled high-risk for a widening array of conditions, the social costs of screening practices fall on workers, their families, and the public. Individuals identified as high-risk may find themselves virtually uninsurable or unemployable or be stigmatized in their personal lives, which can make it difficult for them to be perceived as normal again (see Gostin 1995; and Duster 1990). Corporate physicians and employers have nonetheless shown great faith in the powers of new medical screening. The corporate use of screening out workers expands as corporate managers gain more power to define risk in their own terms, and as labor's power declines. Moreover, physicians will be able to target many more predispositions and diseases in individuals as a result of the 15-year, 3-billion-dollar Human Genome Project's effort to map the human genetic structure (Kevles and Hood 1992). Companies that screen will inevitably get positive results, with adverse consequences for individuals who are labelled high-risk. Unintended social consequences will proliferate as "predisposition" becomes understood as "defect" and as physicians and employers perceive an ever-increasing number of people as biologically flawed.

V.I.P. HEALTH

Physicians are obligated to declare employees fit or unfit for work. This obligation, however, does not extend to executives. Whereas physicians who screen workers routinely turn over the information to management, in general they guard information about the health of executives carefully, creating what could be called V.I.P. health care in the workplace. Occupational physicians say they know of few examples in which company doctors have released health information about an executive, even when it might be the right thing to do or the best way to protect the company. On the other hand, their evaluations routinely hamper the careers and employability of lower-level workers who may be at increased risk for future problems. A chemical company doctor said he evaluates employees' risk and relates to them differently, depending on whether they are higher or lower in the company hierarchy:

> Physical workers who lift, push, and pull aren't much of a problem. I would say "Let's take him out of work exposure to hepatotoxic chemicals and put him in another kind of work." Somebody who is lower in the hierarchy *is* more readily exchangeable and the company hasn't made a huge commitment. But you expect senior officers who go to the Far East for three to five years to have a tremendous effect on the company. If I know that an executive who is being considered for a new assignment has a problem but is doing okay today, I do not recall my ever having interceded to disrupt that promotion.

A financial services company physician who routinely screened employees said he was known for keeping the health risks of executives absolutely confidential:

> When I know an executive has a cardiac or neurotic problem or whatever problem but is ready to move up into a job with more responsibility, travel, pressure, and tension, my job is to persuade him to allow me, as his advocate, to go to the person he reports to and explain that he could do that work but that certain accommodations have to be made, and what the reason is for them. I'd keep my mouth shut if he said no, even if I knew that he was heading for serious trouble.

Conglomerate and chemical company physicians emphasized the importance of keeping executive health information absolutely confidential:

> We deal with the CEO and the top three or four layers of the company. Men in corporate America do not have many places they can open up to talk, but people will come to talk if an in-house physician develops a relationship like a Mother Superior with them. We pick up an enormous amount of disease early by doing executive physicals here, so we have a chance to do something and modify behaviors. You lose everything if you lose confidentiality; that's the bottom line.

> In my 18 years with the company, I have never been in a situation where a health issue has been a consideration in advancing an executive—let's say, a vice president advancing to a president—*never*! That's probably an unfounded fear on the part of the executives. I have never heard of a physician reporting on an executive's health to others in the company.

Much of the work of physicians even 10 years ago involved periodic executive medical exams that had a business-related purpose but did not fall under the medical benefit plans. Corporations required their executives to have annual physicals, including a sigmoidoscopy, barium enema, chest X-ray, and EKG. The goal was to detect people with early signs of disease and save money by intervening early and keeping managers healthy. Many companies rejected these tests as not cost-effective; after billions had been spent testing CFOs and CEOs without symptoms, actuarial tables showed that they were not living longer because of it. Although companies increasingly rely on HMOs or company health benefit plans to cover such exams, many doctors continue to do executive physicals of top managers who have little or no exposure to occupational risks. In addition, company doctors sometimes serve as the personal physicians to top executives. A physician with a financial services company said:

> One company I knew had a medical director who was a longtime personal friend of the CEO, who was worried about dropping dead from a heart attack and wanted a physician at his elbow, and decided the physician was a good gin rummy player, so that's that. Many medical directors got their jobs because they were physicians related to the CEO.

Company physicians also act as medical advisers to executives who have their own personal physicians. The medical department generally enjoys more power, status, and resources if it treats the CEO and top executives. The opportunity to advise high-level executives on health matters is especially important for medical directors and physicians who clinically evaluate executives. Physicians who treat executives for health problems, or otherwise advise them, can ask for favors, such as support for an expansion of the company's medical program. Physicians with a chemical and a power company, respectively, said:

> A large corporation is an extremely political environment. We all do personal favors for people, that's how we get things done, to a degree. But physician colleagues in corporate medicine abuse that practice by having a paper occupational health program and for years only taking care of executives and totally ignoring the rest of the program. That happens all the time. If you helped an executive take care of a personal need in the past you can always go in and say, "I want this program." The executive will often get it for you, aside from business merit, because they feel you've done something for them in the past, so it's a tit-for-tat arrangement. I help executives get through the health-care system and choose specialists for them or their families, serving as their advocate in getting what they want done in the medical arena as efficiently and expertly as possible. I'd like to get it up on the table with my management; I'd say, "Look, it's 20 percent or 30 percent of my time, so if you want me to take care of all the health needs of our senior executives, their spouses, and their children, let's talk about it honestly." They can't talk about it honestly, because some benefits laws prohibit giving excessive benefit perks to executives. They're nervous about formalizing that as a function even though we all know that executives in this country get all sorts of benefits and perks, including health benefits.

> My practice includes almost the whole legal department. I take care of all the lawyers, so I have a personal relationship with them. The fact that I see the lawyers in this setting as patients makes them more understanding. They would not dictate to me or interfere easily. If the lawyers were getting health care somewhere else, then they probably would be arbitrary and dictatorial, looking down at the health-care department. But since we take care of them, they want us to do what's best for patients, which is them. So it's more of a hands-off approach and more collegial. This closed system makes the dynamic a lot different. It's extremely significant.

As with other leaders, the health of corporate VIPs conceivably could affect their careers, but physicians tend to prop up their leaders and keep executives' secrets (see Post and Robins 1993). Some doctors have expressed ambivalence about the role of personal physician or medical adviser to executives, as has this chemical company physician:

> Seeing top executives as patients gives you power to "have something" on them, to know something about them, and knowledge is power. It's a double-edged sword to be viewed as the executive doctor. It works *for* us in that we have access to the most senior people in the corporation on a personal level, which is exciting and gives us enormous opportunities. The downside is that we can never be treated as equivalent on the same playing field as other business managers. Some senior executives always view us as the doctor, and it's a very tricky job to be in. You're playing with fire, because you're playing with the bodies, but more so, the psyches of the senior people in the corporation, and they know it and you know it. How you handle yourself in that role and manage the health information affects whether you succeed. Any honest medical director in a Fortune 500 company will tell you that his or her capacity to survive or thrive is highly dependent on personal relationships with senior executives and their function as the executive's personal physician or advocate. That contaminates our capacity to be viewed as a member of a management team.

The special access that many corporate physicians have to executives strains their relationship to other managers. In addition, employers may fear physicians, as a chemical company physician explained:

> The reason medical departments have generally not thrived in corporations is that the current crop of leaders of Fortune 500 companies fears doctors. They are afraid of us. No one other than occupational physicians has the capacity to bear the burden of the secrets of the CEOs' bodies and minds. They are afraid of having the medical department become too powerful. Somehow they think it doesn't fit with their power games and control over employees and that we represent a force they can't quite understand or control as much as other forces within the corporation.

As this argument suggests, managers may fear doctors in part because they stand for employees' health. Doctors have a role as advocates for workers' health, which is threatening to executives who view workers as their adversaries—as they usually do in companies that are highly adversarial in their management-labor relationships. The whole occupational medicine field is founded on a liberal concept of having workers who are healthy. A physician for a conglomerate refers to company doctors as a silent irritant that managers cannot fully trust:

> Management just doesn't trust anybody with an M.D.—somebody who isn't an engineer who has something to do with a product that makes money for you, or a lawyer that keeps you out of trouble, or somebody in finance that helps you keep your money. And we are a burden people—that's the term; indirect, a burden. Burden departments are departments that you must have to function but that don't make a damn thing for you. That's true of occupational medicine and any support function. Perhaps there is reason for their distrust, because, frankly, I still consider myself to have more loyalty to my profession than to the company, and I think that's why I'm paid. You don't want a hack; you want somebody who's a patient advocate who can keep the corporation out of trouble.

In addition, a visit to the occupational physician can challenge an executive's self image. As a chemical company physician said:

> When the CEO and president walk into the occupational physician's office, they are in a dependent situation, which they loathe.

In an unusual but telling case, one prominent physician told top management about an executive's personal health problem that he thought threatened the business. For this he was fired, even though management agreed that the information he provided did in fact help the company. Management saw him as disloyal for betraying the confidence of an executive, and wondered if he would someday pass on information about their own health or personal problems.

Company physicians and top managers sometimes treat lower-level managers much like low-level employees, as when they use medical information to defend their actions in firing a manager for non-medical reasons. A physician in an aerospace company discussed a case in which he defended the employer's interest by withholding important medical information from a lower-level manager, but continued to feel guilty for having done so. Another physician in the company had failed to identify the employee's cardiac problem in the company's annual physical examination. The cardiac problem was causing sleep apnea, and sleep deprivation was causing him to fall asleep in meetings, which was one reason he was fired. The employee had not gone to a private physician, who might have told him what was wrong. The medical director said:

> They brought me the record and asked me what I thought about it after he left the company and filed a wrongful termination lawsuit. So I looked at the data and said, "Well, yeah, there *is* evidence that this difficulty was there." Then I asked the doctor involved, "Did you talk to him about this problem?" He said he didn't. I told the attorneys, "We didn't do a good job; we screwed up." During the trial the company lawyers called me as a witness regarding this medical information and said, "Just answer questions 'yes' or 'no' when you're on the stand." They didn't ask, "Would the very fact that we failed to give him some information have been important?" Then I waited for *his* attorneys to ask me questions, but they didn't. I wanted him to win his suit and succeed over the company, but he ended up losing it.

Medical departments in many companies have remained small or shrunk as corporate legal departments, human relations, and public relations staffs have grown. Although management's primary motivation for cutting in-house doctors is to reduce costs by contracting out medical services, their fear of doctors contributes. The fear and mistrust of physicians may be largely unjustified, however, since doctors generally do not report on the health of executives; once they uncover a physical or psychological problem, they tend to protect the executive's confidences.

IMPLICATIONS FOR SOCIETY AND FOR SOCIAL POLICY

There are three policy implications of this discussion of deviance and conformity in company doctors' treatment of disease claims. These concern taking effective preventive health measures to reduce long-term and social costs, creating social policy protections and organizational incentives that could foster individual accountability and social responsibility, and separating health screening from employer control. Alternative policies could apply medical information in ways that are more protective, equitable, and rational.

1. Effective Preventive Health Measures

Prevention must be institutionalized in society as well as in the workplace through case law and regulations maintaining standards in business. Preventing illness is far less costly in human and dollar terms than acting after the fact. Effectively resolving problems that employees perceive could also increase job satisfaction, transform the workplace into a less stressful environment, and promote worker health generally. At least recognizing ways in which adverse working conditions contribute to job dissatisfaction, drug use, and disease would give less urgency to testing programs and leave more room for alternative policies.

Preventive steps represent a cost for managers concerned with a short time frame and are a special burden in times of corporate retrenchment, when many American corporations are struggling with declining profitability and worldwide market share. Although gaining support for preventive measures is difficult, corporations should be encouraged to create incentives for measures that are cost-effective over the long term and to consider corporations' and society's long-term needs in evaluating managers' job performance, including the need to prevent illness and death. Then the costs and benefits of workplace practices to employees and the public would be likely to be given important consideration.

In *Moral Mazes*, Robert Jackall (1988) analyzes what he calls the bureaucratic ethic of decision making by corporate actors. What he calls a problem of bureaucracy, though, is really insufficient bureaucracy and quasi-feudal loyalty to employers. Corporate actors tend to view their work not through a fixed bureaucratic lens of rules and procedures as much as through a changing web of cross-cutting allegiances within and outside the corporation. Physicians tend to give little consideration to social costs when they take these allegiances into account. Social policy and the law could help insure that their employers would bear most of the financial burden of occupational disease rather than individual workers or society as a whole.

By seeking to identify individuals with specific risk factors, company physicians have implicitly argued that others are safe, and that therefore no further substance regulation or change in company policies is needed. Workplace screening that locates blame in employees should not gain support without careful examination of the evidence. In addition, anti-discrimination laws should extend to employees' pre-existing health conditions and genetic predispositions to guard against individuals being labelled as high-risk and penalized as deviants.[14] National health coverage and a single-payer health care system of government-financed services could mean that individuals and groups considered high-risk would no longer be denied health coverage or affordable medical care. Screening under such a system would have fewer adverse effects on those considered high-risk, who would have less to fear about losing access to medical treatment.[15]

If risk is conceptualized in terms of workplace hazards that all exposed workers confront, then employers should tighten engineering controls, monitor exposure hazards, replace hazardous products, and collect scientific information on risks to populations in order to determine whether working conditions are indeed safe. Corporate enthusiasm for screening, though understandable as a business interest, has a destructive effect on employees and the public and diverts attention from pressing environmental health hazards and problematic management policies. Moreover, coercion arises when individuals with few job alternatives and incomplete information on workplace hazards are pressured to take tests and provide medical information, when they are threatened with losing their employment or insurance, and when they find that the truly voluntary and independent counseling recommended for private patients is unavailable to them (see Caplan 1995 and Mehlman, Kodish, and Whitehouse 1996). The search for high-risk individuals should not limit the use of effective strategies for reducing environmental hazards and disease that are already widely recognized but underfunded (see, for example, Pelletier 1996 and Cushman 1997). Investing in improved management policies and working conditions could prevent disease more effectively than broad employee testing.

2. Legal and Social Policy Protections and Organizational Incentives That Could Encourage Individual Accountability and Social Responsibility

The legal environment affects the ways in which company physicians work and think of themselves as professionals and corporate actors. Over the past several decades, law has dramatically altered the relationship of professionals to colleagues, clients, and the public. It shapes professionals' judgment about what constitutes appropriate professional conduct, such as in informed consent and minimal preventive measures. Professionals follow news stories about litigation involving corporations and talk with others in their workplace and profession about the meaning of court cases and statutory requirements. How corporate professionals interpret the meaning of the law is important, along with the formal letter of the law, in affecting their decision making. They cast social questions and moral quandaries as legal matters. The prospect of a massive lawsuit or a jury trial with a multimillion-dollar award to the plaintiff in many cases affects their work far more than one would expect from the slight probability of such a suit.

Company professionals 40 years ago could expect the law and their corporate employment to protect them from legal action. Employees could not sue company doctors, for example, because they were considered fellow servants or co-agents. Now, however, company physicians are becoming increasingly vulnerable to malpractice and other lawsuits even after they give up the comparative autonomy of private practice. Also, workers' compensation and OSHA regulation are expanding the realm of willful negligence and the possibility that corporations and individual professionals can be held liable for it. The legal environment defines them as corporate functionaries and sometimes as individually accountable. Company physicians now know they can be sued individually, held personally responsible for their actions, and even face criminal charges against them as individuals.[16] This perceived threat of individual legal accountability reinforces professional standards and bolsters independent professional judgment in corporations.

Organizational incentives could encourage professionals and employees to speak up in organizations, government, and in public forums, and those who do so should be protected against retribution for engaging in socially responsible conduct. Managers company-wide should also be held accountable for health and environmental protection. Professional societies and laws can serve to increase appropriate loyalty and the individual accountability of company professionals for hazards and errors. For example, the Corporate Criminal Liability Act of California provides for significant fines (of up to a million dollars for a corporation) and even for imprisoning managers who violate the law, such as those who are found responsible for workers' deaths.[17] Medical malpractice extended to corporate professionals can serve a similar purpose. Conservative analysts bemoan litigiousness in our society, tracing social ills to greedy claimants, zealous lawmakers, and rapacious lawyers.[18] However, the threat of lawsuits has tended to supplant strict regulation in many arenas and can be very useful in expanding individual accountability, getting companies to curtail hazardous conditions, and promoting beneficial social policies.

Physicians generally frame their relations with patients in terms of personal trust and integrity, downplaying any power problems. They are socialized to believe that they have extraordinary power in society and only recently are beginning to realize how little power they have when they are caught between tectonic shifts of the insurance companies, large corporations, powerful medical organizations, and government payers that largely control medical services. It matters little how nice the company physician is in the context of workers fearing getting fired, having no employee organization to appeal to, and having doctors use information against them. A good patient–doctor relationship depends on the larger corporate and social structure. Employee demands could make it easier for physicians to function in the corporation because they could advise employers to act in view of this employee pressure. But rather than pursue that course, doctors instead focus on demonstrating their integrity and trustworthiness to employees and maintain the illusion that they must accomplish health on their own. Physicians admitting that corporate structures largely govern their relationship with patients tends to conflict with their view of themselves because it strips them in their own minds of their own power, which people—especially doctors—do not naturally do. Still, doctors conceivably could seek workers' empowerment as in their own interest as professionals rather than merely seek to apply their own power to employees.

Employees could strive to improve their own health by gaining a greater ability to identify health hazards and influence their working conditions. Company medical programs could be made responsible to the work force as well as to the employer through joint labor–management committees like those General Motors and the United Auto Workers set up,[19] along with other community and labor organizations. Union membership is small and declining—now at an all-time low since the 1930s of only 11 percent of the private sector, which of course limits their influence on company policies. Unions also have been constrained by limited information and lack of power under restrictive labor laws. Moreover, basic economic issues predominate over health and employee participation issues at the workplace, especially in periods of layoffs. Nonetheless, organized labor in heavily unionized industries and workplaces has pressed for specific services, a prohibition on certain tests, more access to information, expanded employee representation, and greater independence of company doctors. Along with public interest and community groups, they have sought transnational mobilization to counteract business's flexibility, wealth, and power in a globalizing economy.[20] However, gaining influential transnational resources is overwhelmingly daunting for citizen groups. It is thus difficult to be optimistic about this prospect of a globalized counterweight to corporate power and control. Much depends on the strength and vigilance of community and labor organizations that make demands for corporations to explain or change their practices.

3. Separate Health Services from Employer Control

Expanding medical information presents important problems of inappropriate or harmful access to medical information by company physicians, employers, and insurance companies. Individuals should have the right for others not to know test results much more often than current laws provide. People also ought to be fully informed about risks, the nature of tests, who will get the results, and what impact they will have. Most employees now have the right to obtain company medical records if they request them, so they can find out what tests have been conducted. Since misrepresentations of information can have devastating consequences for employment, insurance, and stigmatization, people could learn of inaccuracies and uses of the records if they were to obtain their medical records. But they also need information on tests and health hazards that agencies independent of the employer collect so that they can evaluate their employer's warnings or assurances more effectively. Workers need trustworthy information about risks to individuals as well as aggregate data that may reveal patterns of health hazards and groups screened out.

Control over physicians' services remains in management's hands. Services to employees are likely to improve if control over them is separated from employment. They could be contracted out to a third party that both management and employee representatives choose. Effective regulatory power can serve a critical function in protecting health, but regulatory oversight of employee health policies has been limited by cutbacks in enforcement of health protections, along with slow and cumbersome standard setting. OSHA should be modified so that standards and policies would eliminate health risk more effectively. Government also ought to provide greater support to train occupational medicine physicians, thereby encouraging a professional base that can advise companies on reducing work hazards. Most physicians get little medical school training in occupational health, so regional occupational and environmental health resource centers with board-certified occupational physicians could increase their capabilities by offering health consulting services, developing surveillance programs, dispensing information about work hazards, offering physical exams, and evaluating individuals who might be at special risk. These centers could more credibly study hazards and protect medicine from the constraints of employers who need to serve stockholders by maximizing company profits. Companies and government would pay for professional services but not employ doctors themselves or retain a legal right to see any of the center's medical data about employees. Such a system would allow doctors to address health risks without worrying that their employers could question their allegiance or threaten their corporate employment. Science and medicine, then, could potentially be more independent of management control.

CONCLUSION

Most theoretical and empirical work on professionals approaches professionalization and corporatization as if they were two very different and conflicting processes. But in fact, the professionalization process has oriented professionals—especially engineers and professors, but also accountants, doctors, and lawyers—to work in organizations, often large bureaucratic organizations. Professionals identify with their professional reference group while also identifying strongly with, or acquiescing to, corporate goals. *Professionalization and corporatization are intensifying simultaneously*, and in many ways reinforce each other. Corporate professionals are becoming more professionalized even as they cede greater control to their employers. Many professional fields (such as occupational medicine) have been deliberately professionalizing, becoming more powerful and highly trained, and producing higher caliber research. For example, occupational medical journals and professional societies have grown substantially since the 1950s, with greater professional participation by company doctors. Yet corporate pressures on physicians have intensified along with professionalization over the past four decades as lawsuits, publicity of chemical risks, government regulation, and higher insurance and workers' compensation expenses have raised employers' costs from workplace hazards.

The dilemmas that corporate physicians face concerning loyalty, conformity, treatment of deviance, and risk are in part ethical problems. Company physicians sometimes refer to values to rationalize what they do even when values are not salient factors in their decisions, however. Conflicting organizational demands from being both corporate employees and professionals are not necessarily a matter of ethics. The problem of loyalty and professionalism is a social and structural problem, not a matter of a specific personality or type of person. A professional can be well intentioned, competent, and conscientious. But if companies employ them, they usually end up conforming to the corporate culture and advancing the corporation's ends—or not keeping their jobs. Doctors become involved in such activities as controlling absenteeism, determining fitness for work, and reducing disability leave not because they have "bad values," but because they are doing the job they were hired to do. Thus, though white coats' values are different from team players', the working conditions generally determine what the person does. Ethics and values aside, the social context of the workplace and people's structural position in the organization shape the way people approach work and largely determine that company professionals generally are pro-management. Bringing about effective policies therefore requires increasing corporate professionals' and employees' power to protect the long-term interests of the company, its employees, and society—including protecting health and the environment—and facilitating structural change that strengthens safeguards for them when they act to protect such long-term interests.

ACKNOWLEDGMENT

This paper is based on research supported in part by grants from the Russell Sage Foundation and the Haynes Foundation. Here I refer to confidential interviews with informants who requested anonymity. I gratefully acknowledge the contributions to this article by Ida Simpson, G. William Domhoff, and Gene Tanke.

NOTES

1. See Sullivan (1995), Freidson (1994, 1986), Hafferty and McKinlay (1993), Spangler (1986), and Sassower (1993). A few studies have considered the work of physicians in large organizations. Investigators have paid some attention to physicians on the staffs of large hospitals and health maintenance organizations rather than manufacturing companies (see Starr 1982; and Freidson 1986). Field (1966; 1957) examines the work of Soviet physicians, Lifton (1986) analyzes Nazi doctors, Walters (1984) analyzes Canadian occupational physicians, and Walsh (1987) examines physicians who manage corporate medical departments. Yet the number of studies that attend to conditions of corporate employment remains small.

2. For the ethical code of ACOEM (American College of Occupational and Environmental Medicine), see ACOEM (1994). ACOEM's ethics committee is charged with evaluating possible breaches of professional ethics. While professionals themselves express conflict over the difficult decisions they make, professional journals, speeches, and ethical codes often proclaim the independent professional judgment of corporate professionals.

3. Managers' using physicians to label and remove troublesome employees is similar to the treatment of people considered deviant or troublemakers as psychologically or medically sick in the former Soviet Union, where dissidents sometimes were imprisoned in mental hospitals. See Conrad and Schneider (1992) on deviance and medicalization.

4. For discussion of chemical sensitization and psychological explanation of symptoms, see Sparks, Daniell, Black, Kipen, Altman, Simon, and Terr (1994).

5. See Karasek and Theorell (1990) and Macdonald and Roman (1994) for discussion of associations between job satisfaction, control over work, and health outcomes. Low levels of control over work processes, along with performance demands of jobs that exceed individual and social resources for accomplishing the required tasks, increase job stress and are associated with higher risk of cardiovascular and other forms of chronic disease.

6. Wellness programs include health-screening programs such as for breast cancer and hypertension, and health promotion such as smoking cessation and exercise programs. See Conrad and Walsh (1992) and Pelletier (1996).

7. The American Management Association analyzed surveys from about 10 percent (961) of its 9,500 U.S. corporate members, which are relatively large firms that together employ one-quarter of the U.S. work force. The proportion of companies conducting drug testing rose in its annual surveys from 21.5 percent in 1987. Companies reported a positive test rate in 1995 of 4.0 percent among new hires and 1.9 percent among current employees.

8. Aside from the concern with deterring drug users from their own company, some employers are on the moral bandwagon of using workplace testing to stop drug abuse in the country. For a related discussion of the molecular biological bandwagon in cancer research, see Fujimura (1996).

9. See *International Union, United Automobile, Aerospace, and Agricultural Implement Workers of America, UAW et al. vs. Johnson Controls, Inc.*, 499 U.S. 187 (1991). Some employers continue their policies of excluding individuals they consider high risk—even in the face of discrimination suits—because they still fear costly third-party suits on behalf of those damaged by work exposures.

10. In some cases, risks through fathers' exposure to hazards may even be greater than the maternal reproductive risks. For instance, male exposure to ionizing radiation presents a higher risk for genetic mutations and chromosome aberrations than reproductive risk through female workers. See Draper (1993) and Samuels (1995) for discussion of the selective application of fetal exclusion policies.

11. Employers have screened for genetic traits such as G-6-PD deficiency and sickle cell trait in attempts to identify workers who may be at increased risk of becoming sick on the job. Many screening tests suffer from narrow applicability and limited predictive value, but they may give employers and workers a false sense of security by making them think that screened out workers represent the elimination of the health risk. See Andrews, Fullarton, Holtzman, and Motulsky (1994) and Draper (1991).

12. The Americans with Disabilities Act of 1990 (ADA; 42 U.S.C. §§ 12101–12213) protects people who have, or who are perceived to have, physical or mental impairments from employment discrimination (EEOC, Compliance Manual, Vol. 2, EEOC Order No. 915.0002, § 902 (Mar. 14, 1995)). Employers can require physical examinations of applicants after they make an offer and withdraw an offer if they can prove that an applicant cannot do a job even with reasonable accommodations or if candidates pose a "direct threat" to themselves or others on the job. Few cases have been decided under the ADA that deal with discrimination resulting from the belief that an individual with a currently asymptomatic condition will become disabled in the future. See Andrews (1994) and Rothstein (1992). Title VII of the Civil Rights Act of 1964 (42 U.S.C. § 2000e) also limits employers' ability to deprive individuals of employment opportunities or otherwise adversely affect their status as employees through screening programs that treat differently or disproportionately affect a protected class (such as race, sex, or ethnicity).

13. In *McGann v. H & H Music Co.*, a man with AIDS who worked for a small music company in Texas made claims and collected payments from the company's commercial insurance plan. The company became self-insured and decreased the lifetime medical benefit for AIDS-related claims from one million to five thousand dollars after it became self-insured. The *McGann* court held that self-insured companies under the Employee Retirement Income Security Act of 1974 (ERISA; 29 U.S.C. §§ 1001-1381) can change their benefit plans post facto because of an employee's claim or a medical test. Employers can charge everyone with a high-risk profile higher rates, provide inferior benefits, or tell people they are not insurable. See Rosenblatt, Rand, and Rosenbaum (1997, pp. 159–292 and 1001–1037) and *McGann v. H & H Music*, 946 F.2d 401 (5th Cir. 1991), *cert. denied, Greenberg v. H & H Music Company*, 506 U.S. 981 (1992).

14. At least 26 states have statutes that protect against genetic discrimination in employment or health insurance. Federal bills have been proposed before Congress that would prohibit genetic discrimination, but few protections are now in place. See Rothenberg (1995), Gostin (1995), and Pear (1997). For a promising comprehensive effort to protect individuals from unauthorized analysis of their DNA, see the Genetic Privacy Act, a version of which has been proposed in the Maryland Senate (S. 645, Md. 409 Leg. Sess. (1994)). See also Annas, Glantz, and Roche (1995). Companies could

offer individuals at risk an opportunity to move to an equal-status job in another area without any loss of pay, as in the OSHA lead standard (29 C.F.R. § 1910.1025 (1996)), but companies that are small or in a downsizing mode would have difficulty doing this.

15. Despite political obstacles to enacting a national single-payer health care system, political leaders could overcome opposition to reform by educating the public about the expense, gaps in coverage, and inequities of the current health care delivery system. For discussion of insurance companies' efforts to avoid insuring individuals they consider high risk, see Pear (1997).

16. On liability related to occupational health, see Wolkinson and Block (1996), Bixby (1990), and Business Laws (1994). In *People v. Chicago Magnet Wire Corp.*, 534 N.E.2d 962 (1989), five company officers were charged with aggravated battery, reckless conduct, and conspiracy to commit aggravated battery for causing the injury of 42 employees by failing to provide necessary safety precautions. See also *General Dynamics v. Superior Court* 876 P.2d 487 (Cal. 1994), in which the court upheld a cause of action for wrongful discharge by an in-house corporate lawyer who claimed that the employer made illegitimate demands that conflicted with the mandatory ethical norms in the California Rules of Professional Conduct.

17. California Penal Code § 387 (1997), enacted in 1990 and amended in 1994.

18. For discussion of social effects of litigation, see, for example, Galanter (1994) and Huber (1990).

19. The U.A.W. and General Motors provided a good model with their UAW-GM board that meets with scientists acting as adjudicators, information specialists, and facilitators to try to address workplace concerns jointly. The U.A.W. has been particularly successful in negotiations with major auto companies over joint training funds and other issues. OSHA could mandate joint labor-management health committees and occupational medical services for employees nationwide.

20. See, for example, Beck (1992), Brown and Middelsen (1990), and Couch and Kroll-Smith (1991). See Portes (1996) on transnational networks and communities and Rodrick (1997) on effects of globalization, including its undermining domestic institutions, labor rules, and longstanding social contracts.

REFERENCES

American College of Occupational and Environmental Medicine. 1994. "American College of Occupational and Environmental Medicine Code of Ethical Conduct." *Journal of Occupational Medicine* 36: 28–30.

American Management Association (AMA). 1996. *1996 AMA Survey: Workplace Drug Testing and Drug Abuse Policies*. New York: American Management Association.

Andrews, L.B., J.E. Fullarton, N.A. Holtzman, and A.G. Motulsky, eds. 1994. *Assessing Genetic Risks: Implications for Health and Social Policy*. Washington, DC: National Academy Press.

Annas, G.J., L.H. Glantz, and P.A. Roche. 1995. *The Genetic Privacy Act and Commentary*. Boston: Boston University School of Public Health.

Beck, U. 1992. *Risk Society: Towards a New Modernity*. London: Sage Publications.

Bendix, R. 1956. *Work and Authority in Industry: Ideologies of Management in the Course of Industrialization*. Berkeley, CA: University of California Press.

Bixby, M.B. 1994. "Was it an Accident or Murder? New Thrusts in Corporate Criminal Liability for Workplace Deaths." *Labor Law Journal* 45: 421.

Brown, P., and E.J. Middelsen. 1990. *No Safe Place: Toxic Waste, Leukemia, and Community Action*. Berkeley, CA: University of California Press.

Business Laws, Inc. 1994. *Occupational Safety and Health Law*. Chesterland, OH: Business Laws, Inc.

Caplan, A. 1995. *Moral Matters: Ethical Issues in Medicine and the Life Sciences*. New York: John Wiley & Sons, Inc.

Conrad, P., and J.W. Schneider. 1992. *Deviance and Medicalization: From Badness to Sickness*, expanded edition. Philadelphia: Temple University Press.

Conrad, P., and D. Chapman Walsh. 1992. "The New Corporate Health Ethic: Lifestyle and the Social Control of Work." *International Journal of Health Services* 22: 89–111.

Couch, S.R., and J.S. Kroll-Smith. 1991. *Communities at Risk: Collective Responses to Technological Hazards*. New York: Peter Lang Publishers.

Cushman, J.H., Jr. 1997. "U.S. Reshaping Cancer Strategy as Incidence in Children Rises." *New York Times* (September 29): A1 and A13.

Draper, E. 1991. *Risky Business: Genetic Testing and Exclusionary Practices in the Hazardous Workplace*. New York: Cambridge University Press.

Draper, E. 1993. "Fetal Exclusion Policies and Gendered Constructions of Suitable Work." *Social Problems* 40: 90–107.

Durbin, N., and T. Grant. 1996. *Fitness for Duty in the Nuclear Industry: Update of the Technical Issues 1996. (NUREG/CR-6470)*. Seattle: Battelle Human Affairs Research Centers.

Duster, T. 1990. *Back Door to Eugenics*. New York: Routledge, Chapman, and Hall.

Field, M.G. 1957. *Doctor and Patient in Soviet Russia*. Cambridge, MA: Harvard University Press.

Field, M.G. 1966. "Structured Strain and the Soviet Physician." Pp. 194–208 in *Medical Care: Readings in the Sociology of Medical Institutions*, edited by W.R. Scott and E.H. Volkart. New York: John Wiley and Sons.

Freidson, E. 1986. *Professional Powers: A Study of the Institutionalization of Formal Knowledge*. Chicago: University of Chicago Press.

Friedson, E. 1994. *Professionalism Reborn: Theory, Prophecy, and Policy*. Chicago: University of Chicago Press.

Fujimura, J. 1996. *Crafting Science: A Sociohistory of the Quest for the Genetics of Cancer*. Harvard University Press.

Galanter, M. 1994. "The Transnational Traffic in Legal Remedies." In *Learning from Disaster: Risk Management After Bhopal*, edited by S. Jasanoff. Philadelphia: University of Pennsylvania Press.

Gostin, L.O. 1995. "Genetic Privacy." *Journal of Law, Medicine, and Ethics* 23: 320–330.

Hafferty, F.W., and J.B. McKinlay. 1993. *The Changing Medical Profession: An International Perspective*. New York: Oxford University Press.

Hanson, F.A. 1993. *Testing Testing: Social Consequences of the Examined Life*. Berkeley, CA: University of California Press.

Huber, P.W. 1990. *Liability: The Legal Revolution and Its Consequences*. New York: Basic Books.

Jackall, R. 1988. *Moral Mazes: The World of Corporate Managers*. New York: Oxford University Press.

Karasek, R., and T. Theorell. 1990. *Healthy Work: Stress, Productivity, and the Reconstruction of Working Life*. New York: Basic Books.

Kevles, D., and L. Hood, eds. 1992. *The Code of Codes*. Cambridge, MA: Harvard University Press.

Lifton, R.J. 1986. *The Nazi Doctors: Medical Killing and the Psychology of Genocide*. New York: Basic Books.

Macdonald, S., and P. Roman, eds. 1994. *Drug Testing in the Workplace*. New York: Plenum Press.

Mehlman, M.S., E.D. Kodish, P. Whitehouse, A.B. Zinn, S. Sollito, J. Berger, E.J. Chiao, M.S. Dosick, and S.B. Cassidy. 1996. "The Need for Anonymous Genetic Counseling and Testing." *American Journal of Human Genetics* 58: 393–397.

Miethe, T.D., and J. Rothschild. 1994. Whistleblowing and the Control of Organizational Misconduct. *Sociological Inquiry* 64: 322–347.

Millman, M. 1981. "Medical Mortality Review: A Cordial Affair." In *The Sociology of Health and Illness: Critical Perspectives*, edited by P. Conrad and R. Kern. New York: St. Martin's Press.

Mills, C.W. 1956. *White Collar: The American Middle Classes*. New York: Oxford University Press.

Nelkin, D., and L. Tancredi. 1989. *Dangerous Diagnostics: The Social Power of Biological Information*. New York: Basic Books.

Normand, J., R.O. Lempert, and C.P. O'Brien, eds. 1994. *Under the Influence? Drugs and the American Work Force*. Washington, DC: National Academy Press.

Office of Technology Assessment, U.S. Congress. 1990. *Genetic Monitoring and Screening in the Workplace, OTA-BA-455*. Washington, DC: U.S. Government Printing Office.

Pear, R. 1997. "Health Insurers Skirting New Law, Officials Report." *New York Times* (October 5): 1 and 16.

Pelletier, K.R. 1996. "A Review and Analysis of the Health and Cost-Effective Outcome Studies of Comprehensive Health Promotion and Disease Prevention Programs at the Worksite: 1993–1995 Update." *American Journal of Health Promotion* 10: 380–388.

Portes, A. 1996. "Global Villagers: The Rise of Transnational Communities." *The American Prospect* (March-April): 74–77.

Post, Jerrold M., and Robert S. Robins. 1993. *When Illness Strikes the Leader*. New Haven, CT: Yale University Press.

Rodrick, D. 1997. "Sense and Nonsense in the Globalization Debate." *Foreign Policy* (Summer): 19–36.

Rosenblatt, R.E., S.A. Law, and S. Rosenbaum. 1997. *Law and the American Health Care System*. Westbury, NY: Foundation Press.

Rothenberg, K.H. 1995. "Genetic Information and Health Insurance: State Legislative Approaches." *Journal of Law, Medicine, and Ethics* 23: 312–319.

Rothschild, J., and T.D. Miethe. 1994. "Whistleblowing as Resistance in Modern Work Organizations: The Politics of Revealing Organizational Deception and Abuse." In *Resistance and Power in Organizations*, edited by J. Jermier, W. Nord, and D. Knights. London: Routledge, Kegan Publishers.

Rothstein, M.A. 1992. "Genetic Discrimination in Employment and the Americans with Disabilities Act." *Houston Law Review* 29: 23–84.

Ryan, William. 1971. *Blaming the Victim*. New York: Random House.

Samuels, S.U. 1995. *Fetal Rights, Women's Rights: Gender Equality in the Workplace*. Madison, WI: University of Wisconsin Press.

Sassower, R. 1993. *Knowledge without Expertise: On the Status of Scientists*. Albany, NY: State University of New York Press.

Spangler, E. 1986. *Lawyers for Hire: Salaried Professionals at Work*. New Haven, CT: Yale University Press.

Sparks, P.J., W. Daniell, D.W. Black, H.M. Kipen, L.C. Altman, G.E. Simon, and A.I. Terr. 1994. "Multiple Chemical Sensitivity Syndrome: A Clinical Perspective." Journal of Occupational Medicine 36: 718–737.

Starr, P. 1982. *The Social Transformation of American Medicine: The Rise of a Sovereign Profession and the Making of a Vast Industry*. New York: Basic Books.

Sullivan, W.M. 1995. *Work and Integrity: The Crisis and Promise of Professionalism in America*. New York: Harper Collins.

Walsh, D. Chapman. 1987. *Corporate Physicians: Between Medicine and Management*. New Haven, CT: Yale University Press.

Walters, V. 1984. "Company Doctors: Standards of Care and Legitimacy: A Case Study from Canada." *Social Science and Medicine* 19: 811–821.

Whyte, W.H., Jr. 1957. *The Organization Man*. Garden City, NY: Doubleday and Company, Inc.

Wolkinson, B.W., and R.N. Block. 1996. *Employment Law: The Workplace Rights of Employees and Employers*. Cambridge, MA: Blackwell Publishers.

DEEP IN THE HEART OF TEXAS AND CALIFORNIA

SAVINGS AND LOAN FRAUD IN TWO STATES

Kitty Calavita

ABSTRACT

This chapter focuses on savings and loan crimes in Texas and California, the epicenter of the thrift crisis of the 1980s. I argue that three criminogenic factors—the deregulation of state-chartered institutions which were nonetheless protected by federal insurance, "good old boy" networks, and a political system conducive to bribery and collusion—help account for the extensive fraud in these states. The data for this study come from government documents, statistical data sets from federal agencies, and interviews with regulators and others responsible for the thrift clean-up. The chapter concludes with a brief discussion of policy implications.

INTRODUCTION

The epidemic of frauds in the U.S. savings and loan industry in the 1980s constitutes one of the most dramatic examples of workplace crimes in this century. As

Research in the Sociology of Work, Volume 8, pages 73-92.

ISBN: 0-7623-0608-4

fraud permeated one thrift[1] after another during the course of almost a decade, the financial carnage piled up quickly. By the time the thrift debacle had run its course, the cost to American taxpayers had reached almost $200 billion. When interest on the government bonds used to pay this tab are considered, it may cost up to $1 trillion (National Commission on Financial Institution Reform, Recovery, and Enforcement [NCFIRRE] 1993; Day 1993; U.S. General Accounting Office [GAO] 1996).

There is much agreement that policy decisions in the early 1980s set the stage for the savings and loan crisis. Experts and commentators from a wide variety of political perspectives and academic disciplines point to the fatal combination of broad deregulation of the thrift industry on one hand, and increased federal insurance for deposits on the other (NCFIRRE 1993; Akerlof and Romer 1993; Barth 1991; Day 1993; Ely 1990; Grundfest 1990; Lowy 1991; Mayer 1990; Pizzo, Fricker, and Muolo 1991; White 1991). There is little doubt that this package of free-market deregulation of investments, combined with stepped-up government protection of deposits, increased investment risks while eroding investor accountability.

Despite this consensus, and the wide coverage given to these factors in the evolution of the crisis, two aspects of the debacle have been relatively neglected. The first is its distinct regional character—the most costly thrift insolvencies were overwhelmingly concentrated in a few states, with Texas and California the leaders. Second, most recent explanations for the crisis have downplayed the role of deliberate fraud, and have focused instead on excessively risky (but not illegal) investments and/or inopportune economic forces such as declining real estate markets (White 1991; Ely 1990; Litan 1993; Samuelson 1993).

My co-authors and I have argued elsewhere that extensive evidence points to the central role of deliberate fraud and wrongdoing in the decimation of the thrift industry (Calavita, Pontell, and Tillman 1997; Black, Calavita, and Pontell 1995). I will focus here then on the regional contexts within which the crisis was embedded, concentrating on Texas and California, highlight the criminogenic nature of those contexts, and touch briefly on the forms of fraud they spawned. I will argue that three components of the criminogenic environment in which the thrift industry operated in Texas and California in the 1980s—the deregulation of state-chartered institutions which were nonetheless protected by federal insurance, the prevalence of "good old boy" networks, and a political system conducive to bribery and collusion—virtually ensured that fraud would be rampant. Further, I will point out that the primary forms of thrift investment were quite different in these two states, as was the economic climate in the mid-1980s, with Texas suffering a serious recession, while California was still booming; nonetheless, the losses were extensive in both states, confirming the importance of fraud and the impact of broad criminogenic features in the regional environment.

The data for this chapter come from a variety of sources. First, I use extensive government documents, including Congressional Records, Hearings, and

Reports, as well as studies and reports of the U.S. General Accounting Office (GAO), the Resolution Trust Corporation (RTC), and the National Commission on Financial Institution Reform, Recovery, and Enforcement (NCFIRRE). Second, I rely on interviews that my co-authors and I conducted with government regulators and other officials responsible for the thrift clean-up. These interviews with 105 government officials took place between 1991 and 1994, primarily in Washington, DC, Florida, Texas, and California. Finally, I refer to statistical data from the Resolution Trust Corporation, the Office of Thrift Supervision, and the Executive Office of the U.S. Attorneys. These agency data sets are a unique source of information about the amount and types of crimes committed and the government response. While each of these primary and secondary data sets has its own limitations, together they provide a reasonably reliable and comprehensive profile of the genesis, evolution, nature, and consequences of S&L fraud.[2] Before proceeding, a brief introduction to the thrift industry and its regulatory apparatus will be helpful.

A BRIEF HISTORY OF S&L REGULATION AND DEREGULATION

The savings and loan system was established in the early 1930s to encourage home construction during the depression and to protect against the kind of financial panic that followed the stock market crash of 1929. The Federal Home Loan Bank Act of 1932 (12 USC 1421 et. seq.) created the Federal Home Loan Bank Board (FHLBB) in order to make mortgage money available for home financing and to oversee federally chartered savings and loans. The National Housing Act of 1934 (12 USC 1724 et. seq.) established the Federal Savings and Loan Insurance Corporation (FSLIC) to insure deposits in this newly created savings and loan system.

The FHLBB was the primary regulatory agency responsible for federally chartered savings and loans for more than 50 years (It was replaced in 1989 as a result of the thrift bailout legislation). The FHLBB oversaw 12 regional Home Loan Banks which served as conduits to the individual savings and loan institutions that comprised the industry. These 12 regional banks provided funds for their member institutions at below market rates, in order to disburse loans and cover withdrawals. In 1985, the FHLBB delegated to these district banks the job of examining and supervising the savings and loans within their region. Thus, while the FHLBB was responsible for promulgating regulations, the district banks oversaw the thrifts' operations and had the authority to impose corrective measures, and to notify the Bank Board of wrongdoing.

In the early years, thrifts were heavily regulated. Their sole purpose was to provide home mortgages, and they were limited to the issuance of home loans within fifty miles of their office. The 1960s brought a gradual loosening of these restraints, but the fundamental protection/regulation formula was not substantially changed. That is, in exchange for government insurance on deposits, the thrift industry continued to be subject to substantial regulation.

A number of economic factors in the 1970s radically altered both the fortunes of the savings and loan industry and its *modus operandi*. Locked into relatively low-interest fixed mortgages from previous eras, limited by regulation to pay no more than 5.5 percent interest on new deposits, and with inflation at 13.3 percent by 1979, the industry suffered steep losses. With new investment vehicles available to middle-income investors, and with inflation outpacing the meager interest on deposits that thrifts were authorized to pay, they found it difficult to attract new money and were subject to massive withdrawals from existing accounts. When the Federal Reserve Board tightened the money supply in an effort to break the back of inflation, and thereby contributed to a serious recession, thrifts were faced not only with increasing competition from high-yield investments given the new hikes in the interest rate, but defaults on loans and foreclosures of properties due to the recession. The net worth of the industry fell from $16.7 billion in 1972 to a negative net worth of $17.5 billion in 1980, with 85 percent of the country's savings and loans losing money (NCFIRRE 1993; Pizzo, Fricker, and Muolo 1991, p. 24).

The political appeal of deregulation coincided with these economic forces. The problems of the thrift industry seemed to confirm the prevailing notion that government regulations imposed an unfair burden on thrifts, precluding them, for example, from offering adjustable rate mortgages (ARMs) or competitive interest rates for deposits. In a few bold strokes, policymakers undid most of the regulatory infrastructure that had kept the thrift industry together for four decades.

In 1980, the Depository Institutions Deregulation and Monetary Control Act (DIDMCA; P.L. 96-221) began the phasing out of limits on interest rates for deposits, and all geographic restrictions on investment activity. It also authorized thrifts to make commercial real estate loans and consumer loans for the first time, and to purchase corporate debt instruments, or "junk bonds." Curiously, the move to the free market model that provided the ideological justification for this massive deregulation was accompanied by a decisive move in the opposite direction: At the same time that the law unleashed savings and loans to compete for new money, it *increased* the federal protection accorded these "free enterprise" institutions, raising FSLIC insurance from a maximum of $40,000 to $100,000 per deposit.

DIDMCA was followed by ever higher losses in the thrift industry. Savings and loans did attract more new money at the higher interest rates they could now offer, but the discrepancy between the high rates they had to pay to attract short-term deposits and the low rates at which they had invested in long-term home mortgages widened. Predictably, the law's primary effect was to precipitate larger losses on more money.

The Garn-St. Germain Depository Institutions Act of 1982 (P.L. 97-320) pushed deregulation even farther, dramatically expanding the investment powers of savings and loans, and moving them farther and farther away from their traditional role as a provider of home mortgages. Thrifts were now authorized to offer consumer loans up to a total of 30 percent of their assets; make commercial, corporate or business loans; and invest in nonresidential real estate worth up to 40 percent of their total assets. Furthermore, the Garn-St. Germain Act allowed thrifts to provide 100 percent financing, requiring no down payment from the borrower, in an apparent effort to attract new business to the failing industry.

The FHLBB also began deregulating the thrift industry in 1980, eliminating the five percent limit on "brokered deposits." These high-interest "jumbo" deposits were made by brokers who grouped individual investments into certificates of deposit (CDs) of $100,000 each (the limit on deposit insurance). So attractive was this system to all concerned—brokers who made hefty commissions, investors who received high interest for their money, and thrift operators who now had almost unlimited access to funds—that between 1982 and 1984, brokered deposits as a percent of total assets increased 400 percent (GAO 1985, p. 7). In 1982, regulators opened the door for a single entrepreneur to own and operate a federally insured savings and loan, when they eliminated the requirement that thrifts have at least 400 stockholders with no one owning more than 25 percent of the stock.

Despite these efforts to reverse the declining fortunes of the industry, losses continued to mount. Indeed, the pace quickened. In 1982, the FSLIC spent more than $2.4 billion to close insolvent savings and loans, and by 1986 the federal insurance agency was itself insolvent (U.S. Congress. House. Committee on Banking, Finance, and Urban Affairs. Subcommittee on Financial Institutions Supervision, Regulation, and Insurance 1989, p. 286). While the number of bankrupt and ailing thrifts climbed, the FSLIC began to slow the pace of closures, due to its own inadequate resources to pay off depositors. During the first six months of 1988, the industry lost an unprecedented $7.5 billion (Eichler 1989, p. 119).

There is no question that extensive deregulation, combined with the enhanced protection of deposit insurance, intensified the problems of the industry and vastly increased the cost of its bailout. As we have shown elsewhere, there is also little doubt that these misconceived policies opened the way for an epidemic of fraud and abuse (Calavita, Pontell, and Tillman 1997; Black, Calavita, and Pontell 1995). Often neglected in this scenario, however, is the way in which the dual system of federal and state charters exacerbated this already criminogenic environment, and helps account for the regional character of the escalating crisis. The remainder of this chapter focuses on Texas and California, tracing the regional effects of deregulation within this dual system, the role played by local networks of "good old boys," and the political connections that facilitated these conspiracies.

THE HEART OF THE CRISIS

Deregulation in Texas and California

While the S&L crisis may have had roots in Congressional decisions and national economic forces such as high inflation, its development was disproportionately concentrated in two states. More than one-third of the almost 400 failed banks and thrifts under FBI investigation by 1988 were in Texas and California, with Texas alone accounting for 85 cases (U.S. Congress. House. Committee on Banking, Finance, and Urban Affairs 1990, p. 166). Of the 26 most costly thrift failures examined by the GAO in 1989, 10 were in Texas and eight were in California. Of the thrifts placed in Resolution Trust Corporation (RTC) conservatorship in its first year of operation in 1989, four times as many were located in Texas as in any other state, followed by California (RTC 1989, p. 12). Together these two states accounted for 36 percent of all referrals of suspected thrift fraud among these RTC institutions, and 59 percent of losses due to fraud. By far the most extensive amount of crime was reported at Texas thrifts: Fully 54 percent of losses due to fraud at thrifts taken over by the RTC were reported at Texas institutions (Calavita, Pontell, and Tillman 1997, p. 37).

There is some evidence that this concentration of fraud and insolvencies was at least in part the consequence of deregulation, as it took effect within the dual system of federal and state charters. There were in essence two parallel and overlapping systems of regulation—one at the state level and the other (the one described above) federal. State-chartered thrifts were regulated by state regulatory agencies, but could be insured by the FSLIC if they paid the insurance premiums, which most did. (By 1986, 93% of savings and loans were insured by FSLIC [Federal Home Loan Bank System 1987, p. 11]). This dual structure had disastrous consequences for certain regions within the context of federal deregulation. Because the funding for state regulatory agencies was provided in large part from state-chartered thrifts, agencies that were perceived as more rigorous or enforcement-oriented than the federal system risked losing their funding as thrifts increasingly turned to federal charters to capitalize on the less stringent regulations.

The California case highlights this dynamic and its consequences. Beginning in 1975, the California Department of Savings and Loans had been staffed by no-nonsense regulators who imposed strict rules and exercised rigorous oversight. When federal regulations were relaxed beginning in 1980, state-chartered thrifts in California switched en masse to federal charters, which they correctly perceived would free them from the rigors of California regulations (U.S. Congress. House. Committee on Government Operations. Subcommittee on Commerce, Consumer, and Monetary Affairs 1987, pp. 12–13). As a result, the California Department of Savings and Loans lost more than half of its funding, and more than half its staff. In 1978, the California agency had had 172 full-time examiners;

by 1983, the number had shrunk to 55 (U.S. Congress. House. Committee on Government Operations 1988, p. 62).

In part to save the state agency (and to retain access to the industry's lobbying dollars for California state politicians), California launched "me-too" deregulation. On January 1, 1983, the Nolan Bill (Cal. Stats. 1983 c. 1091) passed with only one dissenting vote, making it possible for almost anyone to charter a new savings and loan, and eliminating most limitations on investment powers. The former commissioner of savings and loans in California said later of this period, "All discipline for the savings and loan industry was pretty well removed" (U.S. Congress. House. Committee on Government Operations. Subcommittee on Commerce, Consumer, and Monetary Affairs 1987, p. 21). Consultants held seminars for real estate developers on how to buy their own "moneymaking machines" (p. 18). One participant at such a seminar (whose newly acquired thrift soon failed) was reported to have exclaimed incredulously, "My God! This is what I've been waiting for all my life!" (Pizzo, Fricker, and Muolo 1991, p. 36). By the end of 1984, the California agency had received 235 applications for new thrift charters, most of which were quickly approved.

Similar state legislation around the country followed the federal deregulation. But, as Pizzo, Fricker, and Muolo (1991, p. 34) put it, "Texas and California outdid them all, grabbing the lead in deregulation one-upmanship." Texas already had thrift guidelines that were even more lax than the new federal (de)regulations (GAO 1989, p. 25). Thrifts in Texas had enjoyed substantial deregulation since 1972 and had been freed from almost all remaining restrictions with a state law passed in 1981.

In this environment, not only did the number of thrifts grow rapidly, but their size ballooned. By the second quarter of 1984, California and Texas, respectively, had 74 and 62 thrifts growing at 50 percent annually, totaling over $75 *billion* in assets (Strunk and Case 1988, pp. 132–134). A study of the so-called "Texas 40" (the 40 worst thrift failures in Texas) found that on average they had grown more than 300 percent between 1982 and 1986—more than five times the industry average nationwide. Some California and Texas thrifts grew by over 1,000 percent each year (U.S. Congress. House. Committee on Banking, Finance, and Urban Affairs 1989, pp. 576–595; Barth 1991, p. 66; Pizzo, Fricker, and Muolo 1991, p. 37). As they grew, their nature changed as well. The following examples, by no means atypical, illustrate this metamorphosis.

When Erwin Hansen bought Centennial Savings and Loan in Northern California at the end of 1980, it was a conservative thrift with a net worth of less than $2 million. Several days after the Nolan Bill deregulated California thrifts, Centennial purchased a construction company by exercising a stock option held by Hansen's high-financier friend, Sid Shah. Suddenly, the small-town thrift became a development conglomerate. Hansen circumvented the rule against loaning money to his own development company through "linked financing" or "daisy chains": He received loans for his construction company to pursue commercial development from his friends at other California thrifts, while reciprocating with loans for their favorite projects. As Pizzo, Fricker, and Muolo (1991, p. 50) describe it, "Immediately money began to flow like artesian spring water among the main players."

As the money flowed, one of the thrift industry's most expensive shopping sprees began. Hansen threw a $148,000 Christmas party for 500 friends and guests that included a 10-course dinner, roving minstrels, court jesters, and pantomimes. He and companion Beverly Haines, a senior officer at Centennial, travelled around the world in private jets, purchased antique furniture, and renovated an old house in the California countryside at a cost of more than $1 million, staffing it with a gourmet chef at an annual salary of $48,000. A fleet of luxury cars was put at the disposal of Centennial employees, and the thrift's offices were decorated with expensive art (Pizzo, Fricker, and Muolo 1991, pp. 41–54; GAO 1989, p. 22).

Centennial's collapse in 1985 cost the FSLIC approximately $160 million (U.S. Congress. House. Committee on Government Operations 1988, p. 38). The day before Hansen was scheduled to appear before the Department of Justice to negotiate testifying against Sid Shah, he was found dead, apparently of a cerebral aneurysm. Haines was convicted of embezzling $2.8 million and spent 67 days of a five-year sentence in prison. Shah was not criminally prosecuted for his Centennial activities, but was sentenced to seven years in prison for money laundering.

Don Dixon operated Vernon Savings and Loan in Texas using many of these same strategies. Dixon was a developer before buying his savings and loan, and he used Vernon largely as a way to provide funding for his commercial real estate projects. When deregulation removed the five percent limit on brokered deposits, thrift owners like Dixon had an almost unlimited source of cash—albeit at exorbitantly high interest rates—with which to fund their investment projects and finance their shopping sprees. Officials later charged that Dixon used Vernon to funnel money from brokered deposits into his holding company, Dondi Financial Corporation. At Dondi, Dixon used federally insured deposits to fund whatever venture he and his associates chose, usually adding commercial real estate to the already glutted Texas market. When Vernon was finally taken over in 1987, at a cost of $1.3 billion to taxpayers, 96 percent of its loans were in default (Black 1993a).

Charles Keating, like Dixon, started out as a real estate developer and in 1984 purchased Lincoln Savings and Loan in Irvine, California through his development company, American Continental Corporation (ACC). He quickly transformed Lincoln from a thrift with 50 percent of its assets in traditional home mortgage loans, into a giant conglomerate specializing in commercial real estate ventures and other direct investments. In the first year, Keating invested $18 million in a Saudi bank, $2.7 million in an oil company, $132 million in a takeover bid, $19.5 million in a hotel venture, and $5 million in junk bonds. Two years later, 10 percent of Lincoln's assets—or $800 million—were tied up in junk bonds, most purchased from his associate Michael Milken at Drexel. Much of this investment activity violated the 1985 limit on direct investments, a rule Keating circumvented by backdating and fabricating documents and records while fighting the FHLBB to have the rule rescinded (Pizzo, Fricker, and Muolo 1991; Black 1993a).

Loan swapping was central to Keating's operations. As money came in the door from depositors, it went out in loans to Keating's associates in commercial real estate and junk bonds. Not only did this net him handsome upfront fees, points, and dividends, but the favor was returned in the form of loans for his own projects. To cite but one example, Keating associate Gene Phillips owned Southmark Corporation and its subsidiary San Jacinto Savings and Loan in Houston, Texas. Keating loaned $129 million to Southmark in late 1985 and early 1986, and in January, 1986, Southmark loaned a Keating enterprise $35 million. At the same time, Keating and Phillips exchanged about $246 million in existing mortgages, booking $12 million in accounting profits from the swap. During the five-year period of Keating's control of Lincoln, he and his family, all of whom were on the payroll, took home more than $41 million in salary and perks. When Lincoln was taken over in 1989, it cost more than $3 billion to resolve (U.S. Congress. House. Committee on Banking, Finance, and Urban Affairs 1990).

While the deregulation of the industry—particularly in Texas and California—allowed thrifts to engage in nontraditional investment activities within which this extensive fraud was embedded, intricate networks of partners and associates widened their scope and inflated their costs.

"Good Old Boy" Networks

A memo circulated among the Senate Banking Committee and staff delineates the four most common forms of fraud found at the center of the thrift debacle (Alt and Siglin 1990). These four essential types of fraud—the permutations of which are almost infinite—were land flips, nominee loans, reciprocal lending arrangements, and linked financing. Investigators and regulators reported finding these four basic scams repeatedly in their autopsies of insolvent savings and loans. As one regulator put it, the pattern was repeated so often "it was as if someone had found a cookie cutter" (personal interview). As we see below, each one of these schemes required a network of participants.

In a land flip, a piece of property was sold back and forth between two or more partners, inflating the price each time and refinancing the property with each sale. It was not unusual in the mid-1980s for partners to "flip" a property in one afternoon until its "value" had increased several times over. The final loan could then be defaulted on, leaving the partners with hefty profits, and the lending institution with short-term points and fees (but holding grossly inflated real estate). The jargon for this scheme was "cash-for-trash," and the defaulting loans were "drag-away loans." By definition, this scam required a network of participants—at a minimum, two "borrowers," an appraiser, and a thrift operator or loan officer.

Erwin Hansen of Centennial used land flips to increase the value of one property by almost 1,000 percent. In another case, loan broker J. William Oldenburg bought property for $874,000, and sold it two years later after a number of flips, when he had the land appraised for *$83.5 million*. He then bought a thrift for $10.5 million, and sold his property to the thrift for $55 million. In 1985, the thrift went under, leaving FSLIC responsible for $416 million in outstanding deposits (U.S. Congress. House. Committee on Government Operations 1988).

Don Dixon reportedly "flipped land deals [like] pancakes." (O'Shea 1991, p. 75). He and associates at Sunbelt Savings and Loan in Dallas (nicknamed by regulators "Gunbelt"), and Texas developer Danny Faulkner, used land flips among other schemes to develop hundreds of miles of condominiums on I-30 northeast of Dallas. Officers at nearby Empire Savings and Loan financed the land flips that provided the collateral for the condo development loans despite an already glutted Dallas real estate market. Faulkner and his partners hosted weekend brunches at Wise's Circle Grill in the I-30 corridor. Invited guests included officials from Empire Savings and Loan, investors, appraisers, and increasingly, politicians who drew huge campaign contributions from the events. Over breakfast, properties quickly changed hands and millions of dollars of phony profits were made in a few hours (personal interview; O'Shea 1991).

A Faulkner associate describes one incident where land flips were conducted in the hallway of an office building in Dallas: "The tables were lined all of the way down the hall, and the investors were lined up in front of the tables. The loan officers would close one sale and pass the papers to the next guy, who would close another sale at a higher price. It was unbelievable. It looked like kids registering for college. If an investor raised a question, someone would come over and tell them to get out of the line, they were out of the deal" (O'Shea 1991, pp. 34–35).

Nominee loan schemes involved loans to a "straw borrower" who was affiliated in some way with the institution. They were generally used to disguise violations of the regulation limiting unsecured commercial loans to thrift insiders. Don Dixon was particularly adept at setting up nominee loans, allowing him to raid his own piggy bank. The nominee loan schemes spun by Dixon were carried out within a network of more than 30 subsidiary companies established for the express purpose of making loans to himself and other insiders.

Ranbir Sahni operated his American Diversified Savings Bank in Lodi, California, in a similar way. Sahni bought American Diversified in 1983 and quickly turned it into a mega-thrift. First, he stopped writing home loans entirely, then closed the teller windows, and finally shut down the storefront bank, opening up instead ninth-floor office space for the receipt of brokered deposits and transacting his many investment schemes (Mayer 1990).

Most of the thrift's investments were in two Sahni-owned subsidiaries and a collection of tax-shelter partnerships. Through his ownership of American Diversified and access to its high-interest brokered deposits (American Diversified paid the highest interest rates on deposits in the country during this time), Sahni had acquired a risk-free money machine for his development companies; looked at the other way around, these companies acted as straw borrowers for Sahni.

Sahni invested in a windmill farm in the desert; a chicken farm designed to process chicken manure into methane energy; shopping centers and condominiums; and, $300 million in worthless junk bonds. He was a partner in virtually all of the real estate deals and alternative energy projects his thrift invested in. The insider dealing and brokered deposits through which it was financed made American Diversified the fastest growing thrift in the country. When it collapsed, it left almost $1 billion in government-insured losses. As one observer described the life course of American Diversified, "With perhaps $500,000 in equity, it destroyed $800 million of insured deposits, a kill ratio of 1,600 to 1.... This anecdote is tantamount to a news report that a drunken motorist has wiped out the entire city of Pittsburgh" (quoted in Mayer 1990, p. 9).

In Santa Ana, California, Duayne Christensen and Janet McKenzie wove the same kind of complex nominee loan schemes. Former dentist Duayne Christensen opened North American Savings and Loan in Santa Ana in 1983. In partnership with real estate broker Janet McKenzie, Christensen used the thrift to make loans to his own real estate projects and to participate in land flips, through a real estate company owned and controlled by McKenzie. In one scheme, a straw borrower purchased property brokered by McKenzie's company and financed by North American. The borrower then immediately resold the property at an inflated value to his own holding company. Fees and commissions poured into McKenzie's real estate brokerage. North American made upfront points and fees, but apparently never saw the proceeds of any of the properties' resales. North American was taken over in 1988, at a loss of $209 million (U.S. Congress. House. Committee on Government Operations. Subcommittee on Commerce, Consumer, and Monetary Affairs 1987).

Reciprocal lending was another way of circumventing restrictions against insider borrowing. Instead of making a loan directly to oneself, which would have sounded the alarm among regulators, two or more insiders at different thrifts made loans to each other. Making loans to each other is not in itself illegal, but making loans solely or primarily on the basis of a reciprocal loan is fraud. These "daisy chains" often involved multiple participants, and unraveling them sometimes took investigators far afield of the original institution. A macabre variation on reciprocal lending involved the trading not of loans, but of bad assets. In this arrangement—the evocative jargon for which was trading "dead cows for dead horses"—savings and loans traded their non-performing loans back and forth to each other, temporarily getting them off the books and artificially enhancing their picture of financial health. These transactions were central to keeping "zombie" institutions open well after their insolvency so they could be further looted, increasing the final cost of the bailout substantially. In one case, 19 of the largest thrifts in Texas sent representatives to a secret meeting in Houston in 1985 to exchange "dead cows and horses" for the explicit purpose of keeping regulators at bay (Personal interview; Pizzo, Fricker, and Muolo 1991, pp. 277–278).

Finally, linked financing involved depositing money in a thrift, with the understanding that the depositor would receive a loan in return. Don Dixon was an expert at linked financing. He and his CEO Woody Lemons, for example, established the Moonlight Beach Joint Venture in Encinitas, California, north of San Diego, developing a condominium project adjacent to an exclusive beach club. When the beach club decided to expand, it needed funding to acquire the Dixon/Lemons property. Dixon and Lemons suggested to the club that Vernon depositors were a good source of new members, and hence, revenue. O'Shea (1991, pp. 110) explains how it worked: "Pretty soon, big customers seeking loans at Vernon Savings started hearing about this great beach club near San Diego.... No one said a $10 million loan request for a shopping center would be denied if the developer didn't join the beach club. But everyone got the message."

Networks involving land flips, nominee loans, reciprocal lending, and linked financing became so intricate and involved so many interconnections that flow charts recording the activity are virtually indecipherable. Arthur Leiser, an examiner with the Texas Savings and Loan Department for 35 years, kept a diary and noted the interrelationships among savings and loan operators, developers, brokers, and a variety of borrowers. One network he describes included 74 participants. According to his network analysis, practically all the insolvent thrifts in Texas were involved. Others have attempted to simplify things by organizing their charts around only the so-called "high flyers" (See Adams 1990, pp. 270–271).

According to journalists Pizzo, Fricker, and Muolo (1991, p. 35), "Banking had for years been done differently in Texas. Typical features of the state thrift business included risk-taking, wheeling and dealing, and domination by a good-old-boy network that had close ties to the most powerful Texas politicians." With deregulation complete by 1982, these networks were free to weave schemes as intricate as they could conjure up. In this process, they were aided and abetted by enduring connections to the state's "most powerful politicians."

The Political Connection

There is some evidence of collusion between the regulators and the thrifts they were meant to oversee. Don Dixon at Vernon, for example, was reported to have hired two senior officials from the Texas Savings and Loan Department, and according to one California regulator, "provided prostitutes along the way" (personal interview).

More important than these relatively infrequent forms of outright collusion between local regulators and thrift owners were connections between thrift industry executives and key elected officials. The ties between former House Speaker

Jim Wright, Rep. Tony Coelho, and Texas thrift executives are a good example. Rep. Coelho of California was Chair of the Democratic Congressional Campaign Committee (DCCC) in the mid-1980s. In this capacity, it was his job to solicit funds to finance Congressional Democrats' campaigns. Coelho regularly went to the savings and loan industry as a major source of these funds.

Tom Gaubert, owner of Independent American Savings Association in Texas, became one of the first members of Coelho's "Speakers' Club," which for a contribution of $5,000 provided members with "personal assistance in Washington" (Jackson 1988, p. 98). Gaubert wrote checks for more than $15,000 in his first six months as a member of Coelho's "club." When Texas Rep. Jim Wright was up for re-election, Gaubert established a political action committee (PAC) called "East Texas First," with offices located in a Dallas savings and loan. The PAC raised money from 66 Texas thrift owners and borrowers, primarily Dallas developers who had received hundreds of millions of dollars in loans (Pizzo, Fricker, and Muolo 1991, p. 287). The *Wall Street Journal* reported that the directors of one Texas thrift were given "subsidies" by its owner to make $1,000 contributions to the PAC (cited in Jackson 1988, p. 266). In 1986, Gaubert became Treasurer of the DCCC, raising $9 million in that capacity (*Newsweek*, cited in Pizzo, Fricker, and Muolo 1991, p. 287). The following year, he chaired a fundraiser that brought in $1 million for Jim Wright.

During this period, Gaubert was under investigation by the FHLBB. By the end of 1984, thrift regulators had forced Gaubert to resign from Independent American, which had a number of criminal referrals for serious regulatory violations. Two years later, he was permanently barred from operating a federally insured thrift. Jim Wright intervened on Gaubert's behalf, threatening FHLBB chair Ed Gray that if he did not stop the investigation of Independent American, he would table the urgently needed FSLIC recapitalization bill before Congress, which would have provided additional funds to the FSLIC and allowed for the closing down of insolvent savings and loans (personal interview). Gray refused, and the recapitalization bill was tabled (U.S. Congress. House. Committee on Standards of Official Conduct 1989; hereafter referred to as Phelan Report 1989).

Wright also intervened on behalf of Craig Hall, Dallas-based real estate syndicator and Chair of Resource Savings Association of Dallas. In 1986, Hall was unable to meet payments on the many loans he had from thrifts in California and Texas, and tried to negotiate a "global restructuring" of the loans. Westwood Savings and Loan in Los Angeles refused to restructure the loans on Hall's terms, which FHLB representative Scott Schultz had advised them was not in their best interests, and instead initiated foreclosure proceedings on Hall's properties. Wright once again attempted to blackmail Ed Gray by putting a hold on the FSLIC recapitalization bill until something was done to accommodate Hall. As the Special Counsel report on Wright's ethical violations described it, "Gray and Fairbanks [FHLBB Chief of Staff] thus determined that if they were to obtain a recapitalization bill, they would have to facilitate a restructuring of Hall's loans"

(Phelan Report 1989, p. 21). Reluctantly, Gray replaced Schultz with a FHLB representative who agreed to the restructuring.

Don Dixon also received special treatment from Wright. As early as 1983, examiners reported that Vernon had engaged in "significant regulatory violations, unsafe and unsound practices, [and had] lending deficiencies, inadequate books and records, and control problems." In 1986, it was revealed that Vernon kept two sets of board minutes, one for internal purposes and one for the examiners. By then the institution was deeply insolvent and was placed under the supervision of the Texas Savings and Loan Department. Regulators considered Vernon (which they referred to derisively as "Vermin"), "the worst-run, worst-managed debacle...in the savings and loan industry" (Texas Examination Report, quoted in Phelan Report 1989, pp. 260–262).

Despite this reputation and the substantial evidence of wrongdoing at Vernon, Coelho advised Wright to intervene on behalf of Dixon. Again, he called Ed Gray and asked him to "look into" Dixon's case. Vernon was eventually put into receivership, and Dixon was convicted of criminal misconduct. As the Phelan Report concludes, "It is clear that Wright was willing to intervene on Dixon's behalf without performing even a rudimentary investigation of Dixon's dispute with the Bank Board." And, "[I]n Vernon's case, Wright could not have picked a more unseemly beneficiary of his influence" (Phelan Report 1989, pp. 268–269).

Texas thrifts were by no means alone in enjoying important political connections. Charles Keating, owner of Lincoln Savings and Loan in Irvine, California, contributed heavily to political candidates at the state and federal levels and to both political parties. At the national level, Keating and his associates contributed almost $2 million to political candidates, most of which went to the five senators who are known as the "Keating Five" (Waldman 1990, p. 95). Reporters once asked Keating if he thought this money bought him special treatment; he minced no words in his reply: "I certainly hope so!" (quoted in Pizzo, Fricker, and Muolo 1991, p. 410).

Keating had been charged by the Securities and Exchange Commission in 1979 with siphoning funds from a Ohio bank. In spite of this charge—which Keating settled—he was granted a charter in 1984 to operate Lincoln. When the FHLBB limited speculative investments such as junk bonds, Keating sought an exemption. Alan Greenspan, former chair of the Council of Economic Advisers under President Ford and later head of the Federal Reserve Board, wrote a letter to the FHLB in San Francisco supporting an exemption for Lincoln, on the grounds that the institution was financially sound. Keating paid Greenspan $40,000 for his support (Mayer 1990, p. 140).

In early 1987, Lincoln was investigated by the FHLB in San Francisco for poor underwriting and investment irregularities. In April 1987, Senator DeConcini called Ed Gray to his office. Senators McCain, Glenn, and Cranston were also at the meeting, all of whom had received substantial campaign contributions from Keating. DeConcini, referring to Keating as "our friend at Lincoln," proposed that

Lincoln might offer more home mortgages, in exchange for which Gray would strike the direct investment rule and call off his investigation of Lincoln (Waldman 1990, p. 96).

The San Francisco regulators were soon called to meet with the Senators, this time joined by Senator Riegle, who was to become Chair of the Senate Banking Committee and who also had received donations from Keating. These "Keating Five" tried to convince the regulators of Lincoln's financial soundness and the lack of evidence of misconduct. Ed Gray was soon replaced by M. Danny Wall as Chair of the FHLBB. One of Keating's lawyers subsequently assured him, "You have the Board right where you want them.... I have put pressure on [M. Danny] Wall to work toward meeting your demands and he has so instructed his staff" (quoted in Waldman 1990, p. 97). In one of his first official actions, Wall moved the investigation of Lincoln to Washington DC, out of the hands of the "hostile" San Francisco regulators. The institution was not closed for two more years, a delay that cost taxpayers an estimated $2 billion.

The ties that bound thrift owners and operators with key elected officials were facilitating factors in the thrift debacle, shielding those intent on fraud and postponing for several years the bail-out and clean-up of the industry. Of course, this political collusion was not unique to Texas and California; there is evidence that this kind of "political fraud" greased the wheels of financial fraud in every state where thrift crime was extensive (Calavita, Pontell, and Tillman 1997). Perhaps it should not be surprising then that this political connection was so pronounced—and its impact so costly—in Texas and California, where the thrift debacle was overwhelmingly concentrated.

Discussion

These criminogenic factors played out in different ways in the two states. For one thing, the specifics of typical thrift frauds differed. In California, a potpourri of investment schemes characterized the industry. So-called high-flyers in California, for example, put their money in junk bonds, windmill farms, commercial real estate ventures, takeover bids, resorts, and a myriad of other direct investments. Texas high-flyers instead concentrated to a greater extent on so-called Acquisition, Development, and Construction (ADC) loans.

These speculative deals typically involved making a 100 percent loan (i.e., no money down) to a real estate developer to purchase and develop property for commercial real estate development. If the project made money, the thrift got repaid and made a profit; if it failed, as it almost always did in the mid-1980s glut of commercial real estate in Texas, the developer defaulted on the loan and the thrift took a loss. The beauty of these large loans from the point of view of a thrift intent on fraud was that the ledger showed a rapidly growing enterprise. More important, because interest payments for the first few years were often structured into the original loan, the institution could advertise record "profits," from which lucrative salaries and bonuses for the thrift's top management could be extracted before the inevitable collapse of the house of cards.

Not only did typical thrift scams vary between Texas and California, but their economic environments were dramatically different. While Texas was experiencing a serious slump in its economy—particularly the real estate sector—California was at the height of its boom, with real estate providing one of the most lucrative investments, bringing wind-fall profits to large and small investors alike. While some financial experts and economists (Litan 1993; Lowy 1991) argue that the S&L crisis was primarily the result of inauspicious economic forces, such as falling real estate values in Texas,[3] this explanation for the crisis is conspicuously unable to account for the billions of dollars lost by thrifts in California at a time of unprecedented economic growth. Indeed, the fact that Texas and California thrifts registered similar magnitudes of losses despite the dramatic differences in economic climates in this period, points once again to the role of fraud in generating these losses, and the criminogenic features shared by the two states.

CONCLUSION

Needleman and Needleman (1979) point to the importance of "criminogenic" environmental factors in the proliferation of white-collar crime. Elsewhere, we have highlighted the criminogenic combination of deregulation of the thrift industry in the early 1980s and its continued protection through federal deposit insurance. This combination of factors, however, does not by itself explain the concentration of thrift insolvencies and fraud in a few states, most notably Texas and California.

I have argued here that in those states where thrift fraud proliferated, three additional factors enhanced the criminogenic nature of the environment. First, not only did the federal deregulation of the industry in the early 1980s set the stage for fraud, but perhaps more importantly, the deregulation of state-chartered institutions in key states like California and Texas encouraged the rapid entrance into the industry of thousands of entrepreneurs for whom thrifts represented little more than riskfree money machines, or as one former regulator has called them, "cash cows" (Black 1993b). *Business Week* (1985, p. 78) described these "Go-Go Thrifts" in an ominous report on the "casino society": "Start an S&L. Offer a premium interest rate and watch the deposits roll in. Your depositors are insured by Uncle Sam, so they don't care what you do with their money. And in states like California, you can do almost anything you want with it."

Second, networks that linked the banking industry to developers, land speculators, and real estate brokers greased the wheels. In Texas, as Pizzo, Fricker, and Muolo (1991, p. 35) point out, these networks had always been a central component of doing business, its *modus operandi*. In California, such alliances quickly emerged to take advantage of the new (deregulated) investment rules in a soaring real estate market. The product of one such massive network is said to have triggered Ed Gray's rebirth as a re-regulator. Watching a videotape of miles of abandoned, unfinished condominiums east of Dallas, Gray (who at the time was Chair of the FHLBB) was appalled and sent his federal regulators to Texas to see first-hand what was going on. As one of these regulators tells it: "I went down there and this Texan showed me this piece of land and told me how this guy had sold it to that guy, and that guy had sold it again, until it had been sold about six times, and I said, 'Oh, my God. That's terrible,' and he said, 'Only if you're sixth.'" The high-flying thrifts that had financed these deals were consistently "sixth," absorbing the loss when the loans were defaulted on; taxpayers of course were "seventh."

These networks extended to, and contained as pivotal players, the political elite. Texas and California not only had among the fastest-growing thrifts in the most de-regulated climate, but they also boasted a host of local politicians in key Congressional positions who looked out for their benefactors in the banking industry. For example, Jim Wright, Speaker of the House from Texas, had long been a friend of the banking and thrift industry in that state. California Congressman Tony Coelho was the House Majority Whip and Chair of the Democratic Congressional Campaign Committee. Senator Alan Cranston of California was a senior member of the Senate Banking Committee.

The point here is not that these elements were unique to California and Texas. But, the constellation of these ingredients as they permeated the environment in these two states—within the larger context of federal deregulation, deposit insurance, and the influence of monied interests in American politics—go far in explaining the regional concentration of thrift losses. Furthermore, this concentration, despite the substantial differences between California and Texas in terms of the specific types of deals at the center of their S&L debacles and the prevailing economic climate in each state, confirms the overriding importance of these factors they shared and the role of fraud in the ensuing collapse.

Several policy implications follow from this analysis, and from the savings and loan experience more generally. First, while deregulation has wide political appeal, its consequences can be disastrous. The continued deregulation of the private sector suggests the urgency of establishing a set of policy guidelines or lessons to be learned from the S&L fiasco. At a minimum, such deregulatory policies should be scrutinized with an eye for their potentially criminogenic features, and must be accompanied by a system of rigorous oversight. More broadly, the thrift debacle underlines the need to revisit the central role of money in the political process. One senior regulator told us, "It was always the worst [most corrupt] S&Ls in America that were able to get dramatically more political intervention," based on their generous campaign contributions (Personal interview). Unless the ability to buy such political intervention is limited, future debacles—perhaps even dwarfing the S&L crisis—are inevitable.

ACKNOWLEDGMENTS

This research was funded by grants from the University of California, Irvine, and the National Institute of Justice, U.S. Department of Justice (90-IJ-CX-0059). Points of view expressed here are those of the author and do not necessarily represent the official position of the U.S. Department of Justice.

NOTES

1. The terms "savings and loan" and "thrift" are used interchangeably to refer to those financial institutions whose raison d'être, as established in the 1930s, was to provide a stable source of home mortgages, but whose nature and function changed rapidly in the 1980s, as described below.
2. For a more detailed discussion of these data, see Calavita, Pontell, and Tillman 1997.
3. It has been suggested by some that the plummeting market in commercial real estate in Texas was in part the consequence of bad lending practices and fraud (personal interviews).

REFERENCES

Adams, J.R. 1990. *The Big Fix: Inside the Savings and Loan Scandal*. New York: John Wiley and Sons, Inc.

Akerlof, G.A., and P.M. Romer. 1993. "Looting: The Economic Underworld of Bankruptcy for Profit." *Brookings Papers on Economic Activity* 2: 1–73.

Alt, K., and K. Siglin. 1990. Unpublished Memorandum on Bank and Thrift Fraud to Senate Banking Committee Members and Staff, July 25.

Barth, J.R. 1991. *The Great Savings and Loan Debacle*. Washington, DC: AEI Press.

Black, W.K. 1993a. "The Incidence and Cost of Fraud and Insider Abuse," Unpublished Staff Report No. 13, National Commission on Financial Institution Reform, Recovery, and Enforcement.

Black, W.K. 1993b. "'Cash Cow' Examples." Unpublished Staff Report No. 6, National Commission on Financial Institution Reform, Recovery, and Enforcement.

Black, W.K., K. Calavita, and H.N. Pontell. 1995. "The Savings and Loan Debacle of the 1980s: White-Collar Crime or Risky Business?" *Law and Policy*. 17: 23–55.

Business Week. 1985. "The Casino Society." September 16, 1985: 78–90.

Calavita, K., H.H. Pontell, and R.H. Tillman. 1997. *Big Money Crime: Fraud and Politics in the Savings and Loan Crisis*. Berkeley: University of California Press.

Day, K. 1993. *The S&L Hell: The People And The Politics Behind The $1 Trillion Savings And Loan Scandal*. New York: W.W. Norton and Company.

Eichler, N. 1989. *The Thrift Debacle*. Berkeley: University of California Press.

Ely, B. 1990. "FSLIC's Losses—When and How They Accumulated." Alexandria, VA: Ely & Company, Inc. Unpublished report, October 16.

Federal Home Loan Bank System. 1987. *A Guide to the Federal Home Loan Bank System*. Washington DC: Federal Home Loan Bank System Publishing.

Grundfest, J.A. 1990. "Son of S&L—The Sequel: The Conditions that Caused the Crisis are Still With Us." *The Washington Post* June 3: D1.

Jackson, B. 1988. *Honest Graft: Big Money and the American Political Process*. New York: Alfred A. Knopf.

Litan, R.E. 1993. "Deposit Insurance, Gas on S&L Fire." *Wall Street Journal* July 29, 1993: A10.

Lowy, M.E. 1991. *High Rollers: Inside the Savings and Loan Debacle*. New York: Praeger.

Mayer, M. 1990. *The Greatest Ever Bank Robbery: The Collapse of the Savings and Loan Industry.* New York: Charles Scribner's Sons.

National Commission on Financial Institution Reform, Recovery and Enforcement (NCFIRRE). 1993. *Origins and Causes of the S&L Debacle: A Blueprint for Reform.* A Report to the President and Congress of the United States. Washington, DC: Government Printing Office, July.

Needleman, M., and C. Needleman. 1979. "Organizational Crime: Two Models of Criminogenesis." *The Sociological Quarterly* 20(Autumn): 517–539.

O'Shea, J. 1991. *Daisy Chain: How Borrowed Billions Sank a Texas S&L.* New York: Pocket Books.

Pizzo, S., M. Fricker, and P. Muolo. 1991. *Inside Job: The Looting of America's Savings and Loans,* second edition. New York: Harper Collins Publishers.

Resolution Trust Corporation. 1989. *Annual Report.* Washington, DC: Resolution Trust Corporation.

Samuelson, R.J. 1993. "S&Ls: Much More Than Sleaze." *Washington Post* July 7: A21.

Strunk, N., and F. Case. 1988. *Where Deregulation Went Wrong: A Look at the Causes behind Savings and Loan Failures in the 1980s.* Chicago: U.S. League of Savings Institutions.

United States Congress. House. Committee on Banking, Finance, and Urban Affairs. 1989. "Investigation of Lincoln Savings and Loan Association." Hearings before the Committee. Part 2. 101st Congress, 1st Session.

United States Congress. House. Committee on Banking, Finance, and Urban Affairs. 1990. "Effectiveness of Law Enforcement Against Financial Crime." Hearings before the Committee, Dallas, Texas. Part 1. April 11. 101st Congress, 2nd Session.

United States Congress. House. Committee on Banking, Finance, and Urban Affairs. Subcommittee on Financial Institutions Supervision, Regulation and Insurance. 1989. "Financial Institutions Reform, Recovery, and Enforcement Act of 1989 (H.R. 1278)." Hearings before the Subcommittee. Part 1. 101st Congress, 1st Session.

United States Congress. House. Committee on Government Operations. 1988. "Combatting Fraud, Abuse, and Misconduct in the Nation's Financial Institutions: Current Federal Efforts are Inadequate." Report by the Committee. House Report No. 100-1088. October 13. 100th Congress, 2nd Session.

United States Congress. House. Committee on Government Operations. Subcommittee on Commerce, Consumer, and Monetary Affairs. 1987. "Fraud and Abuse by Insiders, Borrowers, and Appraisers in the California Thrift Industry." Hearings before the Subcommittee. June 13. 100th Congress, 1st Session.

United States Congress. House. Committee on Standards of Official Conduct. 1989. "Report of the Special Outside Counsel in the Matter of Speaker James C.Wright, Jr." Report to the Committee by Special Outside Counsel, Richard J. Phelan. February 21. 101st Congress, 1st Session.

U.S. General Accounting Office. 1985. "Thrift Industry Restructuring and the Net Worth Certificate Program." Report to the Congress. September 24. GAO/GGD-85-79. Washington, DC: GAO.

U.S. General Accounting Office. 1989. "Failed Thrifts: Internal Control Weaknesses Create An Environment Conducive to Fraud, Insider Abuse, and Related Unsafe Practices." Statement of Frederick D. Wolf, Assistant Comptroller General, before the Committee on Criminal Justice, House Committee on the Judiciary. March 22. GAO/T-AFMD-89-4. Washington, DC: GAO.

U.S. General Accounting Office. 1996. "Financial Audit: Resolution Trust Corporation's 1995 and 1994 Financial Statements." Letter Report. July 2. GAO/AIMD-96-123. Washington, DC: GAO.

Waldman, M. 1990. *Who Robbed America? A Citizen's Guide to the Savings & Loan Scandal.* New York: Random House.

White, L.J. 1991. *The S&L Debacle: Public Policy Lessons for Bank and Thrift Regulation.* New York: Oxford University Press.

Statutes Cited

Garn-St. Germain Depository Institutions Act, Pub L No 97-320. 96 Stat 1469 (1982)
Depository Institutions Deregulation and Monetary Control Act of 1980 (DIDMCA;PL96-221).
12 USC Section 1421
12 USC Section 1724
18 USC Section 215
18 USC Section 652.961c
18 USC Section 1344
18 USC Section 1001
18 USC Section 1005
18 USC Section 2371
Cal. Stats. 1983 c. 1091

A MULTI-LAYERED SOCIETY IN CONTEMPORARY RUSSIA

CRIMINALS AND OLIGARCHES AS ITS MAJOR ACTORS

Vladimir Shlapentokh

ABSTRACT

In this paper, the author suggests that post-communist Russia can not be described in the terms of the systemic–integrative approach, which is so popular in contemporary social science. As the author contends, Russia is divided into four relatively autonomous layers with their respective elites, economic and political basis, ideologies, and forms of protection in a society with an extremely weak state. The layers include: authoritarian, criminal, liberal, and oligarchic. The central theoretical concepts used to explain the interaction between the four layers are the activities of "rent seeking" and "rent giving." Oligarches are the main rent seekers, while the bureaucracy and criminals serve as the rent givers. This activity permeates Russian society and is a major obstacle to economic and political stability.

Research in the Sociology of Work, Volume 8, pages 93-115.

ISBN: 0-7623-0608-4

WHY IS IT SO DIFFICULT TO UNDERSTAND CONTEMPORARY RUSSIA?

In the recent past, many Western politicians and experts viewed the world through a "systemic dichotomy" (a premise which recognizes societies as either authoritarian or democratic) and tended to classify Russia as democratic. For example, in June 1997, the U.S. Government and its allies recognized Russia as a democratic society and invited Boris Yeltsin to join the G-7 as a full-fledged member.

Meanwhile, the vast majority of Russians (excluding the public statements of Russian officials) strongly disagree with this Western assumption and do not label their society democratic or liberal capitalistic.

In summer 1997, I visited Russia and talked with various politicians and scholars as well as ordinary citizens. When describing how they identified their country, none of them used the terms "democratic," "capitalist," or "liberal." Most were inclined to label their society "oligarchic."[1] Many members of the Russian media use variations of the same term, such as "nomenclature capitalism" and "criminal capitalism." Some Russians talk about "the dominance of seven bankers," an allusion to the infamous government of "seven boyars" (feudal lords) in the beginning of the seventeenth century which handed the power in the country to Polish invaders. In the summer of 1997, Boris Nemtsov, first deputy of the premier minister, publicly declared that "bandit capitalism" dominates Russian society, a view which was accepted by Russian society as a "fait accompli."[2] Many Russian journalists and politicians define oligarchy as "the rule of the few," a characterization introduced by Aristotle (1884) more than years ago.

2,000 Why do the views of Western politicians and scholars deviate from the perceptions of Russians when it comes to defining post-communist Russian society? The answer may be found in one of the fundamental problems facing the study of contemporary Russian society, a difficulty which stems from the use of the integrative-systematic approach.

TWO APPROACHES TO THE STUDY OF POST-COMMUNIST SOCIETY

Indeed, there are two contradictory approaches to the study of society. One insists that each society has "a grand integrative system" composed of consistent elements that obey the fundamental principles of the system. The integrative-systemic method suggests that all political, economic, and social institutions are harmonically interrelated on the basis of the common culture and ideology. In such a system, people interact on the basis of common values and social norms. This approach is accepted by many contemporary Western scholars who follow Talcott Parsons[3] and his predecessors of the holistic vision with its strong belief in universalism as a major trend of contemporary society.

Those who operate with the "integrative–systemic" approach propose that any given society can be politically classified as either democratic or authoritative. During the second half of the twentieth century, this dichotomous approach became entrenched in the minds of most politicians and intellectuals around the globe (in the West as well as in Russia, China, and other countries) because of the confrontation between Nazism, communism, and the countries that supported democracy (Macridis 1986; Nagle 1985; Curtis, Blondel, Brown, Fewsmith, Kanet, Kommers, McNelly, Needler, Reshetar, and Wright 1990, pp. 3–15).[4]

The systemic–integrative approach also concludes that totalitarianism can only be replaced by liberal capitalism, that this transition is the only conceivable prognostication of change (Fukuyama 1992).[5] Such a viewpoint only solidifies the two-sided, Parsonian approach to society.

The second approach rejects the integrative–systemic treatment and contends that society can never be completely integrated. As a rule, societies are divided into segments, each of which has its own economy, culture, value system, norms, and political institutions. These groups coexist in an environment of constant struggle because of limited natural resources. At the same time, each segment is in contention for the prevailing influence over the population.

While the segments (or layers) of society do share the same area (or territory) as well as the same language and history, the society itself can not be considered integrated. The layers as a whole represent more of an ecological system in which the layers interact, but do not share common values or norms. Like biological species, each layer is forced to adjust to the diverse behavior, values, and rules of the other layers.

FOUR RUSSIAS

In 1996–1997, Russians may have been closer to understanding their society than Western politicians and experts. Much of the public defined their society as essentially oligarchic. Certainly, it is impossible to dispute the leading role of the oligarchic layer in Russian society. However, if we were to simply classify the society as "oligarchic," we would be making the same "systemic" mistake as Western politicians who recognize post-communist Russia as purely "democratic." In order to understand Russian society, it is necessary to recognize not one (oligarchic Russia), but four Russias: oligarchic, authoritarian, criminal, and liberal. Each layer (also called sectors or segments) has its own economic and political basis.

FOUR ECONOMIES

Each sector of society has its own economy, a postulate that challenges the dominant view of contemporary economics which operates with two types of economy: market and command.[6] The same concept goes against so called "transitional economics" which assume that the command economy can move only toward a market economy (Nee 1989, pp. 663–681; Buravoy and Krotov 1992, pp. 16–39; Nee and Mathews 1996, pp. 4101–4135).

A few economists have only recently begun rejecting the concept of "one economy in one country." They tend to operate with the concept of a "mixed" economy (market and state economies). While attempts are being made to classify various types of capitalism, economists are still refusing to consider the "oligarchic" (or monopolistic) and criminal economies as autonomous types of economic activity.[7]

The economy of any given country differs from the next in its specific make-up, or combination of the four economies. In Russia, the liberal and state economies are not the only forces that shape the economic landscape. Two other economies, the "oligarchic" (monopolistic or oligopolistic) and the criminal economy, also play an extremely important role.

The state economy in Russia is based on enterprises which belong (fully or at least partially) to the state as well as the financial resources which the state collects in taxes and customs. In 1996, the state employed 37 percent of the active labor force (Goskomstat Rossii 1996, pp. 82).

The oligarchic economy controls most of the extractive industry, metallurgy, the chemical industry and financial institutions. This economy employs approximately 38 percent of the work force in Russia.[8] It is remarkable that only 12 firms pay two-thirds of all taxes collected in the country (Interfax 1998).

The liberal economy is based mostly on small and mid-sized businesses. Twenty-five percent of the active labor force are involved in small and mid-sized businesses.[9]

The size of the criminal economy is very difficult to assess accurately. According to various estimates, the criminal economy produces about one-third of the Russian GNP.

THE FOUR LAYERS OF CONTEMPORARY RUSSIA

The Oligarchic Layer: The "Rent Seekers"

The core of the oligarchic layer is made up of wealthy individuals who are able to buy services from all levels of government (from the president to local politicians) as well as from criminal organizations. The crucial element of the oligarchic layer is the activity of "rent seeking." The term "rent seeking" can be defined as a firm's attempt at receiving extra profits by becoming an exclusive, politically backed monopoly. Rent seeking stands in dramatic opposition to the conditions of fair economic and political competition (Buchanan 1980, p. 3). Legally run institutions (private and public firms and companies) strive for (or "seek") privileges from the state as well as from criminal structures which will help them generate the power and control of a monopoly. The actual methods and instruments of rent seeking and giving are designed to be concealed. They range from outright bribery to the sales of subsidies, tax privileges, price supports, tariffs, farm or import quotas, and licenses.[10]

The exchange of wealth for political power is a well-known phenomenon for those who write about and study the behavior of the Russian oligarchy (Kryshtanovskaia 1995). However, the basic idea of exchange does not adequately explain the relationship between political power and big money. The term "exchange" implies that the participants are both losing and receiving something simultaneously. In the case of "rent seeking", however, the partners only gain: bureaucrats receive monetary support which perpetuates their political power, while oligarches procure special privileges which generate wealth and power far greater than the oligarch's initial payoff to the bureaucrat.

Rent seeking, and the corruption that stems from it, is a universal phenomenon. Many American economists, for instance, have studied the effects of rent seeking in the United States. However, most experts consider the current level of rent seeking activity in Russia to be comparable only with Colombian corruption. Among the most successful rent seekers are the companies vying for special state privileges in foreign trade, the extracting industry, and the financial sector.[11] Every major corporation has its "own people" in the government and the Duma as well as in local governments.[12] It is remarkable that in 1997, even an international organization like the World Bank, which almost blindly accepted privatization and the free market as the irrefutable keys to making any society "normal" and healthy, began to pay close attention to corruption and "robber capitalism" or "crony capitalism" as formidable obstacles to social and economic progress, obstacles which can not be autonomically overcome by market forces (World Bank 1997; Heller 1997).

Buying Offices

One of the most important features of an oligarchy (Aristotle 1884) is the purchasing of political positions which, in turn, bolsters the oligarch's economic and political power. This practice not only allows for additional pecuniary revenue, but enhances the social prestige of the buyer. Purchases range from buying nobility titles, as was common in the Middle Ages, to buying ambassadorial offices in the United States with lavish donations to a successful contender in the presidential elections. The buying and selling of political offices escalated in post-communist Russia.

The career of Boris Berezovsky (1996–1997) can be cited as a classic example of how money can buy political power. Berezovsky was appointed as a deputy Secretary of Russia's Security Council despite a myriad of obstacles that stood in his way, including: his double citizenship (Russian and Israeli) which the law prohibited for state employees of such a high rank; the evident anti-Semitic sentiments in the State Duma and the security forces; and the top clearance that the job demanded. The debunking of his reputation and more importantly, his sources of wealth (an article in *Forbes* magazine's December 1996 issue held the title "The Godfather of the Kremlin"), in no way shattered Berezovsky's standing in the Russian political establishment. Berezovsky continued to combine his commercial and political activities until his showdown with Chubais at the end of 1997, which he lost, and was subsequently fired by Yeltsin (*Izvestia* 1997; *Nezavisimaia Gazeta* 1997a).

Potanin's career is also of interest. As the head of an enormous financial empire, he was invited to the government as deputy premier minister and served in this capacity for one year (1996–1997). By the end of 1997, Potanin's people were confident that he had a chance at the Russian presidency (*Nezavisimaia Gazeta* 1997b).

How Oligarches Protect Themselves

When a society has a weak authoritarian layer and a strong criminal sector, oligarches and their people do not receive enough protection from state agencies. After 1991, the murders of businesspeople, political officials, and journalists became a regular phenomenon in Russia. Between 1995 and 1996, roughly 200 bankers and businesspeople (including the prominent American businessman Paul Tatum), along with dozens of journalists were murdered. None of these murders, which had been well publicized in the media, were solved and no one was brought to justice. This also holds true for the perpetrators of various terrorist acts in Moscow's streets, squares, and parks. By 1997, violent crime and murder in Russia no longer attracted much public interest. The media's coverage of violent crime was minuscule compared to the coverage from 1992 to 1994.[13] Today, ordinary Russians are indifferent, if not completely unsympathetic, toward the violent tribulations of oligarches.[14]

With the growing awareness of the state's unwillingness or inability to protect society, large and small businesses have resorted to three methods of protection which date back to the middle ages: (1) develop a link with the criminal layer by hiring criminals to provide a "roof"; (2) garner the support of people from legitimate law inforcement offices by paying them salaries which greatly surpass their official incomes; (3) create a professional (private) guard or small army. (Similar developments are also occurring in several other countries, but to a lesser degree). Large corporations usually rely more on their own resources of defense, though even some of the biggest banks do not completely dismiss their contact with criminals who provide protection.[15] According to data provided by Nikolai Kovalev, head of the Federal Security Service (FSB, formerly the KGB), each of the 2,000 commercial banks in Russia have their own security services. Some of the private security services are comparable in size and composition to the regional office of the FSB.[16]

The members of these private armies are recruited from the former police force and KGB, as well as from professional athletics (mostly sports related to unarmed combat). Most security forces are headed by experienced military leaders, usually former officers or generals.[17] Regardless of how well equipped these private armed services are, they must entertain good relations with criminal structures and observe the rules of the game.

In Russia, "hired guns" are now considered a "normal" occupation. At the same time, bodyguarding is becoming a very popular profession. According to some sources, there are no fewer than one million bodyguards in Russia. Hiring private bodyguards is already a deeply rooted custom for prominent Russians.[18] This phenomenon is completely alien to the past. In Soviet times, only members of the Politburo had personal wardens.[19] The skyrocketing number of bodyguards and the prevalence of private security forces in post-communist Russia is an accurate barometer of the level of fear. Some bank buildings, such as Menatep, resemble castles ringed with gun-toting sentries waiting for the imminent frontal attack.

The Criminal Layer: Control Over Economics and Politics

The core of the criminal layer (or criminal Russia) is composed of various illegal organizations ranging from illegal firms to criminal mafias. Organized crime is the crucial element of the criminal layer. Mafias can be found in every part of the country, with criminal networks reaching into every city and village.

Criminal organizations control many small and mid-sized businesses and a significant number of big businesses. The criminals themselves often work within the targeted bussiness or firm; they might have an administrative or executive position. Control of businesses may also be maintained by criminal orgainizations through direct ownership of a substantial share of stocks in the company.

The shadow economy is another very important part of criminal Russia. It is said to produce around 30 to 40 percent of the GNP. In the opinion of Igor Sundiev, an expert on criminality in Russia, 90 percent of street trade in Moscow as well as 60 percent of "shuttle trade" (trade based on the trip of individual merchants–shuttlers–to neighboring countries) can be considered criminal or semicriminal activity (Sundiev 1997).

Almost every small to mid-sized business, as well as several large companies, have what is known as a *krysha* (or roof).[20] A *krysha* is a service provided by a criminal organization which usually receives 10 to 20 percent of the profits from each business it works for in exchange for "protection" or a "roof" from other mafias.[21] What is more, this service offers the only real option to resolve disputes with clients who refuse to pay for delivered goods, or with companies that do not pay off their debts.

During the past few years, the power and control of criminal organizations has gone far beyond economic matters. Criminal organizations have started taking control of political institutions, particularly the police, courts, and procurators, as well as certain mayors and local Dumas. These organizations use threats, bribes, and even murder to achieve their goals.[22]

A number of authors (Stanislav Govorukhin for example) have attempted to emphasize that Russia has been "a criminal society" since 1992–1993 (Govorukhin 1993, p. 126; Handelman 1997; Waller and Yasmann 1995). Govorukhin's book, *The Great Criminal Revolution* and other articles about the effects of the criminal layer on Russia have all been rejected by the Kremlin as rude exaggerations. However, in a radio conversation at the end of 1997, Yeltsin himself talked about "the intentions of criminal structures to take control of the country" (Russian Radio 1997).

Criminals are active participants in the election process. In 1997, several individuals with serious criminal records were elected to various positions, from mayors[23] to deputies of local parliaments.[24]

Certain state and regional members of parliament are well-known for their direct connection to criminal organizations. Criminal organizations control local administrations; they dictate the selection of "cadres"; they control business policies; and they protect themselves from legal prosecution.[25]

The Authoritarian Layer: "Rent and Immunity Givers"

There are two types, or classes, of the authoritarian layer: "strong" and "weak." The "strong" type is characterized by the ability of its leader to control bureaucracy (particularly regional) and law enforcement agencies. In a totalitarian society, "strong" authoritarism reaches its highest level. Even in Brezhnev's time, when the central administration was much weaker than during Stalin's regime, the Kremlin still had complete control over all levels of the nomenclature (Shlapentokh, Levita, and Loiberg 1997).

"Weak" authoritarianism has a significant dependence upon the bureaucracy, particularly the regional bureaucracy. With its inability to satisfy the basic needs of the population, the center is forced to expand the power of the regional elite and acquiesce to the authority of the local bosses.[26]

While the central authorities in post-communist Russia were seen as weak, local bosses acquired a great deal of power—more than they had in the whole of Russian history since the emergence of the Russian National State in the sixteenth century. In 1996–1997, the degree of gubernatorial control over the developments in the territory surpassed much of the authority of the Kremlin.

In both cases (strong and weak authoritarianism) the authoritarian layer reveals itself through the tendency of its leader and bureaucracy to control the country, while minimizing the influence of democratic institutions, ignoring laws and controlling elections in the interests of those who possess the power.

After 1993, the authoritarian regime defied the law on a countless number of occasions. In 1996, it lavishly financed Yeltsin's election campaign with state money and exploited its position by demanding money from private institutions. The Kremlin forced the media, particularly the television media, to serve its needs in this election campaign as well. Yeltsin even openly proclaimed that governors and presidents of the national republics were directly responsible for the outcome of the elections (Shlapentokh 1997).

The most important issue pertaining to weak authoritarianism in post-communist Russia deals with the rent giving behavior of the bureaucracy. The bureaucracy has become a giant network of rent givers which distributes privileges among economic oligarches (rent seekers).

Strong authoritarianism operates with only one leader and a limited number of his friends and relatives who have the right to distribute privileges among rent-seekers.[27] Weak authoritarianism, on the other hand, provides tight relations between the leaders of political clans (rent-givers) and their oligarches ("rent-seekers," such as banks, trade companies, oil and gas producers, and the mass media).[28]

In 1997, the degree of corruption in Russia, by all accounts, reached a very high level. A prominent Russian liberal and leader of the party, "Yabloko," publically declared that "the Russian government is a government of thieves" (Yavlinskii 1997). It was clear that Yeltsin did not want to pit himself against the rent givers. Despite the arrests of a few highly ranked officials, none of those accused of corruption were brought to trial in Moscow.[29] What is more, any accusation made in Russia is almost always followed by a counter accusation. In other words, both the accused and the accuser are usually guilty of some form of corruption. As a Moscow political observer reasonably noted, the constant exchange of "kompromat" (compromising materials) among the members of the Russian elite demonstrates that practically everybody has a record of criminal actions. "They all should be in prison," exclaims the author (Pavlovsky 1997). The cooperation of the authorities with the criminal sector, particularly law inforcement agencies, has become a serious problem in Russia, especially at the local level.[30] Various sources suggest that collaboration between criminals, officials, and businesspeople is prevalent in Krasnoiarsk, Kursk, Ekaterinburg, Petersburg, Cheliabinsk, Soch,i and several other cities.[31] The link between these layers fortifies crime in the country as criminals receive immunity.

Liberal Layer: Weak But Promising

The greatest achievement of the post-Communist era is the emergence of the liberal layer (or liberal Russia). The liberal layer plays a serious role in Russian life and is highly regarded by those who believe in the ultimate triumph of democracy and the market economy. Democratic institutions such as the Parliament, the judiciary, and a free mass media along with free market institutions like private property, free competition, commercial banks, mutual funds and exchanges make up the core of the liberal layer.

A number of polls have shown that the majority of Russians support liberal values and political freedoms. The "Fund of Public Opinion" survey, held in 1997, showed that 91 percent of those who responded greatly appreciated the freedom of the press; 82 percent supported the freedom to move and travel abroad; and 81 percent were in favor of free presidential, parliamentary, and gubernatorial elections. A majority also supports the idea of private property and laws protecting one's private life from state intrusion (Fund of Public Opinion 1997a).

At the same time, liberal Russia is the weakest of the four layers. Democratic institutions are very fragile and unstable, particularly in the provinces (regions). Although democratic institutions have made some important improvements, they are often unable to oppose the executive authority when in conflict.

The Russian economy is still far from being regulated by market laws. In 1996–1997, 40 percent of all contracts were based on the barter exchange. Thousands of Russian firms and most regions issued their own private currency (a sort of IOU), the market value of which depends greatly on the reputation of those who issue it.

Economic competition is restricted by the power of national and regional monopolies. The freedom of Russian businessmen is also quite limited and the number of new small businesses has begun to decline after its upward trend between 1990 and 1995. {3}*Liberal Layer: Attacked From All Sides*

Despite its minimal influence, the liberal layer is being systematically attacked by the other three layers. The Kremlin constantly humiliates liberal institutions. For example, since the first free election, the Kremlin has kept the Russian parliament in permanent fear of disbandment. In 1993, the Kremlin not only dissolved the parliament, but shelled the parliamentary building, killing more than 100 people. The President wanted to oust the parliament even earlier, in March 1993, when it threatened impeachment; the effort failed because Yeltsin's enemies could not garner the necessary number of votes (Korzhakov 1997, pp. 156–200).[32] In spring of 1996, on the eve of the presidential election, Yeltsin considered canceling the elections and by all means would not have left the Kremlin if he had lost (Korzhakov 1997).

Local governors are also powerful enemies of the liberal sector. Before they were elected (or appointed by the president), however, they were less authoritative and more sensitive to public criticism. Most governors were elected with the use of the local bureaucratic apparatus as well as the support of business and even some criminal structures. Their elections provided them with the feeling of invulnerability with respect to the Federal administration and the masses. In those regions where the candidates for the position of governor (1997) were incumbents, the elections were comparable to those carried out in Soviet times.[33] It is only natural that in most regions, particularly in the national republics, the leaders of the provinces nearly reduced the role of local parliament to nonexistence. In 1997, the provincial leaders held strict control (reminiscent of the Soviet era) over the elections in the local Dumas to enure complete obedience.[34]

Oligarches in their own turn have downgraded the fledgling Russian democracy immensely—a tendency which is true for other countries (including Western countries) as well. Oligraches cynically exert direct control over leading television channels and newspapers.[35] The problem with media objectivity was considered bad following the summer of 1996, but only worsened in 1997 during the "bank war." Consequently, many Russians consider the present media just as restricted as the Communist media of the past.

Oligarches make it very difficult to carry out a fair election campaign. It is commonly believed that just about anyone could win an election with the right financial backing. The impact of wealthy individuals on the outcomes of elections is particularly strong at the local level. There are two major motivations for entering politics (i.e., local parliaments): (1) to increase political leverage for "rent seeking," and (2) to gain immunity from potential criminal persecution. Local parliaments became especially attractive to businesspeople when (under their influence) the parliament began permitting deputies to combine their businesses and their duties as deputies. Following the election of local legislatures in 1997, a Moscow political scientist noted, "the actual regional parliaments in Russia come up as nothing more than an oligarchic organization, free from professional legislative responsibilities" (Afanasiev 1997).

As previously mentioned, like the oligarchic layer, criminal structures also denigrate democratic institutions. Criminals have penetrated all levels of the liberal layer, taking leading positions as deputies of parliament (national and local) as well as administrative positions.

The criminal layer also has a negative effect on the Russian market. Natural competition is hindered by various criminal activities. Free competition between small and mid-sized businesses is practically impossible. Organized crime has a hand in the redistribution of state property.

Quite possibly the most dangerous threat to the liberal sector, ironically, comes from the liberal sector itself. The majority of the parliament is inclined toward authoritarianism as the deputies are more worried about keeping their seats than supporting democratic institutions. As a result, they often abuse the power of their positions.

Moreover, many Russians intellectuals who, in the recent past, favored democratic principles, lost their faith in the ability of their nation to forge a democratic society. Intellectuals see the population as incompetent and full of bias and therefore unable to make correct decisions during the election process. In effect, intellectuals directly or indirectly support the oligarchic ideology. Some intellectuals backed the idea of postponing the presidential election in the summer of 1996, when threatened with the possible victory of the Communists. However, even more dangerous for the liberal sector is the political apathy and sometimes hostility of the masses toward democratic institutions.

INTER-LAYER CONFLICTS

The relationship between layers are very contradictory and combine fierce struggle with collaboration. One of the deepest conflicts is now taking place between the liberal layer and authoritarianism. The fights, between 1993 and 1997, between the executive power and the parliament at all levels of Russian society were among the most important developments of post-communist Russia. In most cases, the executive power has prevailed over the parliament. At the same time, however, the authoritarian layer is in serious contention (along with collusion) with both oligarchs and criminals.

The position of oligarchs toward the authoritarian sector is quite contradictory. They are torn between two mutually exclusive desires. On one hand, oilgarchs want a well ordered society. They fear an unsteady political environment. For example, most oligarchics united in the summer of 1996 when they lavishly supported Yeltsin against the Communists. Oligarchs as a group support the existing state of lawlessness and obstruct the attempts of people such as General Alexander Lebed to seize power. At the same time, however, oligarchs prefer a weak state so they can continue their rent seeking activity. If a strong state took control, the power and authority over rent seeking could change dramatically.

There are incongruities within the authoritarian layer as well. The executive power is torn between cordial cooperation with oligarchs (which yields considerable benefits) and the desire to dominate the country. Due to various ever-changing circumstances (for instance, the alignment of different factions in the presidential administration and the government) the relationship between the Kremlin and oligarchs remains in a state of permanent flux. In 1996, during the presidential election campaign, this relationship reached the peak of cordiality. Then, in the second half of 1997, relations became strained and conflicts between the government and some oligarchs emerged. Boris Nemtsov and Chunbais persuaded Yeltsin to curb the rent giving activity of the bureaucracy and the arbitrariness of oligarchs, particularly Gusinsky and Berezovsky. The battle that roared between Chubais and Berezovsky in 1997 was at the center of political life in the country.[36]

Another conflict arose between Nemtsov and "Gasprom" which is partially owned by the government and whose stocks also belong to the Chernomyrdin family.[37] By the end of 1997, however, most of the friction between the government and the oligarchic layer abated and the oligarchs retained their power.

INTRA-LAYER CONFLICT

Conflicts within each layer are very important for forecasting the future of any given society. Deep intra-layer conflicts have a negative effect on the layer's position in the struggle against other layers. The conflicts inside the authoritarian layer are usually manifested in the struggle between factions, often with different ideological overtones, which compete for the influence over the ruler. During Yeltsin's regime, there was a clash between pro-liberal and anti-liberal (Communist and nationalist) factions as well as between groups with different allies among oligarchs. These struggles became the most important developments within the authoritarian layer.

Inside the liberal sectors, in the 1990s, there was a struggle between consistent (or "old") liberals and statist (or "new") liberals. By the end of the decade, the statists evidently prevailed.[38]

Conflicts in the oligarchic layer (among rent seekers) are particularly bitter because of the government's limited resources available for redistribution. Oligarches compete for a favorable influence over the central administration. However, this is far from the "perfect competition" of the neo-classical model. This form of competition involves only "the few" and there is a strong restriction against the entrance of new actors.[39]

The battles (and collusions) between the empires of Berezovsky and Gusinky; Smolenskii and Potanin; and Potanin and Berezovsky are only a few examples of the many internal conflicts raging within Russia's oligarchic layer.[40] The hottest area of competition among rent seekers revolves around the auctions organized by the government selling chunks of state property. There is a great deal of evidence that confirms that, during the auctions in 1995–1997, Russian officials were in collusion with some of the bidders.[41] Another important conflict is the battle that pits Moscow financial and political groups against the regional oligarchs (Kryshtanovskaia 1995).

There is not much detailed information available about the collaboration and conflicts among Russian mafias, although their conflicts clearly have ethnic overtones.[42] However, the stream of murders and violent activities among mafias certainly indicates some level of struggle among criminals.

For supporters of the liberal layer, serious intra-layer conflicts within the oligarchic and criminal layers are considered rather positive events. For example, Russians clearly understand that without inter-layer conflicts among oligarchs, the problems pertaining to the ligitamacy of the mass media would only grow worse. At the same time, battles between oligarchs have been so intense that Russian politicians and journalists recognized, in 1997, that an all-out war between the oligarchs could threaten the existence of Russian statehood. The conflicts involved almost every political actor in the country (Tretiakov 1997).

COMMON CULTURE AND CRIMINALIZATION OF PUBLIC MENTALITY

Although Russian society is divided into layers with diverse ideologies and interests, there is a common national culture with one language as well as common values and traditions. This common culture, as previously mentioned, has a limited effect on the behavior of the four layers. What is more important, however, is the direct influence the layers have on the mentality of the population.

The criminal layer has a particularly strong influence on the behavior of the population. This layer has created new standards and morals for the Russian people. For example, the "khaliava mentality" is now prevalent throughout Russia. The term, "khaliava," means to receive something without work, payment, or effort (a sort of "rip-off"). "Khaliava" has become a key term for millions of active Russians who are influenced by the oligarchic ideology and its rent-seeking goals. Here, it should be noted that the "khaliava mentality" was evident during the Soviet period as well. However, in the past, this mentality was countervailed by the official glorification of work and the state's encouragement to be socially useful.

The current official ideology (with its blatant disregard for the value of work) only perpetuates the spread of the "khaliava mentality." After being asked about what it takes to be wealthy in Russia, only five percent responded, "talent and hard work," while 44 percent pointed to "financial speculation," and 20 percent responded, "laundering of the mafia's money" (VTSIOM 1997, pp. 42, 79).

The border between legal and illegal activity is virtually non-existent in the minds of even the most refined intellectuals and politicians. The glamorization of the criminal layer and the view that criminals make the most effective managers has spread throughout the country.[43]

In 1996–1997, criminals began to receive respect and prestige. They were often seen as resolute and competent leaders who keep their promises and are willing to help the people. The Russian media, in 1996–1997, published several articles in which the authors proposed that the authorities should go into open cooperation with criminal leaders, promising that this "brave" measure would help the country restore order and promote prosperity.[44] Sviatoslav Fedorov, a popular political figure, defended Ivan Iaponchik (1997) on Russian television as a modern-day Robin Hood. Iaponchik is a notorious Russian criminal, accused of many crimes including murder (Russian Television 1997). Currently, Iaponchik is serving time in an American prison.

The election success of numerous individuals with serious criminal records, particularly elections at the local level, is another evidence of the growing role of the criminal layer in the life of post-communist society.[45] Mikhail Afanasiev, a Moscow political scientist, wrote, "Russians elect criminals, 'tough benefactors' who promise to feed and protect them" (Afanasiev 1997). Russians, particularly women, often regard criminals as brave, sober, and strong men, a vivid contrast to the way they see bureaucrats as selfish and corrupt, and the bulk of Russian men as mostly drunkards and loafers (Pisigin 1997, pp. 125–157). Vladimir Bondarenko, a radical nationalist, wrote, "in our upside down Russia, criminal talents and former convicts are often times more clean and reliable than former members of the Politburo[46] and former generals of the KGB" (Bondarenko 1997). According to the surveys of Vladimir Spiridonov, three groups of Muscovites (students, bank employees, and governmental officials in 1997) all have nearly 100 percent postive attitudes toward bribes (the author did not mention the sample size of the survey). What is more, "bribe takers" and "bribe givers" were regarded by almost all respondents as "active people" who deserve respect and even envy from those who are unable to perform one of these two roles (Spiridonov 1997).

Another good indicator of the influence of the criminal ideology is the massive inclusion of criminal jargon ("four-letter words") in the everyday speech of "normal" people, including politicians and intellectuals. Major Russian television channels are cluttered with such language.[47] The criminal ideology has an especially strong influence on the youth. In many cases, they not only consider criminal professions "normal," but even desirable. The fact that high-ranked officials sometimes use criminal jargon only justifies the reckless attitudes toward moral values and rules.

RUSSIANS PERCEIVE THE FOUR LAYERS

As previously mentioned, the absolute majority of Russians refuse to label their society as liberal or democratic. In fact, by 1997, most realized their society was composed of four autonomous layers. They discuss and evaluate each of the four layers (the Kremlin, the parliament, owners of banks, and the criminal sector) on a regular basis. Most Russians ascribe the dominant role in their society to criminals, corrupted bureaucrats and oligarchs, while only a slight minority points to the prevalence of democratic institutions.[48]

By 1996–1997, Russians had no illusions about the character of each of the four layers of their society. Most Russians believe that their officials (from the president to the local athorities) do very little, if anything, for the economic progress of the country because they export their capital abroad instead of investing at home.[49] Oligarchs are seen by the public as selfish individuals who are unconcerned with the conditions of the country and indifferent toward important national issues such as science, education, and culture. The majority of the population is certain that the union of oligarchs and bureaucrats will continue to be the predominant source of ruling power in the country. In 1997, the "Fund of Public Opinion" survey revealed that 77 percent of the population believes that "corruption" will continue (Fund of Public Opinion 1997b).

With all the pessimism about the future of liberalism in their country, Russians are forced to rethink the authoritarian alternative. However, they are not, by any means, in favor of the authoritarian alternative represented by Yeltsin's inept regime. Russians want an efficient state with a constructive regulatory role in all spheres of social life. It should come as no surprise that this trend of regression to the ideals of socialism has been on the rise for the last year. Between 1995 and 1997, the number of those who prefered socialism to capitalism (despite official propaganda) was around 50 percent. Only one-third prefer the Western model.[50]

Certainly, many Russians are aware that even "efficient" authoritarianism in its socialist or nationalist forms is much worse than democracy. They also understand that a strongly regulated economy can not compete with a market economy, but like Hobbes, they assume that even despotic order is better for the economy and all other spheres of social life than anarchy and criminality. However, Russians also doubt that an effective autocratic state could emerge in Russia. Even those who regularly cast their ballots for the communists do not believe that the communists are able to create a strong and proficient authoritarian state.

CONCLUSION

As previously mentioned, the major problem of the study of contemporary Russian society stems from the use of the integrative-systematical approach. This approach is not suitable for the study of practically any country in the world. The integrative–systematic approach simply should not be employed.[51]

In fact, only from the "anti-systemic methodology" can we form a genuine picture of contemporary society. The so-called "deviant" layers of society (oligarchic and criminal) must be considered "normal." It also must be understood that the liberal layer is under constant pressure from the other three layers, particularly the state (or authoritarian layer).

Like other countries which have yet to reach a level of relative stability, Russia's future depends on the dynamics within society and the changing roles of each of the four sectors. The intereaction between and within layers as well as the composition of society itself will determine the success or failure of Russia in the years to come.

In 1997, Russians were certain that the dominance of oligarchy would persist. However, today, they still do not exclude the potential of communists and nationalists to seize control and restore the despotic state by using among other things, the deep conflict between the army and the Kremlin. Some Russians predict that criminal gangs will take control of the country in the next few years. It is, however, most likely that the existing alignment of social forces in Russia will remain more or less the same for the next decade.

ACKNOWLEDGMENT

The author wishes to thank Joshua Woods. His meticulous editing and helpful suggestions improved this manuscript.

NOTES

1. The evolution of Egor Gaidar's vision of Russian society has been very typical. In 1992–1993, Gaidar, leader of the Russian liberals and architect of reforms, foresaw a "normal" and "civilized" society right around the corner and asked the people to be patient for only a short period of time (see, for instance, Egor Gaidar, "Chtoby ne Bylo Bednykh", *Literaturnaia Gazeta*, January 3, 1993). However, by 1994–1996, Gaidar had already labeled Russian capitalism as "bureaucratic," as "bad state capitalism," as "corrupted bureaucratic capitalism," and as "extremely unsympathetic" (see his *Besedy s Izbirateliami*, Moscow: Evrasia, 1995; his *Dni Porazhenii I Pobed*, Moscow: Vagrious, 1996 and "Ia Stal Vliatelnei Chem Do Prezidentskih Vyborov", *Segodnia*, October 23, 1997). In his book, "Anomaly of Economic Growth" (Moscow: Evrasia, 1997), Gaidar spoke about the actual Russian society as being "oligarchic" and suggested that "imperial policy, adventurous economic activity and high-scale stealing have chances of becoming long-term factors of the Russian reality." Gaidar repeated the same gloomy diagnosis about the Russian oligarches in his interview with *Moskovskii Komsomolets* (April 15, 1997).

2. For more about Boris Nemtsov, see his interview with *Moskovskii Komsomolets*, August 19, 1997; see also *Komsomolskaia Pravda*, July 29, 1997.

3. Talcott Parsons is the emblem of an overreaching "systemic, or holistic approach" to society (see Talcott 1951, 1971).

4. Some authors use other typologies of government, but they are not popular typologies in contemporary political science. For example, see Crick's division of all regimes into autocratic, totalitarian, or republican (Crick 1973). Blondel operates with five types of systems: liberal–democratic, egalitarian–authoritarian, traditional unegalitarian, populist, and authoritarian–inegalitarian (Blondel 1990, pp. 3–15).

5. See the critique of this view in Gray (1995a, 1995b).

6. Most contemporary economists operate with only two types of economy: market and command. See the very popular textbooks: Mankiw (1997); Dryden (1997, p. 9); and Case and Fair (1996, pp. 41–44). See also Przeworski (1991); Bornstein (1994, p. 16); and Schnitzer (1994, pp. 3–21). Paul Samuelson uses the same position in all editions of his famous textbook. In the 1973 edition, he dealt with "one capitalism" and "several socialist-ommunist economies" (British, French "indicative planning," Stalinist, Yugoslav, Maoist, Soviet) (Samuelson 1973, pp. 867–886).

7. Case and Fair write, "The differences between command economies and laissez-faire economies in their pure forms are enormous. But in fact these pure forms do not exist in the world; all real systems are in some sense mixed." That is, individual enterprise exists and independent choice is exercised even in economies in which the government plays the major role (see Case and Fair 1996, pp. 41–44). Morris Bornstein also deals with capitalism and socialism as two types of contemporary economies, but recognizes that "intragroup differences are frequently so great that prototypes (he means the Unites States versus the Soviet Union) are different in regard to certain characteristic or performance criteria" (Bornstein 1994, p. 16).

8. Boris Berezovsky boasted in his notorious interview in December 1996 with *Financial Times* that seven bankers possess "half of the Russian wealth" (*Izvestia*, December 24, 1997).

9. A remarkable section of small to mid-sized business is made up of the notorious group of merchants known as "shuttlers." These merchants travel back and forth between neighboring countries to buy and sell small amounts of goods. There are approximately 1 million traveling vendors who bring

in 15 to 29 percent of Russian imports (mostly consumer goods like clothing) see Leonid Nikitinsky, "Iz Sveta v Ten Pereletaia," *Moskovskie Novosti*. December 28, 1997.

10. "Rent seeking is usually defined as the political activity of individuals or groups who devote scarce resources to the pursuit of monopoly rights granted by governments. The actual methods and instruments of rent seeking and giving are designed to be concealed. They range from outright bribery to the sales of subsidies, tax privileges, price supports, tariffs, farm or import quotas, and licenses. The benefits that go to officials are usually in the form of higher salaries and perquisites" (Mitchell, W., and M. Munger. 1991. "Economic Models of Interests Groups: An Introductory Survey." *American Journal of Political Science*, 35: 525). Another author asserts, "rent seeking is wasteful from a societal standpoint" (Parker 1996, p. 22). See also Buchanan, J., R. Tollison, and G. Tullock (eds.). (1980. *Toward a Theory of the Rent Seeking Society*. College Station, TX: Texas A&M University Press.); and Krueger (1994, pp. 86–89).

11. Leading corporations in Russia (1997) include: financial empires such as "Most," headed by Vladimir Gusinskii; "Logovaz," headed by Boris Berezovsky; "Menatep," headed by Boris Khodorkovsky; "Oneximbank," headed by Vladimir Potanin; and "Stolichnyi Bank," headed by Alexander Smolensky.

"Gasprom" is another well-known corporation, often referred to as the "cash cow." Its market capital consists of tens of billions of dollars, with sales approaching $20 billion. "Gasprom's" gross profits exceed $3 billion, and it employs nearly 400,000 people.

For data on the concentration of capital in the Russian economy see Goskomstat Rossii (1996, p. 499).

12. By the end of the 1990s, it was admitted in Moscow that "Gasprom" is under the special protection of premier Minister Chernormyrdin who was a former boss of this corporation, and who, by all accounts, had a great deal of valuable stock in this company. Furthermore, Chernormyrdin's two sons openly worked for "Gasprom" (*Izvestia*, January 5, 1997).

First deputy, Chubais, as well as a few other high officials were linked to "Oneksimbank" which, by using a variety of tricks (non-interest loans, excessively high honorariums, and other methods) provided them with various perks. Facts discovered by the media (which served the interests of the rivals of Oneksimbank) led to a huge political scandal in Moscow in the second half of 1997 (see *Novaia Gazeta*, November 17 and December 1, 1997; and *Moskovskie Novosti*, November 11, 1997; *Moskovskii Komsomolets*, December 17, 1997).

13. The murder by hired gun of the vice Governor of Petersburg and chairman of the State Property Committee, Mikhail Manevich, in August 1997, only attracted public interest for a few days, after which, the story was completely forgotten, along with the murder of several other prominent business-people (*Moskovskie Novosti*, August 31, 1997; *Segodnia*, August 19, 1997).

14. As Oleg Poptsov, a prominent writer and politician, noted, "a murdered banker or entrepreneur does not arouse public compassion" (see "Iz Nichego v Nikuda," *Literaturnaia Gazeta*, December 10, 1997).

15. In 1997, Igor Sundiev, vice president of the Russian Criminological Association, contended that "in Russia, it is difficult to find banks that do not have criminal roofs" (Igor Sundiev, "Krov I Nerv Kriminalnogo Mira", *Literaturnaia Gazeta*, August 27, 1997).

16. As Kovalev said, one of the biggest banks in Russia almost completely imitated the composition of the Moscow regional branch of the FSB (Nikolai Kovalev, "My Otbrosili Britanskuiu Razvedku Na 20 Let Nazad," *Nezavisimaia Gazeta*, December 19, 1997).

17. For example, the financial complex, "Most," has a private army for its protection. One of the army's commanders was none other than General Bobko, former deputy of the KGB.

18. Today, bodyguards trail their masters everywhere, including the bathroom.

19. According to Vladimir Semichastnyi, former head of the KGB in the 1960s and 1970s, personal guards had only been used for the members of the Politburo—no more than 11 to 12 people (see Semichastnyi, Vladimir. 1997. "Mne Nesterpimo Bolno," *Zavtra* 25).

20. For more on "roof" as an important social phenomenon, see Vladimir Shlapentokh's "Feudalism as the Best Parallel for Contemporary Russia," (1996. *Europe-Asia Studies*, 48(3) (Spring): 339–411); and his "Russia: Privatization and Illegalization of Social and Political Life in Russia," (1996. *The Washington Quarterly* 19: 65–85).

21. Russian businesspeople work with six commandments of foreign business. The second commandment is, "find roof" (see Vladimir Skosyrev, "Kto Smel, Tot I s'el", *Izvestia*, August 12, 1997).

22. For more about the collaboration of criminals and law enforcement agencies in Orel, see Alexander Vasinskii, "Thieves and Procurators" (*Izvestia*, December 9, 1997).

23. For example, Gennadii Koniukhov was elected mayor of the mid-sized city, Leninsk-Kuznetsk, in Kuzbass. In Krasnoiarsk, an individual with an even darker past, named Bykov, was elected to the regional Duma. He collected more votes than all other deputies. Terentiev with four pending criminal cases was elected as mayor of Artem, a city in the Maritime Territory (*Izvestia*, November 14, December 10, 11, 25, 1997).

24. Even in the elections of the local Duma in Moscow, "many individuals with criminal pasts" participated, as was noted by the Moscow journalist, Mikhail Shevelev (see "Teni Zabytykh Vyborov," *Moskovskie Novosti*, December 21, 1997). For more about the role of criminals in the election in Novosibirsk, see Valerii Vyzhutovich, "Poslednii Vagon s Severa", *Izvestia*, December 18, 1997; about the election in Krasnoairsk, see Grigorii Kakovkin, "Tak golosuiut Obmanutyie", *Izvestia*, December 17, 1997.

25. As an example, see how local mafias run a district in the Tula Region (Sergei Zhdakaiev, "Perestreliaem Vsekh", *Izvestia*, January 13, 1998).

26. The history of post-communist Russia is full of examples of confrontations between local leaders and the Kremlin. Yurii Luzhkov, Moscow's mayor, reminds one of a baron from the middle ages. He takes special delight in the permanent conflicts with the Kremlin. In 1993–1997, he ferociously attacked almost all major economic innovations of the Kremlin: privatization, and the reforms in the financing of residential maintenance. Evgenii Nazdratenko, Governor of the Maritime Territory (Far East), was also quite insolent toward Moscow during the same period of time. All of Moscow's attempts to dislodge Nazdratenko, particularly Chubais's endeavors in 1996, failed.

27. The auctioning off of state owned stocks in oil companies is a good example of "rent giving." As a rule, these auctions are a formality because most of the buyers have already been assured the stocks. (See the description in *Moskovskii Komsomolets*, July 17, 1997, that elaborates on the stock auction of the Tiumen oil companies. The author of the article, "Corruption," directly accused Anatolii Chubais and his lieutenants of rigging the auction in favor of Aven, the head of the Alpha financial empire).

28. In the summer of 1997, a few good examples of the rent giving activity emerged. The Russian media documented some interesting exhibits of Chubais's behavior. In the first half of 1996, the foundation, "In the Defense of Private Property," headed by Chubais was given a large non-interest loan which was used for financial speculation and finally as a source of income for Chubais himself. In order to make this possible, Chubais gave up his position temporarily (from December 1995 to July 1996), but was later reinstated in the government. (*Izvestia*, July 1 and 5, 1997). Another major rent giver, Andrei Vavilov, who served as deputy Finance minister, aided various Russian banks and even helped some (Unikombank, among others) participate in fraudulent operations with budget money (*Izvestia*, July 15 and 16, 1997). Alexander Starovoitov, the head of the Federal Agency of Governmental Communication and Information was also accused, along with his colleagues (one of them was arrested in 1997), by the media of corruption (see *Moskovskii Komsomolets*, August 22, 1997).

29. One of several revelations about the vast extent and intensity of corruption at the highest levels of the Russian hierarchy (including within Yeltsin's family) was presented by Yuri Boldyrev, vice chairman of the Counting Chamber of the State Duma and a very respected person in the country, during a radio interview with "Echo of Moscow." He declared that his office prepared a great deal of material which confirmed the corruption of various high-ranked officials in Moscow. He also claimed that the general procurator, Skuratov, ignored his data as well as other information about corruptions

in relation to the "big shots" in Russia (*Nezavisimaia Gazeta*, August 19, 1997). About the corruption in the Russian government, see the series of articles in *Moskovskii Komsomolets*, August 6 and 7, 1997.

30. There have been numerous rumors in Russia about the connection of the Kremlin with criminal organizations, particularly in relation to Alexander Korzhakov, the former head of Yeltsin's security, and the Solnstev gang.

31. See Vladimir Vasiliev's (deputy Ministry of Internal Affairs) article on the power of criminal structures (*Moskovskie Novosti*, January 4, 1998). See about Kursk in *Komsomolskaia Pravda*, August 12, 1997; about Petersrburg and Ekaterinburg in *Moskovskii Komsomolets*, July 12, 1997; and about Sochi in *Literaturnaia Gazeta*, June 25, 1997.

32. Alexander Korzhakov recounts in his book when, in March 1993, the Russian parliament came within inches of voting to impeach president Yeltsin. At this time, Yeltsin ordered his retinue to prepare the arrest of the entire parliament in the case of impeachment. What is more, he planned to use chemical gases to smoke the deputies out of the building. Fortunately for the deputies, the impeachment vote never came. Similarly, in the election year of 1996, Yeltsin had no intention of leaving the Kremlin and was prepared to take any action to ensure his continued presidency. According to Korzhakov, in the summer of 1996, Yeltsin and Prime Minister Viktor Chernomyrdin seriously debated canceling the presidential election. (Korzhakov 1997, pp. 156–200).

33. In Orel and Kemerovo, for example, governors Egor Stroiev and Aman Tuleiev were elected without serious opposition, gaining about 95 to 97 percent of the votes.

34. The elections of 27 local parliaments in 1997 were particularly indicative of this tendency. Almost everywhere the majority of the deputies turned out to be local directors and businesspeople. Representatives of political parties (with the exception of Communists) in most cases could not get elected (Afanasiev 1997).

The most shameful were the elections of the Moscow Duma. Moscow's mayor Luzhkov, in blatant violation of law, was directly involved in the election process and managed to block those candidates of whom he disapproved from entering the elections. What is more, there are serious doubts about the validity of the Moscow election. However, since Luzhkov has a great deal of control over all Moscow political institutions, it is almost impossible to file complaints (see *Nezavisimaia Gazeta*, December 19, 1997).

35. For more about the distribution of the Russian media among major oligarches, see Yurii Zainashev's article, "The Fourth Power is Becoming the Second Oldest Profession" (*Moskovskii Komsomolets*, August 12, 1997). One of the oldest and most respected newspapers, *Izvestia*, fell victim to oligarchic take over. Oneximbank, a leading financial monopoly, bought out the stock and became the owner of the newspaper. Since Potanin, the head of this bank, supported Chubais in his struggle against Berezovsky the editor of *Izvestia* was replaced because he published materials which denounced Chubais as well as the premier Minister Chernomyrdin. The new owners openly ousted the chief editor, Igor Golembiovsky, in August 1997 (about the scandal, see *Novaia Gazeta*, August 18, 1997; *Ogoniok*. 1997. 31: 26–27). Since the time of the scandal, the newspaper has published articles only praising the government.

36. This conflict had two dimesnions. On one hand, it was connected with the competition between Berezovsky and Potanin whom Chubais supported. On the other, there was a struggle between the state and the oligarchs who wanted to control the President, whom they had helped to be elected in 1996. Chubais, of course, focused on the second aspect of this struggle, presenting himself as a politician who wanted to save the state from the control of oligarchs (see Mikhail Berger, "The Battle for 'Sviazneft': Waterloo or Austerlitz of the Government," *Izvestia*, July 31, 1997; see also *Komsomolskaia Pravda*, August 20, 1997; *Izvestia*, December 24, 1997).

Both conflicts initially ended with some success on the part of the government (Berezovsky lost his position in the Security Council while "Gasprom" and a few other big companies were forced to pay their taxes, at least partially), but it was evident that with their great wealth still intact and their control over the media, the oligarchs would regain practically all of their might by the beginning of 1998.

37. See Nemtsov's interviews with *Moskovskii Komsomolets*, August 19, 1997 and December 20, 1997; and with *Izvestia*, December 24, 1997.

38. The leader of the "old" liberals was Egor Gaidar, while the most prominent ideologue of the second group was Boris Nemtsov who was joined in 1996–1997 by several former "old" liberals. Even Chubais, with his focus on the role of the state in this period, evidently moved to the "new liberal" camp (see Viacheslav Nikonov, "Post-Liberal Era," *Izvestia*, January 13, 1997).

39. The ethnic factor has played a role in some oligarchic conflicts. Supposedly, there is fierce competition between "Jewish" (Gusinsky, Berezovsky, Smolenskii, Khodorkovskii) and "Russian" (Vladimir Vinogradov, Vladimir Potanin, Lebedev and others) oligarchs. See the description of this struggle in ethnic terms by Vladimir Vinogradov in his interveiw with *Nezavisimaia Gazeta*, December 25, 1997.

40. For more about the battle between the alliance of Berezovsky and Gusinnky (in the past, ardent ennemies) and Potanin's group, see Denis Babich, "Privatizatsia Kak Zerkalo Rossiiskoi Blagogluposti", *Nezavisimaia Gazeta*, August 15, 1997; and *Moskovskie Novosti*, August 3, 1997.

41. The battles for control over two big state companies (the communication company "Sviainvest" and "Norilsk Nikel") in 1997, resonated the bitterness and deep animosity between the rivals thorughout the country (this time Gusinky and Berezovsky were on one side, and Potanin was on the other). The media played a big part in the conflict as each side tried to compromise the integrity of the other.

At the end of 1997, a new battle among major corporations emerged. This time the struggle focused on a big oil company called "Rosneft" which the state decided to sell (see *Moskovskie Novosti*, December 28, 1997; and *Nezavisimaia Gazeta*, January 23, 1998).

42. Most gangs operating in Russia have ethnic specificity. Besides "Russian" there are Chechen, Azerbaijan, Tartar, Georgian and several other gangs.

43. As Nikita Pokrovskii, a shrewd sociologist noted, "in 1997, Russia was moving quickly toward switching off the button of morals." He also pointed to the spread of the anarchic tendency in the country, observing that the so called "shuttler" (a merchant who goes back and forth to neighboring countries to buy and sell small quantities of goods, each time, making small violations of law) has become the symbol of Russian society (see "Bolshaia Rossiiskaia Igra", *Nezavisimaia Gazeta–Stsenarii*, December 9, 1997).

44. In 1997, *Izvestia* published the article, "Power Might Cooperate with the Leaders of the Criminal World." The author of the article praised criminal leaders as "having an entrepreneurial knack and organizational skills" and contended that they should be recruited by the authorities as "directors of enterprises and as captains of regional and federal structures" (S. Gabrov, "Vlast Mogla by Sotrudnichat s Liderami Prestupnogo Mira," *Izvestia*, December 6, 1997). Irina Medvedeva and Tatiana Shishova in their article, "Shadow Culture" praised the criminal culture with its solidarity values, a culture which they compare to the degenerating official culture with its abandonement of justice and fairness (*Nezavisimaia Gazeta*, July 2, 1997).

45. After publishing a number of drastic articles revealing the criminal past of one of the candidates in the elections of the Krasnoiarsk duma, the publication *Izvestia* noted that the articles depicting the criminal deeds of the candidate only helped him gain the election. "People are now attracted to criminals" (December 25, 1997).

46. The author is clearly alluding to Yeltsin.

47. The author of an article in *Izvestia* noted with sadness that the use of "bad words" among Russians has greatly increased in post-communist society. This language became "normal" among children in elementary schools as well as among college students (December 25, 1997).

48. The following data comes from the Institute of Sociolgy of Parlimentarianism (October-December 1997). After being asked, "who runs Russian society?": 51 percent pointed to criminals; 25 percent said the president and bureaucrats; 26 percent responded oligarchs; and only 7 percent pointed to liberal institutions. (Note: respondents were allowed to choose more than one response). (*Izvestia*, January 23, 1998).

49. In the winter of 1997, a survey asked the question: What is the biggest influence on the Russian president? Forty eight percent replied, the desire to retain his power; 34 percent said, the desire to please the leading Western circles; 33 percent reported, the desire to please his retinue; 26 percent said, to further the position of bankers and entrepreneurs; 20 percent responded, the state appartatus; 14 percent said that the president is influenced most by his family; 13 percent said, his personal views on the developments; 12 percent responded, the opinion of the government; 11 percent, his personal mood; 10 percent, the national interests of Russia; 6 percent, the State Duma; and 4 percent reported, public opinion. (Note: respondents were allowed choose more than one response). (*Izvestia*, January 23, 1998).

50. See the data from the Fund of Public Opinion published in *Segodnia*, May 7, 1995; *Izvestia*, December 7, 1996; and *Nezavisimaia Gazeta*, April 10,1997.

51. Segmentary or particularist approaches to cultural-ethnic form were actively defended in the 1960s through the 1990s by supporters of the "cultural diversity movement" and by post-modernists with their focus on the influence of power and the enviroment in general on the mentality of people.

REFERENCES

Afanasiev, M. 1997. "Golos Grazhdanskogo Obshchestva Stanovitsia Vse Tishe." *Izvestia*, December 25.

Aristotle. 1884. *The Politics and the Constitution of Athens*. Cambridge: Cambridge University Press.

Blondel, J. 1990. *Introduction to Comparative Government*. New York: Harper.

Bondarenko, V. 1997. "'Russkoie Zoloto' Napugalo Ameriku." *Zavtra* 52.

Bornstein, M. (ed.). 1994. *Comparative Economic Systems, Models, and Cases*. Burr Ridge, IL: Irwin.

Buchanan, J. 1980. "Rent Seeking and Profit Seeking." P. 3 in *Toward a Theory of the Rent Seeking Society*, edited by J. Buchanan, R. Tullison, and G. Tullock. College Station, TX: Texas A&M University Press.

Buravoy, M., and P. Krotov. 1992. "The Soviet Transition From Socialism to Capitalism." *American Sociological Review* 57: 16–39.

Case, K.E., and R.C. Fair. 1996. *Principles of Macro Economics*. Fourth Edition. Englewood Cliffs, NJ: Prentice Hall.

Crick, B. 1973. *Basic Forms of Government*. London: Macmillan.

Curtis, M., J. Blondel, B. Brown, J. Fewsmith, R. Kanet, D. Kommers, T. McNelly, M. Needler, J. Reshetar, Jr., and S. Wright. 1990. *Introduction to Comparative Government*. New York: Harper.

Fukuyama, F. 1992. *The End of History and the Last Man*. New York: Free Press.

Fund of Public Opinion. 1997a. 11.

Fund of Public Opinion. 1997b. *Bulletin* February 27.

Gaidar, E. 1997. *Anomaly of Economic Growth*. Moscow: Evrasia.

Gaidar, E. 1996. *Dni Porazhenii I Pobed*. Moscow: Vagrious.

Gaidar, E. 1995. *Besedy s Izbirateliami*. Moscow: Evrasia.

Goskomstat R. 1996. *Rossiiskii Statisticheskii Ezhegodnik*. Moscow: Logos, p. 82.

Govorukhin, S. 1993. *Velikaia Kriminal'naia Revoliutsiia*. Moscow: Andreevskii Flag.

Gray, J. 1995a. *Liberalism Edition*. Second Edition, Buckingham: Open University Press.

Gray, J. 1995b. *Enlightenment's Wake: Politics and Culture at the Close of the Modern Age*. London, New York: Routledge.

Handelman, S. 1997. *Comrade Criminal*. New Haven, CT: Yale University Press.

Heller, J. 1997. "World Bank Thumbs Robber Capitalism." *Moscow Tribune* August 27.

Interfax. 1998. January 9.

Izvestia. 1997. February 14.

Korzhakov, A. 1997. *Boris Yeltsin: Ot Rasveta Do Zakata*. Moscow: Interbuk.

Krueger, A. 1994. "Economists' Changing Perceptions of Government." Pp. 86–89 in *Comparative Economic Systems, Models, and Cases*, edited by M. Bornstein. Burr Ridge, IL: Irwin.
Kryshtanovskaia, O. 1995. "V Chikh Rukakh Sobstvennost." *Argumenty I Fakty* 15.
Macridis, R. 1986. *Modern Political Regimes*. Boston: Little, Brown.
Mankiw, N.G. 1997. *Principles of Micro Economics*. First Edition, Dryden Press, p. 9.
Nagle, J. 1985. *Introduction to Comparative Politics*. Chicago: Nelson-Hall.
Nee, V. 1989. "A Theory of Market Transition: From Redistribution to Markets in State Socialism." *American Sociological Review* 54: 663–681.
Nee, V., and R. Mathews. 1996. "Market Transition and Societal Transformation in Reforming State Socialism." *Annual Review of Sociology* 22: 4101–4135.
Nezavisimaia Gazeta. 1997a. May 31.
Nezavisimaia Gazeta. 1997b. July 29.
Parker, G. 1996. *Congress and Rent Seeking Society*. Ann Arbor, MI: University of Michigan Press.
Parsons, T. 1951. *The Social System*. Glencoe, IL: Free Press.
Parsons, T. 1971. *The System of Modern Society*. Englewood Cliffs, NJ: Prentice-Hall.
Pavlovsky, G. 1997. "Voina Elit Chuzhimi Rukami." *Nezavisimaia Gazeta*, December 5.
Pisigin, V. 1997. "Puteshestvie iz Moskvy v Sankt-Petersburg." *Oktiabr* 12: 125–157.
Przeworski, A. 1991. *Democracy and Market*. Cambridge: Cambridge University Press.
Russian Television. 1997. May.
Russian Radio. 1997. November 15.
Samuelson, P. 1973. *Economics*, Ninth Edition. New York: McGraw-Hill.
Schnitzer, M. 1994. *Comparative Economic Systems*. Cincinnati: South-Western Publishing.
Shlapentokh, V., R. Levita, and M. Loiberg. 1997. *From Submission to Rebellion; the Center Versus the Provinces in Russia*. Boulder: Westview Press.
Shlapentokh, V. 1997. "Bonjour Stagnation: Russia's Next Years." *Europe-Asia Studies*, 49(5).
Spiridonov, V. 1997. "Dat I Vziat." *Nezavisimaia Gazeta*, December 25.
Sundiev, I. 1997. "Krov I Nerv Kriminalnogo Mira." *Literaturnaia Gazeta*, August 27.
Tretiakov, V. 1997. *Nezavisimaia Gazeta*, December 31.
VTSIOM. 1997. 2: 42, 79.
Waller, M.J., and V.J. Yasmann. 1995. "Russia's Great Criminal Revolution: The Role of the Security Services." *Journal of Contemporary Criminal Justice* 11(4) (December).
World Bank. 1997. *The State in a Changing World*. New York: Oxford University Press.
Yavlinskii, G. 1997. "To Begin, We Must Remove Thieves From the Government." *Yabloko Podmoskovia*, April 22.

STRUCTURE AND CONTROL

"DEVIANCE" IN POLICE ORGANIZATIONS

Peter K. Manning

ABSTRACT

Police deviance arises from the structure of police work. The police are agents of a government charged with enforcing laws to maintain order and protect citizens and their property. The state gives the police broadly defined authority that empowers them to take immediate and decisive actions, without hesitation, as the occasion demands. This work expectation of taking action on the spot enables the police to do their work, but the expectation's generality and urgency lay the foundation for ambiguous interpretations of the law that can lead the police to overstep the boundaries of their legitimate authority. The police do not have time for reflection: "something must be done now"; if and when undue force is used or neglect occurs, the imperative of having to take action rationalizes and neutralizes personal responsibility. It also helps to unite the police as a cohesive body to defend themselves and aberrant conduct from criticism. Like other cohesive and societally valued bodies, the police prefer self-governing rules and boards to monitor their conduct and investigate illegal allegations. While a police department has considerable leeway in policing itself, it is still subject to externally imposed rules, regulations, and laws. The extent of deviance among the police is not known, in part because of limitations of the research and because of the autonomous nature of police work, the strong

Research in the Sociology of Work, Volume 8, pages 117-138.

ISBN: 0-7623-0608-4

cohesion among police officers, and also because the police do not always recognize their own violations. When police violations become public knowledge, public reaction tends to polarize around the police and oftentimes embattles the police in political controversy. Since a police department is empowered by the state, political controversy challenges its legitimacy and in turn creates an anomic situation in which the public trust in its efficiency may be undermined.

INTRODUCTION

Police organizations regulate social relations primarily with penal strategy in the name and interest of the state using legitimate violence including fatal force (Weber 1947, p. 152). The police inspect, evaluate, and respond situationally if and when they define matters in need of control; however, they process (formalize or "format") their official responses normatively and describe their decisions employing legal and quasi-legal concepts. This is now assisted and sped up by computer-based information systems. Because they have considerable broad authority, and see the law as a persuasive resource, the police frame many decisions as "law enforcement," even when the legal bases for the decision are culturally nuanced and perhaps subject to another interpretation. The usual guidelines for assessing "deviance" are blurred for those who monitor enforcement themselves, in part because they are granted power and authority to violate laws that are binding upon other citizens. For example, in enforcing laws concerning fraud, vice, and other crimes, they are permitted to create the conditions of crime in order to enforce the law. They may buy and sell drugs, engage in money laundering for criminals as a way to monitor the movement of funds for the purpose of catching criminals higher up the hierarchy, and watch while crimes are committed without intervening in order to follow burglars to locate fences for the goods and to arrest them. Freedom to obtain confessions has been broadened as have the conditions for stops and searches, thus validating what were previously marginal or illegal practices (e.g., gaining a confession in jail by "planting" an informant in the target criminal's cell). The police role and function, embedded in their mandate, shape patterns of police deviance, and these in turn reflect the structure of opportunities in given organizational contexts and socio-cultural environments. Like politics, most deviance is local. The ability of local boards, police commissions, complaint systems and the like to produce accountability has been very uneven, and from a libertarian perspective, an abject failure (Walker and Bumphus 1991).

The patrol officer's role has been the focal concern of a large number of police studies. Bittner's perceptive insights, based on the concept of the role of the police reveal basic police functions (1990, p. 131). He defines policing as the distribution of non-negotiable force in response to an intuitive grasp of situated exigencies. He characterizes the patrol officer's role as requiring watchful attention to situations that might require forceful intervention. The role also requires the management of authority-based, phenomenologically-defined encounters by negotiation, persuasion, violence, or local knowledge. It demands, or is seen as requiring, active and immediate intervention. The police believe that they must assess a situation quickly before it escalates to reduce the potential for further disorder. This emphasis on immediate action justifies many decisions at law, despite the fact that all deciding can be prolonged. Speed is a central aspect of police ideology (Fyfe 1986). It justifies many police practices. Coercion may be applied on the ground that "something had better be done or else...." The police represent the 'or else.' The need to disregard complexity is built into the conditions precipitating police intervention.

This role-based conception of policing provides the *figure* from which most empirical studies of crime control and deviance begin; the ground for which, organization and environment, is developed here. My argument, based on ethnographic work, official statistics, and studies of police violence, connects the structure of police organizations to patterns of police deviance or officially labeled violations of standards, internal and external.

POLICING AND DEVIANCE

The police mandate is a symbolic representation of the moral authority granted police (Manning 1997, Ch. 5). All occupations normalize deviance, accept institutionalized evasions of their own putative standards, insulate practitioners from arbitrary accusations, and rationalize mistakes at work (Hughes 1958), but they are also subject to external standards, periodic audit and review. Insofar as the police represent a conflation of the state, law, and morality, they endure periodic demands for meeting higher standards than other occupations. Police deviance, for reasons reviewed below, is largely invisible, concealed, and difficult to study. It is likely that, as with most organized deviations from known standards, it is not regarded as deviance, but is normalized and concealed, and seldom comes to public attention. Violations of police standards, of civil or criminal law, or of local standards of conduct, are as yet not subject to precise measurement, in part because both conceptual and data gathering problems remain. As one terse and accurate summary stated with respect to the police use of force, "The problems with data collection on such organizationally sensitive and controversial acts suggest the need for standardized measurement and reliable and valid measures" (Alpert and Dunham 1997a, p. 1).

This generalization holds true apparently for all forms of police deviance (Worden 1995, McEwen 1996). Scholars of policing and police violence find generalizing beyond a case difficult, given the local nature of policing, its structure and function, and the freedom granted to the patrol officer to intervene or not, to record or not, in short to make unreviewed decisions (Reiss 1974). In addition, nonstandard modes of data collection, lack of conceptual equivalence and external validity (Alpert and Smith 1994), and varying types and completeness of records frustrate researchers. Experts have bemoaned the lack of data on the use of force for more than 30 years, and this was a theme of the 60-year-old Wickersham Commission report (1931). The absence of data on the use of force reflects the power of the police to shield their conduct.

Clearly, police deviance can be motivated by personal gain (e.g., greed, by intentional criminal motive, ignorance, and loyalty) as when officers track down and kill those who have shot fellow officers. In their efforts to act expediently, the police sometimes violate procedural protections as when a person is seen as guilty and evidence is manipulated to ensure conviction. In their devotion to formal departmental goals and/or duty, the police may overstep their authority, as occurred when Los Angeles police ransacked and destroyed four apartments whose addresses they confused with the address on a warrant (Cannon 1997). When deviant acts occur, the police tend to construct accounts that justify their actions and neutralize their feelings of responsibility (Kappeler, Sluder, and Alpert 1997, Ch. 3). Thus, theorizing about motive and intent does not yield clear-cut typologies and analyses. We need to remember that deviance is a function of reactions to conduct.

Given this pattern of data paucity, dependence on police sources, and serious questioning of the validity and reliability even of large data sets, we consider why data are lacking. What is measured, and why? What is not measured? Like crime statistics, these data represent socially validated concerns and conventional fears. The reification of official statistics on particular kinds of deviance, while ignoring others, parallels the differential attention to the crime that crime statistics report. The legitimation of policing and its targets, strategies, and tactics blinds society to some sorts of excesses and directs attention to others. To understand the difficulty in drawing generalizations about police deviance, a structural portrait of policing is needed (see Manning 1997, pp. 97–106). Following that, we can explore types of deviance and those about which less is known systematically.

Police

American public policing is decentralized; local in focus, style, and tone; and is locally financed. Some 15,000 local, 49 state, and a large, but undetermined number of federal police agencies exist. There are more than 650,000 full-time public officers, some 8.2 percent of whom are federal employees, and another 250,000 part-time officers (Reaves 1996). Civilians constitute 27 percent of police employees and have increased considerably during the 1990s as a ratio of the total population (O'Brien 1996b, 197).[1]

Most police officers work in relatively small organizations of fewer than 30 officers. The 15,000 vary in size from a handful in departments serving small towns and villages to the more than 38,000 officers in the New York City Police

Department (NYPD). Police traditions and practices are locally learned, practiced, and refined, and reflect in some way local standards of decency and propriety. Until fairly recently, police were likely to be born in or near the cities in which they worked, and they lived nearby. From my observations this pattern has changed. Now, police in large cities are recruited nationally, while in smaller cities they are still recruited locally.

The decentralization of the system extends to training and promotion. No national police force, training system, or National Police College exist. Police are trained in cohorts in local academies, and formal training can range from a few days to more than 16 weeks plus later apprenticeships under field training officers. Hiring and promotional standards vary widely, and are little influenced by educational attainment. Promotions in rank are few and arise when exams or board interviews (of ranks above sergeants) are offered.

Policing is shaped by local law and selected federal and appellate decisions concerning civil liberties and liabilities. It is historically a function of the executive branch of government, separated from courts and the legislature. Policing powers, de facto, are quite widespread, and shared among individual citizens, private investigators, citizen self-help groups, private policing agencies and occasionally, the military (national guard, reserves, and regular forces). Territorial limits or jurisdictional boundaries, once binding in Anglo-American policing, now are largely irrelevant at the federal level.[2] Locally, however, agencies serve overlapping jurisdictions—city, township, county, state, and federal—and enforce a maze of contradictory statutes.

Anglo-American police departments grew from the regulation of city life and at their root, are inspectorial bureaus: They are best suited to observing and managing rare events, and to flexible and consistently graded response to episodes. The police locate some 70 to 90 percent of their sworn personnel "on the ground" in shifts of eight to 10 hours at a time, 24 hours a day, through the year. This means, given holiday, overtime and "comp time," (informal time off given by supervisors) as well as disability and sick leave, that roughly four to five times the number of on-duty officers are required to fully staff 24 hour shifts. The police react to calls for service, investigate those that are crime-related, and manifest minimal specialization and a flat hierarchy of few ranks. Some five to eight percent are in detective work and other specialized units. The police are divided into staff and line, with patrol as "line" and staff performed by administration, internal affairs, detectives, and the service division. Most officers prefer to remain in patrol, and city budgets constrain the available slots. Police tend to remain in the organizations they join, with only a few lateral transfers, usually at the chief rank, occurring each year (Reaves 1996).

The police legitimately apply violence; standing symbolically between the "citizens" and the "state," and are granted considerable latitude in enforcement. As an organization employing and symbolizing violence in a society in which violence is denied and publicly denigrated, the American police confront the violence paradox: violence is seen as required yet denied as a feature of everyday life in industrialized societies.

Policing is embedded in the administrative structure of the modern state which holds out violence as a means to coerce compliance only if habit and expediency fail. The police are expected to use the level of force needed to control a situation, yet not escalate disorder. The absence of visible police coercion is a sign of legitimacy and the effectiveness of informal controls (Goode 1973). Police violence is double-edged, as it can be turned against "respectable" citizens, and the state in revolutionary situations. Police hold unique powers, even though fatal force is not restricted to the police in law or by practice, and stand ready to intervene with restraint or levels of force in an infinite range of social situations. Their failure to uniformly apply violence in moderation is often a public issue.

Internally, the basis for compliance to command is a mix of charismatic or personalistic authority, and rational-legal authority based on expertise and experience. Often, tensions arise between these modes of authority, in part because they are unevenly distributed throughout the organization. Considerable autonomy exists within each of the divisions (usually patrol, administrative services, and investigative) and within the occupational culture.

Policing combines a visible and distinctive uniform with an astounding array of tools, including high-powered semi-automatic weapons, and burgeoning information technology (Manning 1997, 102–106). It relies on a basic "technology," interpersonal and communicative skills, and good judgment. Its basic sciences are an admixture of applied social science. Its more obvious and dramatic technology—weapons—are rarely used. Information technology is now widespread, especially computers, both in-car and mainframe, and has as yet unproven effects on police practice (Manning 1992).

Police officers work alone, in partnerships or small groups, and sometimes join in performance-oriented, short-term teams to serve warrants, cordon off an area, make massive traffic stops, or sweeps of areas. In most cities they patrol, ecologically separated in time and space, linked via communications networks, and are rarely directly supervised. Their work is autonomous. Police workloads, "free time," and the composition of work tasks, vary widely by time of day, and day of the week, month, and year, but are shaped by local traditions and conditions (Bayley 1994, pp. 39–44). Studies reveal patterned police tactics for managing citizen encounters (Bayley 1986; Bayley and Garofalo 1989). These patterns suggest conditions under which events may escalate, or require force, although official reports suggest that violent episodes constitute fewer than five percent of police encounters (Alpert and Smith 1994, p. 482). The use of violence, ultimately sanctioned by the state, varies empirically rather than being an "essential feature of the police role."[3]

These structural features of policing, as shall be seen, make data gathering vexing and generalizations about police behavior and misbehavior tenuous. Let us now examine the modes of control and review in place.

Mechanisms of Control of Police

Given that the police are a lighting rod for conflict, and that their conduct is subject to controversy, debate, and varied normative definitions, democratic societies have evolved several modes of review and control of the police (Bayley 1985). Let us begin with police controls and then we will examine external modes of control. These are matters of social structure, politics, and the social organization of policing, and both singularly and through their relations to one another, they suggest why so little is known about police deviance.

The police evaluate, audit, and review their own performance focusing on case-by-case responses to reports of individual officers' misconduct. Police departments have internal affairs divisions designed to audit and investigate violations of rules and regulations, as well as the law. They also have complaints offices to investigate citizens' complaints. Their supervisory style is preventive and rule-oriented, with an emphasis on harsh discipline. Local custom interacts with law and legislation (Reiss 1971, pp. 173–221) to shape departments' managerial mandates.

However, policing in the United States is also held accountable by local means (Bayley 1994, pp. 91–101), but the mechanisms to insure accountability vary from one community to another. Defense attorneys, district attorneys, and judges review legal cases, and civil law provides remedies (del Carmen 1991). External bodies also regulate the police. These include citizens' review boards (Walker and Bumphus 1991), elected or appointed police commissions, "blue ribbon," *ad hoc*, investigative committees such as Knapp [1967] and Mollen [1994] commissions in New York City and the Christopher Commission [1991] in Los Angeles).

Policing is traditionally loosely coupled with the political and legal systems, with a rather broad domain of relatively unaccountable action (Bittner 1990). The police are protected by the courts which are loath to punish police *ex post facto*, and by their traditional quasi-sacred status and legitimacy (Manning 1997; del Carmen 1991). Ostensively high political crimes, such as riotous attacks (Stark 1972), excessive fatal force and violence (as used at Kent State University in 1970), or gathering secret and illegal files (Rothmiller and Goldman 1992) are sanctioned tacitly by the state and often approved in advance. The police role in quasi-revolutionary situations, when authority is broadly questioned, is potentially quite ambiguous.

The most commonly assumed constraint on policc actions is the law. For a number of complex reasons, the law works more as a social fact in the Durkheimian sense than as a set of known, precisely understood and enforced rules. Policing, in Bittner's view, is not powerfully constrained by the courts or by formal law. They are "...involved in activities that cannot be fully brought under the rule of law" (1990, p. 119), and only a limited set of legal strictures can be conditionally imposed upon the police (p. 119). The courts, in his view, are "...in fact powerless vis-a-vis the police establishment" (p. 119). The supremacy of the police derives from their mandate that warrants the application of situationally justified violence, as perceived on the scene, and based on legal rules that are endlessly defeasible.[4] Bittner (1990) partially overstates the case in assuming that the issue is when and how to enforce authority, not what happens as a result of a decision to intervene. There are far too many violations available to react to, even if one wished to, so pragmatism rules in most cases. The evidentiary requirements and procedural guidelines are quite clear after a decision is made to intervene, and the police are quite skilled at meeting them. The law in short provides the conditions under which one can intervene, but not how one must intervene, except in very narrow circumstances such as pursuits and fatal force. The notion of "discretion" assumes the fettering effect of the law, but it does not specify what is at issue or which laws are relevant to the situation at hand. For example, there are no legal specifics on how to handle a loud party in a park, gambling in a bar, or even domestic violence, given the "invisible" nature of these offenses and the difficulty of review in the absence of records of the occurrences. The impact of specific laws on police practice remains debatable (Fyfe, 1988). *Post hoc proper hoc* reasoning guides administrative bodies and courts.

These systems and modes of review, with some exceptions, rely upon materials gathered by the police. Let us examine their modes of data gathering to see how information is filtered, shaped, and monitored to serve internal and external audiences. Data gathering and record keeping, like all other aspects of social life, contain an aspect of impression management and audience manipulation.

Police records of all kinds, like any bureaucratic records, require careful and knowledgeable interpretation. The police maintain an attitude of secrecy and value it because they believe it is essential to the surveillance, investigation, and capture of criminals. This attitude extends to concern for information kept, police records, investigative reports, and individual logbooks, notebooks, and case files. Information is rarely shared widely among officers, and the myriad of stored records are not linked, compatible, nor organized for retrieval. The introduction of new software and hardware packages compound the problem of assembled data sets that were constructed for different computing programs. The result is an archaeology of records with various formats, taking diverse physical forms, and kept in various locations. The growth in data aggregation modalities, such as geocoding of city services, crime-mapping and crime analysis, complaint-tracking systems for city government, and networks of terminals, symbolizes the concurrent and underlying growth of managerial information systems and data control. The information systems are semi-autonomous appendages to the core "technology" that mediates the environment and they serve the senses of individual officers.

In spite of information being valued and essential to policing, police officers are quite ambivalent about keeping written, retrievable, and well-organized records. Top command has long focused on discipline and nurtured and promoted charismatic views of command and control, based on individual leadership. It shares officers' views that much of importance is not and should not be committed to paper. "Real police work" is on the streets, in their eyes, and "paperwork" is a constant irritant and impediment to doing their job. Work is about particular people in particular places, doing particular things.

Reality is not a shared, consistent matter captured uniformly in reports, verbal or written. The meaning varies by context, and by level of the organization. At the very least, a kind of dualism prevails within the police organization. Two kinds of social reality emerge and are sustained. There is the secondary reality of official paper and potentially or could-be-public versions of an event, each of which has its own `spin;' and the primary reality of the informal, understood, unwritten, or tacit reality that is shared among a few, understood by many, and rooted in "normal practices and routines."

The occupational culture of the police is flexible and enduring, protective of individual officers, but it is likely that the degree of secrecy and protection accorded each other vary across organizations. Anglo-American policing is a rather powerful set of ideas, beliefs, values, and artifacts that mediate the experienced and perceived environment for practitioners (Chan 1996, Shearing and Ericson 1991; Manning 1997). Dominated by the practices and beliefs of the patrol division, it is variously closed, parochial, hostile to the public, and defensive. In part, this defensiveness arises out of the risky environment of police work, in which officers feel they must control and prevail. Officers are oriented to the peer culture, sustain a secretive attitude, and guard their discretionary right to implement fatal force. These beliefs and practices give rise to a powerful set of tacit assumptions that are supportive of an infrastructure of deviance, rule evasion, and creativity in problem solving. In so doing, the police culture sustains a contextual view of police conduct. "You had to be there" is the guiding precept.

The occupational culture may be partitioned into at least three segments. Each differentially displays aspects of the culture and is organized around ranks anchored in distinctive social spaces (rank clusters) within the organizational hierarchy. The three segments are the *command* (above lieutenant), the *middle management* (sergeants and lieutenants), and the *lower participant* segment (officers). Each segment produces a perspective that emphasizes different and distinct themes in its work. "Crime on the streets" is the central theme of the patrol officers. Information must flow up, but the primary gatekeepers and sources of information, the patrol officers, are rarely reviewed. Their problems are solved at the lowest level possible, and the top command is both literally and symbolically removed from "the streets."[5]

To summarize briefly, the limits on external regulation of policing are historical and rooted in the common-law freedom granted to police. Internally generated data, often the basis for external reviews, are shaped by the value police put on secrecy, their ambivalence to paperwork and record keeping, and their view that "reality" is on the street. The occupational culture of the police is insular and protective, and it segmentalizes policing, which in turn alters and limits the flow and meaning of information within the police organization as a whole.

DATA CONSIDERATIONS

This review of police structure and function suggests that it is misleading to use "deviance" without specifying the context in which it is being used. Categories, such as crime, civil law infractions, "excessive force," and "incivilities" (Kappeler, Sluder, and Alpert 1997), are indicative of deviance, but are not mutually exclusive. They are logically fuzzy categories, connoting related clusters of similar conduct. These are labels, not incidents; a given incident could be classified in any one or all three; police officers are often subject to internal investigation, suspension and fines, civil law, and criminal prosecution. These are *ex post facto* labels for conduct that could have been sanctioned, positively or negatively. Internal and external standards may vary with respect to gratuities, normal and acceptable violence, lying, or ethical norms. Thus, whether internal or external standards are applied is much affected by the power relations in the situation (Kappeler, Sluder, and Alpert 1997, pp. 18–19).

Criminal conduct as defined by the Uniform Crime Reports (UCR), embezzlement, and other white collar crimes of trust are important, and presumably rare among police. Violations of rules and regulations are frequent, but they vary widely from breaking dress (uniform) rules, tardiness, or leaving one's patrol area to serious violations like discharge of a firearm or lying to superior officers. "Incivilities" are highly contextual in character, probably "part of the territory" as police say about policing, and are defined by those offended. This creates variations by class, race, and gender in reporting complaints and in police investigation of them. Research on incivilities, because they are local, tends to be case studies, or content analysis of newspaper stories. A parallel to incivil conduct are "hate crimes," UCR crimes in which the attributed motive is based on gender, ethnicity or sexual orientation of the offended. Such reports of crimes embody contradictions and inequities (Jacobs and Potter 1998). No data set includes these types of police deviance for a group of police organizations.

It is helpful to recall that citizen behavior considered "deviant" or criminal may be quite acceptable and positively sanctioned. The police, because they are given a mandate to enforce laws, are also permitted to break them. They are indeed encouraged to commit acts in reaction to conduct that would be considered criminal if engaged in by the average citizen, and to use psychological and physical force to apprehend criminals and solve crimes (Alpert and Smith 1994, p. 481). "Criminal" and "deviant" are context-bound notions. Certainly, the law does not define when and how such labels will be applied by whom and to whom. The police role insulates and protects the officers from allegations of misconduct on the job.

These situational features of police work mean that generalizations about police deviance are difficult to draw, whether based on ethnographic work, observational studies, interviews, questionnaires, or social surveys.

The rarest happenings among the police are perhaps the most widely known. Public scandals occasionally occur, especially in large cities such as New York, Philadelphia, Chicago, and Los Angeles. These range from criminal groups within the police department who extort drug money from organized crime groups (New York), commit burglaries (Denver), frame alleged drug dealers (Philadelphia) and fabricate statistics (N.Y. Transit Police) to the solo deviant officer who perjures him or herself, uses excessive force, or engages in a fantastic chase (Riverside). Police deviance is sometimes so dramatically publicized that it becomes a political issue, as happened in the Rodney King beating in Los Angeles, the fatal beating of Malice Green by Detroit police, televised beatings of blacks in Cincinnati (Kaminski and Jefferis 1997), and publicly-known deaths in custody (Lansing, Michigan). Such occurrences are often filmed and so dominate the news as to become spectacles (Manning 1996). Legal and case-based analyses may reveal extreme actions, but as case events they fail to illuminate the routine character of police work in which the deviance is embedded. Singularly dramatic incidents have been well documented (Hersey 1968; Van Maanen 1982; Cannon 1997), but for the most part, journalistic accounts are superficial and hackneyed "exposes" of police deviance (e.g., Maas 1975). Few go beyond the headlines in exploring police scandal. Sherman's work (1978) is an exception.

Studies of "routine" police deviance, on the other hand, that use official records, interviews, social surveys, large data sets, sophisticated statistical techniques, and multiple measurements, reveal substantial unexplained variance. At best, they trace only thin connections between structure, process and outcome (Jacobs and O'Brien 1998; Alpert and Dunham 1997a; McEwan 1996; Worden 1995; Adams 1995). Official data on civilian complaints or internal records of investigations for excessive force are available for a few departments, but are generally kept in confidential and inaccessible files (Christopher Commission 1992). When released, they are rather sterile because portions are blacked out or otherwise edited. They have been crafted carefully with public release in mind.

Some studies using official records where external validation and review are involved are more promising. Data on accidents, occupational injuries, and disabilities (partial, temporary, or full), "blue flu," and "sick outs" as well as malingering in respect to injury, alcoholism, and other drug usage, are rarely analyzed (Brandl 1997). Accidents and illness are more draining on personnel levels and budgets than encounters with citizens that lead to injury. There are few comparative studies of injuries and morbidity among police and analogous occupations such as firefighters. There are a few studies of police accidents. Fyfe (1988) points out that police frequently shoot other officers and themselves; Kappeler, Sluder, and Alpert (1997) report exaggerated claims concerning the danger, stress, and consequences of policing; and Brandl (1997) identifies accidents at work as more consequential than dangerous villains. Police ideology strikingly dramatizes "risk" and "danger" to officers, while undervaluing and minimizing violence that may be done to citizens.

Ethnographic studies of deviance, on the other hand, are windows into processes and situational dynamics, but few have been carried out in the necessary depth and as yet, only a few departments have been studied (Skolnick 1967; Manning 1979; Westley 1970; Dunham and Alpert 1995). Some studies are insightful (Graef 1989; McClure 1980, 1984), but are ethnographies lacking an analytic structure. One anthropologist captures in detail the violence of policing and of drug dealing in New York City (Jackall 1997). His descriptions provide background to the Louima beating by NYPD officers in August of 1997 and the shooting of Diallo in the winter of 1999 that was featured in a cartoon on the cover of *The New Yorker Magazine* (February 22, 1999). The cartoon showed an officer at a shooting gallery offering 41 shots (the number that hit the unarmed Diallo) for five cents. Many rich autobiographical accounts and narratives are fascinating but blend fiction, edited narratives, several kinds of policing (local, state, big city, and federal officers) and conflate persons by attributing several individuals' quotes to only one person (Baker 1985; Fletcher 1990) Two studies are based on detailed interviews with a few officers (Stoddard 1968; Barker and Carter 1994).

Given these limits, the structure and function of policing provide abundant clues to police deviance, but more has been inferred from extant data (Worden 1995) than observed.

POLICE AND DEVIANCE

Three types of deviance that have been responded to publicly and labeled deviant have been carefully studied so that generalizations may be drawn. These are violations of the law; violations of internal rules, regulations, and policies; and violations of incivilities (Barker and Carter 1994, p. 9). In some respects, the types reflect a final disposition of an investigation, rather than a window on the processes of deviation (Alpert and Smith 1994, p. 492). For this reason, we begin with a typology and some description.

Types of Deviance

Three are significant: *Police violations of criminal law* are relatively easy to identify and count, because they are recorded, published, systematized, and routinized in character. But this codification does not mean that these data are readily comparable across sites or easy to gather. A subcategory is police violations of the civil rights of citizens. Data on this first category result from federal convictions. *Violations of internal rules and regulations* are also of questioned validity and reliability, because these data are contextual. They may vary by the rules governing the police and the police department, resources available to the police, and the traditions and ethos of the police organization. *Violations of civilities* are the third type of carefully studied police deviance. Civilities reflect local cultures, and violations *of* them are matters of taste, aesthetics, manners, and morals. They vary regionally. Incivilities that occur on the job stem from the role of the police in the context of the local culture.

Contexts of Deviance

The above types of deviance vary by *context*. Any propositions about the distribution of police deviance must take into account (1) the markets police attempt to regulate or eradicate, (2) the targets of police strategies, and (3) the quality of deviance being studied. We discuss these below.

1. *Markets: Regulation or Eradication?*

Police can either attempt to regulate markets in goods and services, using a model of control and containment that resembles civil regulations, or attempt to eradicate the market through sanctioning (Manning and Redlinger 1977). The patterns of deviance that result vary. In general, the "eradication" or criminal sanctions model produces the greater numbers of actions and the higher rates of deviance, especially in departments that are attentive to such enforcement (Kappeler, Sluder, and Alpert 1997, pp. 52–57).

2. *Types of Policing: Reactive or Proactive?*

The police can either pursue a "deterrence" model of random patrol and subsequent investigation of criminal acts or a target model, employing directed patrol or some form of problem-solving policing (Goldstein 1989). The idea of targeting stands in contrast to the random patrol model of call-driven service, in which officers drive around aimlessly for some 50 to 60 percent of the time, and follow an entreprenurial proactive approach to policing. Some departments use "directed" patrol to draw attention to areas and problems; some use problem-solving, while others use an "overlap" work schedule, in which two shifts work the same time period, often for the purpose of working jointly on projects. The targeting idea is rarely adopted by departments. The targeting model requires strategic allocation of resources directed toward places, other officers, standards of civility, or whatever the target is. Place targeting, also called "hot spots" policing, has short-term effects. It may escalate citizens' reactions to a militaristic defense of their community. Targeting citizens is usually carried out by mobile tactical and "special operations" squads who serve warrants, pursue suspected drug dealers, check alibis, and so on. When special operations work autonomously, they may take on some of the character of a secret police unit, as has been said of the LAPD

(Rothmiller and Goldman 1992). In theory, internal affairs is a proactive, intelligence-driven unit, but in fact it is typically more reactive, investigating citizens' complaints about police misconduct. Sometimes, areas of incivility or disorder (parks, subways, public amusement areas) are targeted for massive and brief attention. Violations of minor crimes may also be selected as targets as a way of publicizing crime suppression, law enforcement, and "crackdowns" (Sherman 1992). In general, when officers are supervised, targeted, and directed, the probability of deviance on the job is reduced.

3. *The Quality of Deviance and Level of Abstraction.*

Police violence can be direct, interpersonal, and immediate, or more erosive, long lasting, and subtle in character. Face-to-face violence is the most frequently studied. It is discussed below.

With respect to police "violence" as a visible threat of force or use of force against another, records are uneven and debatable (McEwen 1996; Fyfe 1988; Jacobs and O'Brien 1998). Debates about "excessive force" cannot be resolved by fiat. "Excessive" is locally defined in standards of practice, legal cases, training, and supervision (Klockars 1995; Worden 1995). Systematic evidence bears on three kinds of violence: shootings of police as victims (Fridell and Pate 1997; Fyfe 1988); shootings by the police of other police and of citizens (Fyfe 1979, 1986, 1988); fatal accidents; and chases (Fridell and Pate 1997; Alpert and Fridell 1992).

a. Shootings by Police. The most systematic research on police shootings is that by Sherman (1983), Sherman and Langworthy (1979), Fyfe (1979, 1988), and Robin (1963). Police shootings have declined relatively (as a ratio to population) as well as absolutely, though the exact statistic is unknown. Data on police homicides come from two different data sets, the FBI reports on homicides and the NCHs data reported by local coroners. Fyfe (1988) points out that figures from the two data sets vary by as much as 50 percent, that both sets of data underestimate the number of shots fired as well as the number of shootings, and both sets of data, most notably the FBI data, are biased in favor of "dead bodies." (See also Sherman and Langworthy [1979] on the NCHS data and Jacobs and O'Brien [1998] on the FBI data.) Fyfe (1988) using New York City data on shooting attempts estimates that one in five shots misses. FBI data from the 57 largest U.S. cities show a decline in the absolute number (not as a percent of all shootings, which is not examined) of justifiable homicides (Matulia 1985) from 1975 to 1983. Large cities are the most likely to have written policies. Written policies are a way to organizationally direct and contrain the police, and as the research of Fyfe (1988) show, they appear to curb trigger-happy reactions. Fyfe (1988) examined the effect of an explicitly written policy on police violence by comparing shootings in Philadelphia, which has little or no policy, with those in New York City, which has an explicit written policy. He found that Philadelphia had higher rates of fatal shootings, shootings in dubious circumstances, and shots fired than New York City. Fyfe's findings make a strong and convincing argument, along with Sherman's (1983), that organizational policies have an immediate, consistent, and altogether humane consequence of reducing shootings.

As we have already noted, when the culture of a community tolerates violence generally, this tolerance seems to enhance police shootings. For instance, police homicide rates are moderately correlated with a community's general homicide rate (O'Brien 1998b; Fyfe 1988). Jacobs and O'Brien (1998), using aggregated city data, including domestic violence, find shootings by police most prevalent in Southern cities in which minority groups are around 40 percent, and have recently grown. Election of a black mayor seems to suppress slightly police shootings. Even if the black mayor did not change policies on shootings, his or her race symbolized a change in community attitudes toward policing, which, in turn, may have contributed to the decline in the police use of violence.

b. Shootings of Police. Shootings of police steadily declined as a rate and in absolute numbers in the 21 years from from 1973 through 1994, from 3.3 per 10,000 officers in 1973 to 1.1 in 1994, according to Fridell and Pate's (1997) analysis of FBI data. Fyfe shows that although African-Americans are both most shot at and most likely to be shooters (by percent of shootings); black officers are also likely to be young, assigned to conflicted and highly violent areas, and live in violent areas in which they are likely to shoot (or be shot) while off duty.

c. Active Pursuits. Departmental policies are consistent predictors of rates of accidents, reported chases, and fatal pursuits (Alpert and Fridell 1992; Alpert 1997). Clear, unambiguous, written polices decrease the number of chases and fatal accidents, while vague policies implicitly validate chases and lead to higher rates (Alpert 1997). These data, from a small sample, are consistent with Fyfe's careful analysis of the use of fatal force. While social structure and community characteristics shape this form of deviance, organizational policies and procedures increase the regularity of the pattern. This correlation assumes that such policies are actually enforced and are followed by officers.

d. Other forms of Police Violence. Other forms of violence, perhaps less visible, are denied publicly but extant nevertheless. Symbolic violence associated with differential enforcement of the law in relation to class, race, and gender is biased in favor of aggressive patrolling of the more subordinate groups. As a result, the weaker groups are sometimes denied protection under the law (Manning 1994; Manning and Singh 1997). The realm of "indirect" violence is social, collective, and categorical as well as being immediate. For example, community policing has created a new category of symbolic violence, including "zero tolerance" policies, drug-free zones, abatement proceedings, and other procedures using the power of the city to destroy questionable buildings, evict people from public housing, and change streets and parks. Law enforcement authority is used to coerce lifestyle differences and reduce "disorder." In policing disorder, standards are more general and abstract than legal and even municipal regulations and zero-tolerance policing raises questions about justice and equity. "Crack houses" are razed and entire public housing units are demolished as a "solution" to drug use.

Studies on police deviance suggest a patterning of deviance by size of organization (Kappeler, Sluder, and Alpert 1998), compositional characteristics of urban areas (Jacobs and O'Brien 1998), micro-environments (Herbert 1997; Klinger 1997), organizational policies (Alpert and Fridell 1992; Fyfe 1988; Fyfe and Skolnick 1993; Dunham and Alpert 1995), and other socio-economic variables, such as the gross crime rate, police budgets, and personnel numbers. In other research, the socio-economic variables were found to have little impact on police homicides (or crime rates) (Bayley 1994, pp. 3–5). Simple and partial correlations between police shootings and the crime rate, police personnel levels, and budgets are weak and inconsistent (Fyfe 1988).

Police behavior is not easily discernible. It is labeled inside the police department, and the decision criteria are invisible to outsiders. Most public reports resulting from these internal decisions are at best only indirect surrogates for the internal processes and controls. We lack a clear definition of what constitutes police deviance, and therefore we cannot know how much of what kinds of deviance occurs. The question remains concerning what behavior is and is not measured and why.

Summarizing these studies, one can see that the focus of police research has been on the concrete, the immediate, and the obvious, such as "violence," "excessive force," or "arrests" (typically undefined) without addressing the community or organizational context or the situation. Thus, the research ignores the question of organizational and local standards about the appropriate level of force. When community structure alone is measured, organizational variation is overlooked, and the connection between the violent act and a policing practice is unexplicated. Evidence suggests that comparative ethnographic research that explores the situation, organizational traditions, and conventions about the use of force (Cancino 1998), and the social structure of the case is needed. Perhaps the most challenging research will need to make conscious and explict the taken-for-granted basis for notions like "order," "disorder," "crime," and the like, and how these are grounded in typifications of social areas, specific places, groups, and persons (Herbert 1997). For example, it is common and sanctioned police practice to create a crash to end a long pursuit, to punish a fleeing felon after a chase, and for police to justify responding violently to "assholes" and violent, disputive citizens. This is "normal" violence within the organization, whether it is sanctioned by supervisors or external standards, and thus stands in the gray area of police conduct. A careful and close analysis of police violence, legitimated by explicit policy or not, might reveal the context within which it takes place and penetrate the official curtain drawn around it. The difficulty is to link the levels of effects to a model of interactional processes (Alpert and Smith 1994).

REFLECTIONS

Clearly, society has granted the police license to broadly define their work. Perhaps the fear of disorder, crime, lurking unknown menaces, and fluctuations in the economy are more salient to the public than police violations of law, civility, and departmental regulations. Like the view of the public on the several "wars on drugs," the outcomes, deterrence, fluctuations in drug markets, number of users, and accuracy of data on these are of far less concern to the public than is media hyperbole. Nor is the public very interested in figures on arrests, known sentences, and the high rates of incarceration of those charged with drug offenses (Tonry 1996). Even the rigorous research on arrest is narrowly focused and limited in scope.[6]

The first area worth further exploration is the role of context (the situation) in the use of force. Context consists of the roles and relationships of the parties in a police encounter (Black 1980, 1984). The role of third parties and the social structure of the case (the social relations of those involved) pattern outcomes of control encounters. Black's theory predicts rates of formal police interventions (governmental social control or "law") to be higher, other things being equal, in violent cultures or subcultures in which social integration is low, unstable, or changing (Black 1984; Cooney 1998). High rates of violence among low-income African-Americans indicate low social integration, but such groups are subject also to high degrees of surveillance, governmental or formal social controls using penal sanctions, and immediate "justice" (i.e., shootings). Because minorities are most socially distant from governmental agents, and there are fewer kin and neighborhood modes of negotiation and arbitration, violence is more likely. Whites are likely to be shot when they are assaultive, are former criminals, or are carrying a weapon, but black citizens are also more likely to be shot under dubious circumstances (Fyfe 1988). These data suggest that the threshold for use of potentially fatal force against blacks is much lower than for whites. The race of the victim and the offender influence the sanction applied.

If one examines the process and framing of interpersonal violence by the police according to self-reports (in two departments), it is patterned by more than the ratio of force used by each party to the encounter (the net effect of scoring police force as + and citizen force as -). Other factors include organizational policies and training, suspect and officer characteristics, officer/suspect ethnic congruity, and the presumed mental state (under the influence, or mentally ill) of the citizen (Alpert and Dunham 1997a, p. 5). The use of this relative measure of force reveals patterns worthy of further investigation. For example, female officers in Dade

County use more force than male officers. Among racial groups, hispanics use less force on members of their own ethnic group than whites or blacks use on members of theirs. The preceived mental state of offenders also affects police use of force. The most force is used with stable, sober citizens and least with "mentals." (Alpert and Dunham 1997a).

Perhaps the most promising finding for future research, in addition to the individual effects of citizens' mental status and ethnicity, is the organizational effect on initial levels of force. Eugene, Oregon trains officers to use more initial force, while Miami-Dade trains for less as suggested by data reported by Alpert and Dunham (1997a). A further inference from these materials is that the process of applying force is sequential and depends on the response of the officer to an initial "violent" or resisting move on the part of the citizen. A second theoretically important finding in this research was that the underapplication of violence in response to citizens tended to lead to violence and injury to officers. These patterns illustrate vividly how apparently anomalous events, such as the beating of King or Green, or the riots touched off by coercive action after "routine" traffic stops, are products of history, training, and traditions rather than the product of "bad apples" in the police barrel.[7]

The problem of police deviance is two-sided. When police violate laws, regulations, or are excessively violent, the society is implicitly both the victim and perpetrator. This duality is perhaps inevitable in a democratic society. For just as the police represent social patterns and conventions, and are given wide latitude and license to command citizens and organizations, their kinds and level of deviance are reflective of the neighborhoods where they work and live. Thus, to rephrase an old cliche, we may not get the police we deserve or even want, but we get what we need.

ACKNOWLEDGMENT

I thank Rosanna Hertz for her insightful comments and suggestions on earlier drafts.

NOTES

1. Recall that police organizations include many occupations. A considerable number of employees are non-sworn, including specialists who look after equipment, especially information technologies. "Deviance" of the patrol and detective divisions is most often studied and given media attention. However, almost nothing is known about "deviance" in managing police budgets and accounting procedures, disability and compensation decisions, record keeping, and routine corruption among middle and senior officers.

2. Some federal agencies have asserted international and border jurisdictions, and enforce American law in foreign countries. Boundaries between different policing units are almost always blurred, even when the units go under different and distinct names: "policing," "peace-keeping," "low-level domestic conflicts," "terrorism," and "war." This overlapping of the police is illustrated by the pres-

ence of U.S. agents and soldiers as "peacekeepers" in Bosnia, and Somalia; DEA and FBI agents operate from embassies all over the world. U.S. Navy and Coast Guard "inderdict" drugs in the South Atlantic and Caribbean, and serve in local disasters such as hurricanes in Florida, floods on the Mississippi, and earthquakes in California (Kraska and Kappeler 1995).

3. A theory of police deviance cannot explain violence if it is assumed to be present in the nature of the case (Reiss 1992). The distribution of violence in a society is a consequence of historic political decisions concerning regulation.

4. The occupational culture of policing may polarize a police force around their support of "legalism" as a cultural theme. Legalism refers to the notions that procedural law constrains, and should constrain, policing; that selective law enforcement is wrong; and that policing rests on police officers' acceptance of the rules and authority of their departments. Legalism tends to be of particular interest to the managerial and command levels.

5. A question that should also be considered is what divides and what unites the police. The segments (and generalist and specialist units) liaise through a set of well-understood transactions that link segments, rank hierarchies, and the specialized units.

6. Let us take as an example how data have superseded conceptual equivalence in research on arrest practices. This research reflects a number of obvious conceptual weaknesses, primarily because, with some exceptions (Chatterton 1982; Black 1980; Reiss 1970; Ericson 1981), it omits analysis of the social context of the arrest. What are the relationships between offender, victim, and witnesses, and the role of the third party, when present, in the event? Most studies of attitudes and arrest behavior, as well as studies of interactional dynamics, tend to be sterile because they are cross-sectional and collapse a variety of situations and role relationships (Mastrofski 1996). Studies using officers' attitudes or other reductionistic measures that focus on "arrest" or non-arrest as binary outcomes (Sherman 1982) yield consistently unsatisfying results. Relevant background factors, such as the social area of an arrest, locale, and attributions that "motivated" the incident initially, and the role relationships of third parties, are omitted (See by contrast Herbert 1997; Klinger 1997).

7. It is almost impossible to disaggregate elements of the self-fulfilling prophecy with respect to enforcement patterns, attitudes, and traditions that associate low income, minority, and relatively disorganized areas as primary loci for police attention and the resultant rates of arrest, conviction, and penal sanctions (Tonry 1996; Miller 1996). There is evidence that some types of crime are in fact higher in these areas (O'Brien 1996a).

REFERENCES

Adams, K. 1995. "Distribution of Force" Pp. 10–37 in *And Justice For All*, edited by W. Geller and H. Toch. Washington, DC: Police Executive Research Forum (PERF).

Alpert, G. 1997. "Pursuit Driving: Planning Policies and Action from Agency, Officer, and Public Information." *Police Forum* 7: 1–12.

Alpert, G., and R. Dunham. 1997. *The Force Factor: Measuring Police Use of Force Relative to Suspect Resistance*. Police Executive Research Forum Publication, pp. 1–24. Washington, DC: Police Executive Research Forum.

Alpert, G., and R. Dunham. 1997a. *Critical Issues in Policing*, 3rd edition. Prospect Heights, IL: Waveland Press.

Alpert, G., and L. Fridell. 1992. *Police Vehicles and Firearms: Instruments of Deadly Force*. Prospect Heights, IL: Waveland Press.

Alpert, G., and W.C. Smith. 1994. "How Reasonable is the Reasonable Man? *Journal of Criminal Law and Criminology* 85: 481–501.

Baker, M. 1985. *Cops*. New York: Pocket Books.

Barker, T., and D. Carter. 1994. *Police Deviance*, 3rd edition. Cincinnati: Anderson Publishing Co.

Bayley, D., and J. Garofalo. 1989. "The Management of Violence by Police Patrol Officers." *Criminology* 27: 1–25.

Bayley, D., and J. Garofalo. 1985. *Patterns of Policing*. New Brunswick, NJ: Rutgers University Press.

Bayley, D., and J. Garofalo. 1986. "The Tactical Choices of Police Patrol Officers." *Journal of Criminal Justice* 14: 329–348.

Bayley, D., and J. Garofalo. 1994. *Police for the Future*. New York: Oxford University Press.

Bittner, E. 1990. *Aspects of Police Work*. Boston: Northeastern University Press.

Black, D. 1980. *The Manners and Customs of the Police*. New York: Academic Press.

Black, D. 1984. *Theory of Social Control*, Two Volumes. New York: Academic Press.

Brandl, S. 1997. "In the Line of Duty: A Descriptive Analysis of Police Assaults and Accidents." Working Paper, University of Wisconsin, Milwaukee.

Cancino, J. 1998. "Violence and the Police Role." Unpublished M.A. thesis, School of Criminal Justice, East Lansing, MI: Michigan State University.

Cannon, L. 1997. *Official Negligence*. New York: Times Books.

Chan, J. 1996. *Changing Police Culture*. Melbourne: Cambridge University Press.

Chatterton, M. 1982. "Police Work and Assault Charges" Pp. 194–220 in *Control in the Police Organization*, edited by M. Punch. Cambridge: MIT Press.

Christopher Commission Report. 1991. *The Independent Commission on the Los Angeles Police Department*. Los Angeles: Los Angeles Police Department (LAPD).

Cooney, M. 1998. *Warriors and Peacemakers: How Third Parties Shape Violence*. New York: New York University Press.

del Carmen, R. 1991. *Civil Liabilities in American Policing*. Englewood Cliffs, NJ: Brady.

Dunham, R., and G. Alpert. 1995. "Controlling the Use of Force: An Evaluation of Street-Level Narcotics Interdiction in Miami." *American Journal of Police* 14: 83–100.

Ericson, R. 1981. *Making Crime*. Toronto: Butterworth's.

Fletcher, C. 1990. *What Cops Know*. New York: Pocket Books.

Fridell, L., and A. Pate. 1997. "Death on Patrol: Killing of American Law Enforcement Officers" Pp. 580–608 in *Issues in Policing: Contemporary Readings*, 3rd edition, edited by R. Dunham and G. Alpert. Prospect Heights, IL: Waveland Press.

Fyfe, J. 1979. "Administrative Interventions in Police Shooting Discretion: An Empirical Examination." *Journal of Crime and Delinquency* 7: 309–324.

Fyfe, J. 1986. "The Split-Second Syndrome and Other Determinants of Police Violence" Pp. 207–223 in *Violent Transactions* edited by A. Campbell and J. Gibbs. Oxford: Basil Blackwell.

Fyfe, J. 1988. "The Police Use of Deadly Force: Research and Reform." *Justice Quarterly* 5: 165–205.

Fyfe, J., and J. Skolnick. 1993. *Beyond The Law*. New York: Basic Books.

Goldstein, H. 1989. *Problem Oriented Policing*. New York: McGraw-Hill.

Goode, W.J. 1973. "The Place of Force in Human Society." *American Sociological Review* 37: 507–519.

Graef, R. 1989. *Talking Blues*. London: Fontana/Harper Collins.

Herbert, S. 1997. *Policing Space in Los Angeles*. Minneapolis: University of Minnesota Press.

Hersey J. 1968. *The Algiers Motel Incident*. New York: Knopf.

Hughes, Everett C. 1958. *Men and Their Work*. Glencoe, IL: Free Press.

Jackall, R. 1997. *Wild Cowboys: Urban Marauders and the Forces of Order*. Cambridge, MA: Harvard University Press.

Jacobs, D., and D. O'Brien. 1998. "The Determinants of Deadly Force: A Structural Analysis of Police Violence." *American Journal of Sociology* 103: 837–862.

Jacobs, J., and K. Potter. 1998. *Hate Crimes*. New York: Oxford University Press.

Kaminski, R., and E. Jefferis. 1997. "The Effect of a Violent Televised Arrest on Public Perceptions of the Police." Paper presented at the American Criminal Justice Society, Louisville, KY.

Kappeler, V., R. Sluder, and G. Alpert. 1998. *Forces of Deviance*, 2nd edition. Prospect Heights, IL: Waveland Press.

Klinger, D. 1997. "Negotiating Order in Patrol Work." *Criminology* 35: 277–306.

Klockars, C. 1995. "Excessive Force." Pp.1–22 in *And Justice For All*, edited by W. Geller and H. Toch. Washington, DC: Police Executive Research Forum (PERF).

Knapp, W. 1972. *The Knapp Commission Report* [on Police Corruption in New York City]. New York: George Braziller.

Kraska, P., and V. Kappeler. 1995. "To Serve and Pursue: Police Sexual Violence against Women." *Justice Quarterly* 12: 85–112.

Kraska, P., and V. Kappeler. 1997. "Militarizing American Police: The Rise and Normalization of Paramilitary Units." *Social Problems* 44: 1–18.

Maas, P. 1975. *Serpico*. New York: Bantam Books.

Manning, P.K. 1979. *The Narcs' Game*. Cambridge, MA: MIT Press.

Manning, P.K. 1992. "Police and Information Technology" Pp. 349–398 in *Modern Policing*, edited by M. Tonry and N. Morris. Chicago: University of Chicago Press.

Manning, P.K. 1994. "Class, Symbolic Capital, and Social Control," Pp. 80–96 in *Inequality, Crime, and Social Control*, edited by G. Bridges and M. Myers. Boulder, CO: Westview.

Manning, P.K. 1996. "Dramaturgy, Politics, and the Axial Media Event." *The Sociological Quarterly* 37: 261–278.

Manning, P.K. 1997. *Police Work*, 2nd edition. Prospect Heights, IL: Waveland Press.

Manning, P.K., and L.J. Redlinger. 1977. "Working Bases of Corruption." Pp. 60–89 in *Drugs and Society*, edited by P. Rock. New Brunswick, NJ: Transaction Press.

Manning, P.K., and M.P. Singh. 1997. "Violence and Hyperviolence." *Sociological Spectrum* 17: 339–361.

Matulia, K. 1985. *A Balance of Forces*, 2nd edition. Gaithersburg, MD: International Association of Chiefs of Police.

McClure, J. 1980. *Spike Island: Portrait of a Police Division* [Liverpool]. New York: Macmillan.

McClure, J. 1984. *Cop World: Inside an American Police Force* [San Diego]. New York: Pantheon.

McEwen, T. 1996. *National Data Collection on Police Use of Force*. Bureau of Justice Statistics. Alexandria, VA: Institute for Law and Justice.

Miller, J. 1996. *Search and Destroy: African-American Males in the Criminal Justice System*. New York: Cambridge University Press.

Mollen Commission. 1994. *The Mollen Commission to Investigate Allegations of Police Corruption in New York City*. New York: City of New York.

O'Brien, R. 1996a. "Police Productivity and Crime Rates, 1973–1992." *Criminology* 34: 183–207.

O'Brien, R. 1996b. "Crime and Victimization Data." Pp. 57–81 in *Criminology*, 2nd edition, edited by J. Sheley. Belmont: Wadsworth.

Reaves, B. 1996. *Local Police Departments*. Washington, DC: Bureau of Justice Statistics.

Reiss, A.J., Jr. 1970. "Police Brutality: Answers to Key Questions." *Society* 5: 10–19.

Reiss, A.J., Jr. 1971. *The Police and the Public*. New Haven, CT: Yale University Press.

Reiss, A.J., Jr. 1974 "Discretionary Justice." Pp. 679–699 in *The Handbook of Criminology* edited by Daniel Glaser. Chicago: Rand McNally.

Reiss, A.J., Jr. 1992. "Police Organization in the Twentieth Century." Pp. 51–97 in *Modern Policing*, edited by M. Tonry and N. Morris. Chicago: University of Chicago Press.

Robin, G. 1963. "Justifiable Homicide by Police." *Journal of Criminal and Police Science* 54: 225–231.

Rothmiller, M., and I.G. Goldman. 1992. *L.A. Secret Police*. New York: Pocket Books.

Shearing, C., and R. Ericson. 1991. "Culture as Figurative Action." *British Journal of Sociology* 42: 481–506.

Sherman, L.W. 1978. *Scandal and Reform: Controlling Police Corruption*. Berkeley, CA: University of California Press.

Sherman, L.W. 1980. "Defining Arrest I." *Criminal Law Bulletin* 4: 376–471.
Sherman, L.W. 1982. "Arrest I" pp. ???? *Criminal Law Bulletin*. New York: Warren, Gorham, and Lamont.
Sherman, L.W. 1983. "Reducing Police Gun Use" Pp. 98–125 in *Control in the Police Organization*, edited by M. Punch. Cambridge, MA: MIT Press.
Sherman, L.W. 1992. "Attacking Crime: Police and Crime Control." Pp. 159–230 in *Modern Policing*, Vol. 12: *Crime and Justice*, edited by N. Morris and M. Tonry. Chicago: University of Chicago Press.
Sherman, L.W., and R. Langworthy. 1979. "Measuring Homicide by Police Officers." *Journal of Criminal Law and Criminology* 70: 546–560.
Skolnick, J. 1967. *Justice Without Trial*. New York: John Wiley.
Stark, R. 1972. *Police Riots*. Belmont, CA: Wadsworth.
Stoddard, E. 1968. "The Informal Code of Police Deviancy: A Group Approach to Blue Collar Crime." *Journal of Criminal Law, Criminology, and Police Science* 59: 201–213.
Tonry, M. 1996. *Malign Neglect*. New York: Oxford University Press.
Van Maanen, J. 1982. "The Moral Fix." Pp. 115–139 in *Handbook of Methods*, Vol. 2, edited by R. Smith and P.K. Manning. Cambridge: Ballinger Law, Criminology.
Walker, S., and V. Bumphus. 1991. *Civilian Review of the Police*. Omaha, NE: University of Nebraska.
Weber, M. 1947. *The Theory of Social and Economic Organization*, translated and edited by A.M. Henderson and T. Parsons. Glencoe, IL: Free Press.
Westley, W. 1970. *Violence and the Police*. Cambridge, MA: MIT Press.
Wickersham Commission. 1931. *National Commission of Law Observance and Enforcement*. Washington, DC: U.S. Government Printing Office.
Worden, R. 1996. "The Causes of Police Brutality: Theory and Evidence on Police Use of Force." Pp. 23–51 in *Police Violence: Understanding and Controlling Police Abuse of Force*. New Haven, CT: Yale University Press.

EXTERNALIZATION AND INTERNALIZATION AS FRAMES FOR UNDERSTANDING WORKPLACE DEVIANCE

THE MANAGEMENT OF ALCOHOL AND DRUG ABUSE

Paul M. Roman and Terry C. Blum

ABSTRACT

While it is widely used in economics, the concept of externalization is rarely found in sociological analyses. Its application to workplace deviance appears promising. Like many types of social groups, organizations react variably to deviants (both within and outside the system) in terms of their exclusion or inclusion. In this chapter externalization is first explored as a sociological variable and is then used to describe organizational reactions to employees' use and abuse of psychoactive substances, wherein the testing of persons for evidence of drug use is widely recognized as the trigger for externalization. This example and the contemporary moral panic

Research in the Sociology of Work, Volume 8, pages 139-164.

ISBN: 0-7623-0608-4

about illegal drugs highlight the importance of societal context, and draw attention to legislative attempts to prescribe workplace "internalization" of persons in certain social categories. Employee assistance programs offer a contrasting illustration of efforts to internalize deviant employees that are undertaken voluntarily by organizational decision makers. A series of hypotheses suggests how the empirical dynamics of externalization and internalization might be documented effectively.

INTRODUCTION

As a nexus where concepts meet from several sociological theories, workplace deviance is a potentially exciting research topic. Given the abundance of sociological interest in work and the parallel abundant interest in deviance, the combination of these topics would be expected to be a center of research activity. Despite these promising features, it is difficult to identify a group of sociological researchers or a body of sociological literature even loosely organized around this topic.

With occasional exceptions, public and governmental interest in workplace deviance is close to minimal. Murder and violence in the workplace have been an emergent media focus in the 1990s. Despite the social drama, the diffuseness and unpredictability of workplace violence has not produced a groundswell of research or design of interventions to curtail these occurrences. With the important exception of sexual harassment, antisocial behavior in the workplace has only recently attracted the attention of organizational researchers (Giacalone and Greenberg 1997) and it is unlikely that funding specifically earmarked for such research could be identified.

Media attention in the 1990s has also been drawn to employers' surveillance of employee behavior, with such surveillance possibly serving to prevent deviance or nip it in the bud (Hubbartt 1998). On closer inspection however, employer surveillance strategies seem less concerned with curbing what might be called events of traditional deviance and more concerned with minimizing shirking, deterring minor theft, and emphatically underlining to workers just who's in charge (Pfeffer 1981).

Despite workplace violence, widely publicized sexual harassment, and revelations of intrusive surveillance by employers, there is little evidence that these events have compelled public concern about workplace deviance. Overall impressions suggest that the mainstream cultural notions envision workplaces as tightly controlled in a relative sense, with detected incidents of deviance leading to rapidly administered discipline, including dismissal. There also appears to be a high degree of public confidence in workplaces' techniques to screen out potentially troublesome individuals from initial employment, that is, workplaces are not seen as "safe harbors" for individuals who are potential threats to others. More globally, these images likely hinge upon the institutionalized rationality of work organizations (Coleman 1993). If work organizations have institutionalized images of being rational systems, then a singular focus on productivity and no-nonsense management of deviant behavior should be captured within these images.

As is established throughout this volume and in other publications, deviance is abundant in workplaces and its management is problematic, in seeming contrast to institutionalized imagery. Occurrences of deviance in workplaces encompass dramatic interfaces between complex bureaucracy and various foibles of the human condition.

The absence of a fertile conceptual framework within which to talk about and study workplace deviance may also hinder research development. At present theories about workplace deviance are borrowed from elsewhere, either "whole cloth" or haphazardly, although some work shows no evidence of theoretical guidance. Given the empirical linkages of workplace deviance to organizations, occupations, and deviance, maybe there is "too much" available in terms of potential theoretical direction. Further, none of these "root" specialties can be described as organized around theoretical paradigms, but are instead miniature Towers of Babel, with cacaphonies of competing approaches as to how empirical worlds should be conceptually organized.

Our ambitions here are to take a first step toward an integrative conceptualization of a major dimension of workplace deviance. The concept of "externalization" shows great promise for describing how workplaces contend with perceived deviance in their own work forces and in the labor force generally. The sociological application of the concept of externalization to work organizations is based in the work of Charles Perrow (1991; 1996). Fundamentally, externalization is the idea that firms move certain costs of production outside their boundaries and impose them elsewhere, often in a subtle or oblique manner.

An apt illustration is where an efficient production method used in a factory results in the pollution of the air, water and/or land in the surrounding environment. The corporation owning the factory collects the profits resulting from the production process whereas the humans, plants, and animals outside the factory suffer a reduction of their quality of life, and through these losses indirectly and involuntarily contribute to corporate profits. This example amply demonstrates the emotional "charge" that the concept can generate. It is clear that the notion of externalization is fundamental to the environmental movement of recent decades, although not articulated as such by sociologists. It is also clear that the social indictments implicit in these observations have overshadowed the possibilities for conceptual analysis.

While the implications of externalization as environmental pollution are profound, the basic idea of externalization may be valuable in other applications to organizational behavior that are not necessarily founded on indictments of corporate actions. The application of the idea of externalization (and its opposite, internalization) to how organizations deal with certain employees or groups of employees shows great promise.

As a starting point, we suggest that externalization of workplace deviance has institutional features in that it describes the core of public beliefs about how these issues are dealt with in American workplaces, that is, managers specifically proscribe certain behaviors, they ferret out persistent deviants, and they dump them into the community. The concept of externalization can frame the basic theoretical questions of "deviance management," namely why, when, and how organizations elect to "externalize" deviant organizational members versus why, when, and how they choose to "internalize" them. This framework helps organize an understanding of how organizations act, as well as linking these actions with broader social processes over time and space. While our focus here is primarily at the level of organizational actions, we propose that this framework also has applications to understanding workplace deviance at the group and dyadic levels.

Our perspective is based on several decades of field research about how workplaces deal with employee substance abuse using survey, on-site interview, and qualitative methods. Some of our attention has been focused on an externalization strategy, workplace drug testing, while we have also done a great amount of research on an internalization strategy, employee assistance programs.

While there are many gaps in the historical record, it is clear that the emergence of the population of work organizations in American culture has been accompanied by waxing and waning of various social concerns centered on psychoactive substances, the presence and attraction of which has marked all of American history, to say nothing of the history of humankind (Rorabaugh 1979; Rumbarger 1989). Thus what we see today needs to be examined in the context of change over time.

The present day is a good time to look at employers' reactions to drug and alcohol use among their workers, because the level of concern is very high, with some characterizing the current cultural response to illegal drugs as "moral panic" (Goode and Ben-Yehuda 1994). Our empirical work has produced two observations that are the foundation of our conceptualization of workplaces' responses to deviance:

First, there has been considerable variation in American history in reactions to alcohol and drugs in the workplace, with waves of emphasis on internalization and on externalization of employees' substance use and abuse problems.

Second, while distinctive "fashions" (Abrahamson 1996), patterns, or trends can be observed in employers' ways of dealing with these issues, there is marked variability in how these interventions diffuse across the population of work organizations, as well as considerable variation in the ways in which some interventions are adopted or implemented.

There are few satisfactory explanations of the historical changes that have been observed, or of the cross-organizational variations in reactions that describe the contemporary scene. Sociologists have shown considerable interest in the former topic and have developed a substantial and fascinating literature on the emergence of patterns of management and social control in the American workplace (Barley and Kunda 1992). Much less interest has been shown in explaining cross-organizational differences in discrete human resource management practices (Kalleberg, Knoke, Marsden, and Spaeth 1996; Bennett, Blum, and Roman 1994) although attention has been focused on the macroscopic emergence of organized practices of personnel management (Baron, Dobbin, and Jennings 1986).

It is not completely clear whether considerations of workplace deviance "fit" within the concerns of general management. In other words, a fundamental issue in management is to direct and motivate workers to work. Measures of average performance always create below average performers, and these performers are principal targets of managerial strategies to enhance and sustain productivity. The question is the extent of commonality between the management of workplace deviants and the management of below average performers. A careful analysis of the published literature will show considerable shifting and ambivalence on this point. Thus an important but unanswered question is whether the management of deviance is "continuous" or "discontinuous" with the general concerns and orientations of organizational and supervisory management toward maintaining adequate levels and predictability of job performance and output.

The explanations of observed patterns of organizational management tend to attribute or imply a high degree of rational planning and action on the parts of employers or managers (Zey 1998). Fundamental to recent sociological analyses of the management of workers are notions of various types of employer "control" (Edwards 1979), posing rather monolithic societal trends in organizational behavior. Like implications of rational choice, these models of workplace social control suggest potent institutional forces that eliminate most managerial discretion. While the conceptual distinctions of different patterns control over time, and their emergence in response to technology, will be enduring contributions to sociological theory, these approaches offer little toward explaining the variation in control strategies across different organizational settings. Further, much of the description of various types of control does not explain the dynamics of control processes.

A closely related perspective draws on several variations of stratification theory, focusing on the differential value employers attach to employees of varying skill levels and educational accomplishment, with different levels of "social desirability" of employer reactions being directly linked to the workers' class status (Tolbert, Horan, and Beck 1980; Falk and Lyson 1988). By implication, internalization of problem employees will dominate in organizations dependent on primary or core labor markets; externalization of such employees will be common among organizations drawing from secondary or peripheral labor markets. A final perspective embeds varying combinations of these ideas wherein high levels of rationality are ascribed to employers who minimize costs and maximize benefits in strategically planned determinations of "what to do" about alcohol, drug use and mental illness in the workforce (Hartwell, Steele, French, Potter, Rodman, and Zarkin 1996).

Previous work has understated the intertwined relationships between employers' reactions to employee deviance and the surrounding institutional structures that are constantly changing. These structures have been seen as determinants of what employers do, but there has been less recognition of the dynamic nature of this relationship, namely that employers' behavior guides and shapes changes in institutional structure (Rumbarger 1989). Further, the inter-organizational dynamics associated with these processes deserves examination: new service or "helping" organizations emerge and existing organizations transform in order to respond to opportunities and provide solutions to organizational alcohol and drug problems (Roman 1981), these solutions typically reflecting contemporary institutional emphases.

Thus, our central focus is on the manner in which workplaces as organizations act in a complex set of ways to develop and implement norms that include or exclude persons whose actions allow that they be labeled as socially deviant. A great deal of sociological interest has focused on the various ways in which work organizations may foster, generate, or enhance deviant activities. Relatively little attention has however been given by sociologists to what organizations "do" about individuals whose behavior fits the several categories of social and cultural proscription that we in American sociology loosely call deviance, namely crime, mental illness, sexual misconduct, and substance misuse.

Employees whose behavior places them in these social categories may be problematic for organizations in four overlapping ways:

The symptoms or "syndromes" of their deviant behavior prevent performance of work role expectations.

The deviant behavior leads to damage, injury, loss, or the threat thereof to others in the workplace, or to material objects in the workplace.

The deviant behavior is disruptive to the work performance of others.

The presence of deviant actors is incongruent with the values and morality that are an overt part of the workplace's culture.

While it is hoped that some of the ideas in this paper will have general application across all four areas of culturally proscribed deviance, our particular focus is on substance misuse. A large literature can be pulled together describing that substance misuse impacts work organizations across all four categories above. Yet, in contrast to what might be expected, organizations do not move quickly to identify and remove all substance misusing employees.

A paradoxical observation is fundamental to much of the discussion that follows: workplaces in the United States engage in activities that serve to exclude persons who are substance misusers and also engage in behaviors that serve to include persons who are substance misusers. In some instances, exclusive and inclusive behaviors toward substance abusers occur within the same workplace.

In the remainder of this chapter, we describe and place in context these organizational behaviors and then offer a series of propositions that can help explain variation in these patterns, as well as serving to organize a broad range of empirical data about workplace deviance.

THE PERROW THESIS

In 1991 Charles Perrow offered a sweeping summary of social science theory about organizations and society. His fundamental proposition is that large organizations have "absorbed" a vast range of activities and services that were formerly provided through families, communities and other social groups. The significant implication of organizational absorption of numerous societal functions is the extent of control over individuals and culture that redounds to organizations as a consequence. In interesting ways, his characterization of contemporary American society resonates with an earlier historical analysis of isolated instances of "greedy institutions" (Coser 1974).

While his causal model is largely implicit, Perrow posits three dimensions of the organizational absorption of functions previously assigned to other institutional structures. These are wage dependence, factory bureaucracy, and the externalization of social costs. While Perrow's essay is not designed as a literature review, it is not novel in assigning importance to wage dependence and factory bureaucracy as bulwarks of workplaces' social control of employees.

Perrow does however offer an important translation into organizational theory of the economic concept of externalized costs, touching upon the recent surge of interest in rational choice within sociological theory (Coleman 1993). While damage wreaked by organizations on the external biophysical environment typifies economists' contemporary use of the notion of externalities, the concept also fits organizations' treatment of persons with undesirable characteristics who are either job applicants or current employees.

While Perrow does not refer to the externalization of deviant employees, his discussion of "absorption" bears upon the potential consequences of such externalization. One of his central contentions is that "large organizations have absorbed society...activities that once were performed by relatively autonomous and usually small informal groups...and small autonomous organizations...are now performed by large bureaucracies" (Perrow 1991, p. 726). He then goes into considerable detail describing the overall control exerted by large organizations across the lives of employees, control which includes the provision of many services and benefits formerly provided by small, autonomous systems. This "absorption" of societal functions by workplaces adds to the jeopardies that are faced by externalized employees. Not only are they left without employment income, but they are excluded from a panoply of "first class" benefits and services that are socially "absorbed" adjuncts of employment provided by workplaces. Such individuals become dependent on unpredictable and unevenly distributed "second-class" charities and services provided in the community to those who are not employed.

EXTERNALIZATION AND THE MANAGEMENT OF HUMAN RESOURCES

The underlying notion of externalization is part of the heritage of the sociology of deviance. Durkheimian theory includes the proposition that communities and groups define their normative boundaries by designating deviance, and by implication, through exclusion or externalization processes. Erikson's (1966) study of the designation of witches in the Puritan colony remains central to the contemporary study of deviance.

Short of executing deviants, human communities have often "passed on" their problematic folk to other groups via the mechanisms of excommunication, banishment, and deportation. Generally, externalization may be the source of all "social outsiders": schools expel incorrigible students, churches excommunicate certain types of evildoers, marital partners struggle to remove from the household spouses who are abusive or nonproductive, with separation and divorce being primary mechanisms for externalizing into the community those who have more or less failed at family roles. It is important to distinguish between these more general processes of exclusion where there is no explicit concern about where people "end up" and those which lead to a specific "relocation" for "correction" or "treatment" through incarceration or hospitalization.

Systematic development of the idea that social groups "externalize" or "internalize" problematic behavior has roots in early studies of family processes that evolve in the identification and external referral of family members who are mentally ill (Clausen and Yarrow 1955), in a descriptive study of the maintenance of deviants within military barracks life as a form of entertainment and maintenance of group solidarity (Dentler and Erikson 1959), and in an analysis of the family forces that work against the externalization of an emotionally disturbed child from the family setting (Vogel 1963). While a multitude of studies have described the extent and variety of nonwork activities and informal social structures within the formal contexts of workplaces, an examination of the management of proscribed deviance in the workplace has generally escaped such attention, with a few notable exceptions (Ames and Delaney 1992; Delaney and Ames 1993; Sonnenstuhl 1996). These studies provide some general frames for understanding why small-scale social systems externalize or internalize deviant members. In our examination we try to stay at a more macrolevel and examine how the environmental context may affect organizational decisions to move in one or both of these directions.

Application of the concept of externalization to the flow of human resources through work organizations requires careful specification. Externalization is not simply the movement of workers out of workplaces. This flow must impose some burden on third parties. Critical to the economists' definition of externalization is that it is an economic "failure" in a perfect market since it imposes an unreimbursed cost on one or another parties as part of transaction costs (Winfrey 1998). Going back to the typical example, externalization does not exist if the impacts of pollution are corrected through payment by the agency of production to others who have an economic interest in the impacted area or resource. Such outcomes likely occur after government intervention has occurred to reduce or eliminate the observed externalization (Winfrey 1998).

As we consider the externalization of human resources, the economists' specification becomes sociologically intriguing in three ways:

First is the extent to which an externalization impact is measured, measurable, or even known. In retrospect it is likely that an unknown proportion of the environmental pollution "discovered" in the recent past occurred unwittingly, that is, substances were disposed of without knowledge of their eventual toxicity or it was incorrectly assumed that these pollutants would be neutralized by natural "absorption" within the environment. This possibility might not be limited to environmental pollution, for workplaces may externalize job applicants and workers without a full understanding of the implications of these exclusion behaviors on subsequent patterns of community life.

A second variable is closely linked to the first, namely the variation in the degree of alliance or bonding among the parties impacted by externalization. It is possible that these parties are or become well organized, and move eventually to demand that the externalization be transformed into an exchange, through either action by the producer or by governmental intervention (Winfrey 1998). However, it is possible that affected parties do not or cannot communicate with each other, and are thus unaware of their shared costs resulting from externalization. It is also possible that despite alliances among "victims," there are few collective resources with which to respond to the perceived impacts. In either case, action toward the producer or attempts at governmental remediation are thus unlikely.

Third, a reverse effect is also possible: externalization impacts may become the province or territory of a set of specialist organizations which develop vested interests around their existence. In such instances, the human resources that are disvalued by workplaces as employees may become values to other organizations as patients or clients.

Turning from impacts to process, externalization of human resources can take one of two general forms: involuntary unemployment and disqualification for continuing employment.

EXTERNALIZATION AS INVOLUNTARY UNEMPLOYMENT

Involuntary unemployment comes about when an organization alleges and/or perceives that it cannot survive without reducing the size of the workforce. Most prominent in recent years has been the phenomena of "downsizing" whereby "excess" personnel (usually in specific occupational categories or organizational units) are terminated in the interest of increasing corporate efficiency (Gordon 1996).

While downsizing has drawn a great deal of attention and alarm as it has penetrated deeply into middle and upper-middle class positions in workplaces, organizations' reductions in force through layoffs, dismissals, or plant closings have a long history of impact in blue collar and working-class segments of the workforce. Of some significance to our discussion is the assumption that downsizing or layoffs are independent of workers' job performance; the position is abolished rather than the person being dismissed. This assumption is reflected in common efforts to transfer displaced workers to open positions elsewhere within the organization. The governing imagery is that external economic forces of various types and combinations have forced the organization to lose totally competent and committed "good people," and that the sacrifice of their positions is for the greater good of the surviving employees and of the survival of the organization.

These actions by organizations are good examples of the externalization phenomenon as it applies to human resources. Generally, organizations are not subject to legal or governmental challenge following downsizing or layoffs, unless specific steps to deal with these exigencies have been *a priori* specified in a collective bargaining agreement.

Instead, government policies address externalization consequences. Several decades ago, in response to the possibility of unemployment and the resulting transactions costs, the government established unemployment insurance funds which are supported by contributions from employers and employees. Availability of these funds to unemployed workers is typically designed as transitional, to support them "between" jobs (with the assumption that any unemployed person can become re-employed within a reasonable period of time). Beyond unemployment payments are welfare programs that are supported by general taxation and which, in the United States, have also been designated recently as "transitional" economic support for many categories of potential workers.

Obviously, unemployment is in many instances an example of externalization as an "economic failure" (Winfrey 1988). The likelihood of unemployment insurance payments providing a smooth, cost-free transition for a person to transit from one job to another appears unlikely. By their very design, unemployment payments do not cover the full wages or salary that the individual was receiving while employed. Thus, transactions costs come to bear upon individuals and their families, to say nothing of the spillover into demands on other relatives, friends, and community agencies. It is also clear that there is no guarantee of re-employment, especially re-employment at the same level of wages and benefits that were previously enjoyed. It appears sound to conclude that any episode wherein numbers of employees are downsized or laid off is an instance of the externalization of transactions costs onto the community. But it is equally important to recognize that these patterns of practice have become institutionalized. While often noted as regrettable, involuntary unemployment and its consequences are nonetheless legitimate in American society.

The institutionalization of layoffs and downsizing provides a critical context for what we examine here as organizations' externalization and internalization of substance abusing employees. These broader actions by employers, and government's reactions to them, establishes the priority of organizational survival, and indeed, organizational profitability, over the consequences that may ensue for "outplaced" human resources. These actions provide the platform for employers' exercise of discretion in dealing with substance abusers.

EXTERNALIZATION AS DISQUALIFICATION FOR CONTINUING EMPLOYMENT

The second context for externalization of human resources is where there is a continuing demand for employees and available positions, but certain individuals are disqualified from employment due to some set of personal attributes. This type of externalization can be broken down into three "socio-behavioral" categories:

1. Employees who are disqualified from their positions by breaching the employment contract through inadequate job performance, including substandard attendance and poor relations with others in the workplace. This type of disqualification is specific to a given work organization and not to the (former) employee's participation in any future work roles.
2. Employees who develop certain patterns of behavior, such as alcoholism, drug dependence, or mental illness, that disqualifies them from continuing employment with a given employer. Depending upon the visibility of the behavior patterns, change in these patterns, or the employees' disclosure of life events to others, such persons may or may not be able to be employed elsewhere.
3. Employees whose chronological age is a proxy for an assumed decline in ability to work up to standards of efficiency and effectiveness, and who retire from organizational positions which continue after their departure as vacancies. Retirement can also take the form of disability retirement where an employee who has accumulated a required period of organizational tenure is judged physically or mentally incapable of continuing employment.

DRUG TESTING AS EXTERNALIZATION OF SOCIAL COSTS

We now examine how externalization mechanisms work relative to workplace substance abuse. Illegal drug use has been defined in this decade as a grave threat to the fabric of American society. Users of illegal drugs are to be excluded from any areas of activities where they may affect the well-being of non-users of illegal drugs. Such exclusion includes work roles. Mechanisms of pre-employment drug screening and its consequences for those detected as illegal drug users seem, on their face, ideal illustrations of workplaces' attempted externalization of a significant part of this social problem.

These emphases did not develop solely or even primarily from employers' initiatives, but were part of a larger "War on Drugs" declared by both Congress and the Executive Branch, a significant part of which called for "Drug-Free Workplaces" throughout America (Roman and Blum 1992). While all employers are urged to implement such policies, and while some governmental programs provide tax incentives for employers' policy adoption, mandated requirements for pre-employment and on-the-job drug screening are limited to the transportation industry and certain security-sensitive occupations.

The controversial nature of drug testing is highlighted by alternative definitions of the meaning of working people's use of illegal drugs, such as a notion that employees' use of illegal drugs is a lifestyle decision irrelevant to the demands of work, or that drug use might be seen as something which workplaces can reasonably deal with and absorb (i.e. "internalize" illegal drug use by ignoring it).

However, as a consequence of positive drug tests, drug-using job applicants are sent "out" into the community. Presumably some of them will be dealt with by other institutional systems supported by community resources, for example, criminal justice agencies, drug treatment programs, or social welfare departments. In other words, pre-employment drug testing leads to the externalization of persons seeking employment who are also illegal drug users, assigning to others whatever costs may be associated with their management.

Workplaces rarely refer drug-positive job applicants to their own EAP services or to specific agencies in the community. This implies that employers who implement pre-employment drug screening assume that drug users are a responsibility of someone or something other than the workplace. However, it is the responsibility of the excluded job applicant to identify this "other" elsewhere in the community.

Organizations' externalization of these human resource-related costs of their activities, that effectively assign these costs to others, parallels externalizations such as environmental pollution or traffic congestion. Such parallels focus upon the normative scope of relationships between employers and employees. Preemployment screening may be seen as underlining both the moral and secular authority of employers, authority that in general has been substantially reduced by both the external and internal bureaucratization of work organizations (Cavanaugh and Prasad 1994; Comer 1994; Pfeffer 1981).

While drug testing may underline employers' rights in regard to employee selection, there have however been counter-forces embedded in sociocultural change and governmental legislation which in turn have mandated "internalization" of representatives of certain categories of applicants on the assumption that their hiring was viewed as producing higher human resources costs relative to other hires. Equal Employment Opportunity and Affirmative Action regulations require that employers offer employment to persons with ascribed characteristics of gender, age, and ethnicity that had been historically associated with the perception and definition of lesser qualifications for employment. Here a portion of costs that were perceived by communities as having been turned back to them by employers' discriminatory practices are now seen as the rightful responsibility of employers.

A more recent counter-force, the Americans with Disabilities Act (ADA), goes beyond ascribed characteristics to affect employment opportunities for persons with a range of physical and mental disabilities. While many disabilities are ascribed characteristics, agency in producing the disability (i.e., personal negligence resulting in injury) does not disqualify the individual from a claim to disabled status. Here again the community appears to be turning back costs to the employer that were previously created by discrimination in employment practices and/or the physical inaccessibility of employment to persons with certain disabilities.

Thus there is a multifaceted context for considering pre-employment drug testing as a means for employers to externalize certain costs of human resources management. In sharp contrast to the examples drawn from legislation requiring employers' inclusive behavior toward groups viewed as problematic in some fashion, we have in the case of illegal drugs strong governmental support for a policy of exclusion of applicants who manifest evidence of illegal drug use. Between these government policies urging in some instances exclusion and in other instances inclusion, there may actually be counterproductive and contradictory outcomes to the extent that persons sharing the same ascribed characteristics are the targets of policy implementation, that is, controversial evidence that African-Americans are more likely selected out of employment by drug testing in the same settings where affirmative action policies are promoting their greater inclusion (Normand, Lempert, and O'Brien 1994; Roman and Blum 1992; Blum 1990).

There are several socio-historical facts that support the argument that pre-employment drug screening is an emergent example of the externalization of social costs, that is, it is a practice that has been deliberately selected by employers rather than being imposed on them by environmental changes or legislative actions. First, workplace drug screening emerged many decades after the drugs of concern were introduced into American culture and used by members of the

American work force (Morgan 1984). Likewise the technology in use today to test for evidence of illegal drug use is not a recent invention, but has been available to the workplace in its basic form for many years (Roman and Blum 1992). Further, there has been a delay of nearly two decades between the widespread adoption of urine-based drug testing and diffusion of evidence that the use of illegal drugs by American adults had escalated rapidly from its previous status as an "underground" behavior. Finally, there has been no subsequent "breakthrough" that has enhanced the efficacy of urine-based drug testing, a change that might explain its rather sudden, widespread adoption.

Thus diffusion and adoption of pre-employment drug testing as a way for employers to externalize social costs of drug users occurred well after the evidence that a problem existed, and well after the invention and availability of drug testing technology. While it can be argued that pre-employment drug testing was adopted in response to the *perception* of a problem, an obvious but subtle point is that the practice replaced an essentially unwritten policy that employed persons who were users of illegal drugs would be managed internally by workplaces. From a different view, it can be asserted that workplaces have recently curbed their societal participation in the management of a particular social problem which has existed and been dealt with ("internalized") by employers for many decades (Morgan 1984), albeit with low social visibility.

EMPLOYEE ASSISTANCE PROGRAMS AS INTERNALIZATION OF SOCIAL COSTS

While externalization has a relatively good fit with recent traditions in sociological characterizations of the workplace, internalization presents more challenges to extant paradigms. It might be argued that internalization strengthens the concept of externalization, but both of these ideas overlap with a plentitude of other frames that have explained employers' apparent beneficience in light of their apparent singular attraction to maximizing ownership gains.

We have already painted part of the picture of employers' reactions to drug abuse. There is another set of social histories about employers' involvement with employee alcohol problems. The internalization of alcohol problems set the stage for the broader base of internalized employee deviance encompassed by EAPs.

Workplaces were the first American institutions to implement the prohibition of alcohol (Rumbarger 1989). Not only was alcohol forbidden in any form in the workplace, but it was not uncommon for employers to forbid their employees to drink on their own time. The principal target of the movement for alcohol prohibition was the saloon, a place of male drinking and entertainment designed to counter the stress of work, but also to exploit the workingman. The central icon of the Temperance movement was the workingman made a drunkard by his habitual frequenting of saloons, ultimately being externalized by his employer and left in the street with his pitiful and hapless family without food or shelter. Thus, there can be no doubt that American culture had a strong tradition of accepting the legitimate externalization of the employee who becomes alcoholic.

The Repeal of Prohibition was accompanied by a gradual rejection of the ideologies upon which the Temperance Movement was based, and perhaps the legitimacy of the externalized alcoholic worker was slowly undermined. In the decades following the 1930s, slow but gradual changes in the institutional responses to alcohol problem issues became evident (Blum, Roman, and Bennett 1989).

This change gained great impetus with the invention of Alcoholics Anonymous (AA), wherein a new focus on changing the alcoholic came to replace the focus on changing the nation's drinking behavior. AA very quickly diffused as a successful recovery modality. It was not, however, until the 1970s that a strong "readiness" to again approach alcohol issues became evident in American culture (Beauchamp 1980).

As the outcome of long-term lobbying by a small but highly energetic and powerful group of AA members organized through the National Council on Alcoholism, key legislation was passed in 1970. This legislation established a federal agency, the National Institute on Alcohol Abuse and Alcoholism (NIAAA). The enabling legislation was rhetorically based on a "new epidemiology" of alcohol problems designed to supplant the Temperance-based idea that alcohol's victims were primarily the down-and-out homeless men that inhabited the "Skid Rows" of American cities (Roman and Blum 1987). Instead, the new model emphasized the widespread nature of "hidden" alcohol problems up and down the social structure.

This new epidemiology instantly located millions of alcoholics within the walls of America's workplaces. NIAAA's initiatives emphasized the urgency for employers to act in order to curb the losses exacted by hidden alcoholics on company payrolls. At the same time, the workplace-oriented campaign emphasized the business wisdom of rehabilitating rather than dismissing these workers or ultimately being forced to place them on disability benefits (Roman 1975, 1981).

Following an unsuccessful effort to diffuse "alcoholism-only" programs to workplaces, NIAAA moved in the mid-1970s toward the promotion of a concept that ultimately became embellished as the philosophy of the EAP (Roman 1975, 1981). This new programming strategy deemphasized the substance abusing employee per se. It instead suggested that work settings are characterized by costly disruptions and productivity loss due to a wide variety of "behavioral-medical problems," of which substance abuse is only one category, albeit a very significant category. In terms of "selling" such a program concept, it might be easy for an employer to deny the presence of alcoholic employees, but it would be much less credible to claim that none of the range of disruptive and difficult-to-handle "behavioral-medical" problems was represented in a workforce of any significant size.

To sidestep employer's problems with empowering their supervisors to identify alcoholism within the workforce, the EAP strategy firmly stated that problem employees were to be identified on the basis of their performance problems, not their behavioral symptoms. Within the EAP philosophy, the emphasis moved away from the supervisor's knowledge of the signs and symptoms of alcoholism. Instead the sorting out of proper referrals was shifted to an EAP expert capable of specifying and diagnosing the nature of employee problems which underlay the job performance problems. These experts could be company staff or external contractors. Upon receiving a referral, the EAP expert was to assess, motivate, and direct those employees to the treatment resources in the community most appropriate for their needs. This program coordinator was then in an ideal position to maintain treatment gains through post-treatment follow-up and support within the work setting.

COMBINATIONS OF DRUG TESTING AND EAPS

Thus far, our discussion of workplace drug testing has been limited to pre-employment screening. The externalization of drug positive job applicants is of a different genre than the externalization of drug positives among the existing workforce. Here we find a split between strategies.

The majority of workplaces which have in place policies for pre-employment drug testing also have policies calling for random testing of current employees and/or for-cause testing of employees who have been in accidents or who show erratic behavior (Bennett et al. 1994). The majority of workplaces with these policies also have EAPs in place. Where an EAP is in place, nearly all policies provide at least "one strike" for a drug positive employee to utilize EAP services and subsequently remain drug-free. Thus in these instances, the use of illegal drugs has been more or less medicalized and is treated in a fashion somewhat parallel to alcohol problems, although there is usually more leniency for "slips" among the employees who have received assistance for alcohol problems.

The residual group of workplaces that have drug testing but no EAP almost invariably dismiss (externalize) employees who are found drug positive in a random or for-cause test (Bennett et al. 1994). Here it can be said that there is logical consistency between the policy implemented for job applicants and that implemented for current employees. It is however important to note that when an EAP is present (which usually predated drug testing), its ideology prevails relative to the management of drug positives among current employees.

EXPLANATIONS FOR ORGANIZATIONAL INVESTMENT IN DRUG TESTING AND EMPLOYEE ASSISTANCE PROGRAMS

As is evident from the foregoing thumbnail descriptions, the governing ideologies behind preemployment drug testing and EAPs are radically different. One poses illegal substance use as so threatening to the fabric of the workplace that no user should be allowed to enter while the other offers the possibility of continuing employment and at least tentative forgiveness for those drug abusers who follow the prescriptions of the EAP.

To conclude this discussion, it may be useful to examine a series of propositions that might explain why employers adopt and utilize pre-employment screening and EAPs. We briefly consider the tenability of each of these ideas.

PROPOSITIONS REGARDING EXTERNALIZATION PROCESSES

Proposition 1. Drug testing is an aspect of organizational rationality, for it has been established that it successfully eliminates illegal drug users from employment.

In terms of typical work performance concerns, drug testing is neither a necessary nor a sufficient mechanism for identifying an individual whose work performance or other behaviors as an employee would not meet normative standards. The actual work performance of drug positive employees has not been studied, except for one project which allowed for the blind employment of drug positives, which did not produce persuasive evidence that their job performance patterns that could be attributed to their drug-using behavior were significantly different from employees who were not drug positive at the time of employment (Normand, Lempert, and O'Brien 1994).

From several other points of view, employers' investments in the drug testing of job applicants and in the implementation of EAPs for current employees are irrational and contrary to organizational goals of minimizing costs and maximizing profits.

First, drug testing is an expensive activity for which nearly all organizations must depend on external vendors. Rough estimates indicate that drug testing costs about $75 per employee tested. Thus the use of applicant drug testing involves a cost outlay that represents an increase in recruitment costs. One way to minimize these costs is to place drug testing at the end of the applicant selection process, increasing the likelihood that the applicant has shown a sustained interest in this particular employment opportunity and will not be rejected on other grounds. A potential side-effect of such a policy is that the employer may have become increasingly attracted to a particular employee by the time positive drug test results emerge, putting some strain on commitment to this policy.

Because of the specialized nature of the techniques involved, the costs of drug testing cannot be absorbed through assignment of these responsibilities to underutilized components of the organization. The singular way of avoiding these costs is to require that they be paid by the job applicant, a reasonable possibility only when the labor market is offering an abundant supply of the categories of workers needed by an organization.

The real economic cost of drug testing is an important context for considering the question of drug testing's effectiveness. Employers are committed to the level of investing "real money" in these programs, and they use the low and declining rates of drug positives as evidence that drug screening of applicants works. Almost never is this assumption linked to data about the actual rates of illegal drug use that subsequently emerge among those employees who are hired. When such data have been examined, they indicate no association between the presence of pre-employment testing and the rates of employee drug problems that are revealed in EAP case loads (Roman 1989). Thus it is difficult to conclude that preemployment drug testing is adopted and maintained on the basis of its proven cost-benefits.

Proposition 2. Externalization through drug testing is actually a flexible tool wherein information about positive test results is withheld from applicants whom employers want to hire, or they are given unexpected "second chances" to repeat the drug tests until they turn out negative.

There is no empirical evidence to support or refute this idea, but it is the case that the employer is in control of the results of drug tests and can use them any way that is seen fit. A prospective employee who is an illegal drug user is not likely to contest a negative drug test. Thus, while great care is taken to sustain a "chain of custody" of urine samples prior to testing (Walsh and Hawks 1986), the control of test results may be open to employer discretion.

Proposition 3. Because of the individualized patterns of pre-employment drug screening, there are no bases for organizing constituencies to oppose the operation of these programs.

Job-seeking is an individualized activity, and applicants do not necessarily obtain full information about the results of interviews or testing. Employers are not required to inform applicants that employment is being denied because of a positive drug test. Given the low likelihood that groups of rejected applicants would have a basis for alliance, there is little likelihood that the apparent "victims" of drug testing would arise to protest it.

Proposition 4. In a culture marked by increasing external control of workplace management discretion in hiring, drug testing represents the symbolic assertion of employers' authority over hiring decisions.

There can be little doubt that employers' discretionary authority over their human resources management practices has been greatly altered by the emergence of legislation mandates at the local, state, and national levels. Exclusion of drug-positive employees is one area is which their control is still allowed, although it is tacitly assumed that they would not exercise discretion and hire drug-positive employees who were otherwise desirable. Given the weak evidence about the economic rationality of drug testing discussed above, its use as a symbolic mechanism (Pfeffer 1981) seems substantially supported.

PROPOSITIONS REGARDING INTERNALIZATION PROCESSES

Proposition 1. EAPs are aspects of organizational rationality, for they are adopted because of their proven cost-efficiency and cost-effectiveness.

There is a minimal amount of research about EAP effectiveness, although the aggregation of studies with widely varying methodology all points in the direction that they are cost-effective (Blum and Roman 1995). It is especially difficult to design and execute research that can be generalized across the wide varieties of structures that are called EAPs.

A method that has not been used in any published research would potentially offer "bottom line" data about EAP effectiveness. Such a study would require sampling across a range of EAPs and could use case-control comparisons to establish the long-term job performance and employment stability of persons who did and did not use EAP services. Presently it is assumed that in the light of fairly good evidence of short-term recovery among persons referred to EAPs with alcohol and drug problems, long-term recovery should show similar patterns.

Proposition 2. The mechanisms of EAP operation allow an organization to selectively internalize and externalize problem employees, depending upon their desirability to the organization.

Proposition 2a. The internal nature of EAPs is non-bureaucratic and discretionary, adding an attractive element to workplaces overwhelmed by externally imposed rules of personnel management.

Proposition 2b. EAPs are actually externalizing devices in that EAP referral is often the first step in ultimately getting rid of troublesome and inconsistently productive employees.

Through strong emphasis on confidentiality and focus on individuals, EAPs are a means to controvert legal structures and disempower employees, resulting in eventual "legitimate" termination or disability retirement.

Proposition 2c. Because of the individualized patterns of case identification and case management, there are no bases for organizing constituencies to oppose the operation of EAPs.

While these ideas should not be pushed to the extreme, they play on the notion of using psychiatric labeling and processing as a means of sociopolitical control. The extreme version of such practice would be the psychiatric incarceration of political dissidents in the former Soviet Union. This concept reintroduces organizational rationality, and suggests that EAPs may actually be extremely expedient mechanisms wherein the organization appears benevolent and humane while it is actually using covert processes of personnel selection. If this proposition is accurate, then there should be numbers of people who were referred to EAPs and who were dismissed from the organization, but who do not have a strong enough perception of injustice to lead to either litigation or attempts to expose what the organization "did" to them.

There is no real evidence of litigation against EAPs for inappropriate practices, and no known published "exposes" by alleged victims of EAPs. Further, nearly all EAPs involve mental health and substance abuse professionals who typically must have access to a broad range of confidential information about EAP client management. This ideological background should direct a large proportion of these workers toward sympathetic stances toward EAP clients in contrast to primary loyalties toward the employing organization. Furthermore, since these operatives are at best occupants of staff (rather than line) positions in organizations, and are commonly employed by external contract service providers, it would seem highly likely that one or more of them would easily slip into the role of "whistle-blower" about the practices suggested by this proposition.

Thus there are strong reasons for rejecting the validity of this proposition. There are however four points that qualify such rejection. First, the visibility of actual practices of selective retention or dismissal are related to the extent of their occurrence. Surely the short-term dismissal of the majority of employees referred to an EAP would quickly challenge its credibility across several constituencies. At the same time, it cannot be expected to "succeed" in retaining the employment of all referrals. Given that it is unlikely that organizations would be faced by large numbers of intractably problematic employees, and given that the majority of EAP usage is through self-referrals where employees present relatively minor difficulties, the externalization of employees with significant behavioral problems whom the employer desires to dismiss could occur without high visibility.

Second, the organizational placement of the EAP specialist in a staff or contractual position is a barrier to this individual's continuous monitoring and ongoing advocacy of employee clients' interaction with organizational forces. Organizations can easily transfer or otherwise move about individuals about whom they desire low visibility. It is clear that these movements could move well beyond the reach of the EAP specialist's communication lines.

Third, official processes of the labeling of deviance have long been believed to have significant impacts on self-concepts, self-image, and self-defense. While Gove (1980) and his colleagues have long argued from empirical data that labeled psychiatric clients are genuinely ill and are more or less appropriately labeled, few data are available that really provide a longitudinal test of labeling processes from their initiation. Thus, labeling impacts remain at the level of hypotheses to a large extent, but it seems credible that a portion of EAP clients are going to concur with the disabling implications of labels that are placed upon them, concurring with the logic for their eventual externalization from the organization.

Fourth, there may be social consensus regarding the externalization of certain deviant employees. This is well documented in the classic study of paranoids reported by Lemert (1962). Persons who ended up with a diagnosis of paranoia had been extremely difficult individuals with whom to work, and part of their paranoid ideation was centered on the genuine attempts of their co-workers and colleagues to exclude them. This escalated their ideation and in turn made interaction more difficult. The relevance of this study to present concerns is that there are likely employees who have no advocates in the workplace and around whom there is consensus that they should be externalized.

Proposition 3. EAPs serve significant functions for organizations, independent of their costs and independent of their impacts on individual employees.

Proposition 3a. EAPs are effective as part of an effort to keep out unions, or to weaken their presence and ultimately get rid of them.

Proposition 3b. EAPs are a means for enhancing the status, power, and influence of personnel departments which were emerging, newly powerful, as human resources management departments during the same time period that EAPs were emerging.

Proposition 3c. EAPs take potentially damaging focus away from both large-scale and group-level work forces that cause substance abuse and mental illness, and essentially blame the victims for these outcomes.

There is no basis for either accepting or rejecting any of these propositions, but each has substantial face validity. There is no doubt that EAPs offer the kind of "caring" about workers that has been traditionally an offering of labor unions. The ongoing decline of union representation in the American work force can be correlated with the increased prevalence of EAPs, but the possibility of a causal connection requires careful study.

EAPs introduce the medicalized management of troublesome employees into human resources management, increasing at least the appearance of rationality in dealing with alcohol, drug abuse, and mental illness in a scientifically and politically correct manner. Finally, the design and operation of EAPs assures that little or no focus will be turned on the internal pathology of the work organization or workgroup relationships. As with pre-employment drug screening, cases are dealt with on an individualized basis, and there is no mechanism for those who perceive "abuse" from the EAP to band together as protestors.

Proposition 4. EAPs are a contemporary manifestation of employers' good will, kindness, and decency toward employees, exemplifying Williams' (1970) key value orientation of humanitarianism embedded in American culture.

EAPs may be direct descendants of "welfare capitalism" (Brandes 1976; Jacoby 1985, 1998). As used by sociologists and most social historians, the concept of welfare capitalism imposes a cynical and manipulative interpretation on any employer effort to provide benefits to employees, increase their morale, or enhance their commitment to the workplace. It is perhaps no coincidence that sociologists' characterization of these outreach efforts by employers is almost precisely identical to the perspectives of labor organizers during the 1940s and 1950s (Fones-Wolf 1994).

This singular and unilateral perspective in the literature ignores the possibility that employers actively desire an organizational environment that might be described as positive, friendly, constructive, team-like, or happy. The perspective also imposes an ultra-rational orientation on top managers. Anything that is "given" to workers beyond the fair market value of their employment is seen as a cynical gimmick to cloud the workers' perception of what is "really going in" in the everyday world of capitalist enterprise.

Contrary as it may be to the extant literature, a fresh examination of the provision of a range of different benefits to employees by employers might be in order. This is an excellent stage upon which to consider the validity of rational choice perspectives in managerial decision-making. Part of this alternative perspective could build upon innovative entrepreneurs who seemed genuinely motivated to improve working conditions for their employees. An excellent example is W.K. Kellogg (Hunnicutt 1996) upon whose biographical facts it seems very difficult to impose a singularly manipulative, cynical, and profit-driven motivation. Without doubt, it is impossible to disprove the projection of secret or hidden motives on decision makers, but the possibility of benevolence among managers might allow for a better understanding of topics such as the one at hand.

Summary Proposition: The combined presence of both externalization through drug testing and internalization through EAPs allows employers to accommodate images of both toughness and humane treatment. These dual and contradictory perspectives are a mirror image of the dual and contradictory perspectives that describe the encompassing culture. By providing this combination of practices, employers increase the likelihood that their workplace is an attractive employment setting for the "mainstream" of American culture.

CONCLUSION

In this paper we have offered some different ways of viewing the management of deviance in the workplace. We have attempted to move beyond the merging of deviance theory and organizational theory, or the additive effort to intertwine the two conceptual areas into a bigger theoretical scheme. The translation of these ideas into empirical projects is a further challenge, and it is there that these ideas will prove their ultimate worth.

An attempt to place a different conceptual grasp around relatively well known phenomena can be enlightening. In this instance we come away impressed by the limitations of much of the dominant thinking about relationships between people in the workplace. We have in this instance borrowed from economics, but not with total success. A tendency that becomes clear in this examination is the excessively rational vision that we place on formal organizations as normative structures. Sociologists have shown great skill in describing the nature of bureaucracy, and of relationships between and even among position occupants operating in contexts of explicit rules directed toward equity. Especially well-described are relationships between superiors and subordinates. Similarly, but lesser so, we have a wide range of descriptions of relationships among groups at different status levels within organizations. The attempt to add richness to organizational life through adding concepts of "culture" is in some ways a welcome addition, but seems quickly to have moved toward another description of structure (history, "stories," rituals, etc.) that elaborates but does not necessarily elucidate.

What is missing is a good understanding of the genuinely human element in organizations, the element that leads to potentially good employees being denied work and well-known poor performers to continue their tenure indefinitely. While in the grammar of rationality these incidents could be described as "mistakes" or "slack," such description misses the essentially deliberate features of these outcomes. Our continuing study of organizational behavior and behavior within organizations needs a new language that captures the full range of human behavior beyond rational choice and beyond simple conformity to or deviation from bureaucratic prescriptions. In particular, such language and thinking needs to capture peer relationships and the quality of group life in organizations, rather than being centered on hierarchical relationships.

ACKNOWLEDGMENT

The authors acknowledge partial support from Grant No. R01-DA-07218 from the National Institute on Drug Abuse and Grant No. R01-AA-10130 from the National Institute on Alcohol Abuse and Alcoholism during the preparation of this manuscript. The comments of Heath Hoffmann are appreciated.

REFERENCES

Abrahamson, M. 1996. "Management Fashion." *Academy of Management Review* 21: 254–285.

Ames, G., and W. Delaney. 1992. "Minimization of Workplace Alcohol Problems: The Supervisor's Role." *Alcoholism: Clinical and Experimental Research* 16: 180–189.

Barley, S., and G. Kunda. 1992. "Design and Devotion: Surges of Rational and Normative Ideologies of Control in Managerial Discourse. *Administrative Science Quarterly* 37: 363–399.

Baron, J., F. Dobbin, and P. Devereaux Jennings. 1986. "War and Peace: The Evolution of Modern Personnel Administration in U.S. Industry." *American Journal of Sociology* 92: 250–283.

Beauchamp, D. 1980. *Beyond Alcoholism*. Philadelphia: Temple University Press.

Bennett, N., T.C. Blum, and P. Roman. 1994. "Presence of Drug Screening and Employee Assistance Programs: Exclusive and Inclusive Human Resources Practices." *Journal of Organizational Behavior* 15: 265–277.

Blum, T.C. 1990. "The Organizational and Structural Context of Employee Assistance Pro-grams." Pp. 321–344 in *Structures of Power and Constraint: Essays in Honor of Peter M. Blau*, edited by C. Calhoun, M. Meyer, and W.R. Scott. New York: Cambridge University Press.

Blum, T.C., P. Roman, and N. Bennett. 1989. "Public Images of Alcoholism: Data from a Georgia Survey." *Journal of Studies on Alcohol* 59: 5–14.

Blum, T.C., and P.M. Roman. 1995. *Cost Effectiveness and Preventive Implications of Employee Assistance Programs*. Washington, DC: Center for Substance Abuse Prevention.

Brandes, S.D. 1976. *American Welfare Capitalism: 1880–1940*. Chicago: University of Chicago Press.

Cavanaugh, J.M., and P. Prasad. 1994. "Drug Testing as Symbolic Managerial Action: In Response to 'A Case Against Drug Testing.'" *Organizational Science* 5: 267–271.

Clausen, J., and M. Yarrow. 1955. "Pathways to the Mental Hospital." *Journal of Social Issues* 11: 25–32.

Coleman, J.S. 1993. *Foundations of Social Theory*. Cambridge, MA: Belknap Press of Harvard University Press.

Comer, D. 1994. "A Case Against Workplace Drug Testing." *Organizational Science* 5: 258–266.

Coser, L.A. 1974. *Greedy Institutions: Patterns of Undivided Commitment*. New York: The Free Press.

Delaney, W., and G. Ames. 1993. "Shop Steward Handling of Alcohol-Related Problems" *Addiction* 88: 1205–1214.

Dentler, R.A., and K.T. Erikson. 1959. "The Functions of Deviance in Groups." *Social Problems* 7: 98–107.

Edwards, R.C. 1979. *Contested Terrain: The Transformation of the American Workplace in the 20th Century*. New York: Basic Books.

Erikson, K.T. 1966. *Wayward Puritans: A Study in the Sociology of Deviance*. New York: John Wiley and Sons.

Falk, W.W., and T.A. Lyson. 1988. *High Tech, Low Tech, No Tech: Recent Industrial and Occupational Change in the South*. Albany: State University of New York Press.

Fones-Wolf, E.A. 1994. *Selling Free Enterprise: The Business Assault on Labor and Liberalism, 1945–1960.* Urbana, IL: University of Illinois Press.

Giacalone, R.A., and J. Greenberg. 1997. *Anti-Social Behavior in Organizations.* Thousand Oaks, CA: Sage Publications.

Goode, E., and N. Ben-Yahoda. 1994. *Moral Panics.* Cambridge, MA: Blackwell.

Gordon, D.M. 1996. *Fat and Mean: The Myth of Corporate Downsizing.* New York: The Free Press.

Grove, W.R. (ed.) 1980. *Labeling Deviant Behavior.* Beverly Hills, CA: Sage.

Hartwell, T.D., P. Steele, M.T. French, F.J. Potter, N. Rodman, and G.A. Zarkin. 1996. "Aiding Troubled Employees: The Prevalence, Cost and Characteristics of Employee Assistance Programs in the United States. *American Journal of Public Health* 86: 804–808.

Hubbartt, W.S. 1998. *The New Battle over Workplace Privacy: How Far Can Management Go? What Rights Do Employees Have?* New York: Amacom Books (American Management Association)

Hunnicutt, B.K. 1996. *Kellogg's Six Hour Day.* Philadelphia: Temple University Press.

Jacoby, S.M. 1985. *Employing Bureaucracy: Managers, Unions and the Transformation of Work in American Industry, 1900–1945.* New York: Columbia University Press.

Jacoby, S.M. 1998. *Modern Manors: Welfare Capitalism Since the New Deal.* Princeton, NJ: Princeton University Press.

Kalleberg, A.L., D. Knoke, P.V. Marsden, and J.L. Spaeth. 1996. *Organizations in America: A Portrait of their Structures and Human Resources Practices.* Newbury Park, CA: Sage Publishing Co.

Lemert, E.M. 1962. "Paranoia and the Dynamics of Exclusion." *Sociometry* 25: 2–25.

Morgan, W.J. 1984. *Drugs and Society: A History.* Syracuse, NY: Syracuse University Press.

Normand, J., R.O. Lempert, and C.P. O'Brien (eds.). 1994. *Under the Influence: Drugs and the American Work Force.* Washington, DC: National Academy of Sciences Press.

Perrow, C. 1991. "A Society of Organizations." *Theory and Society* 20: 725–762.

Pfeffer, J. 1981. "Management as Symbolic Action." Pp. 1–52 in *Research in Organizational Behavior*, Vol. 1. Greenwich, CT: JAI Press Inc.

Perrow, C. 1996. "The Bounded Career and the Demise of the Civil Society." Pp. 297–313 in *The Boundaryless Career: A New Employment Principle for a New Organizational Era*, edited by M.B. Arthur and D.M. Rousseau. New York: Oxford University Press.

Roman, P. 1975 "Secondary Prevention of Alcoholism: Problems and Prospects in Occupational Programming." *Journal of Drug Issues* 5: 327–343.

Roman, P. 1981. "From Employee Alcoholism to Employee Assistance: An Analysis of the De-Emphasis on Prevention and on Alcohol Problems in Work-Based Programs." *Journal of Studies on Alcohol* 42: 244–272.

Roman, P. 1989. "The Use of Employee Assistance Programs to Deal with Drug Abuse in the Workplace." Pp. 271–286 in *Drugs in the Workplace: Research and Evaluation Data*, National Institute on Drug Abuse Research Monograph No. 91, edited by S. Guste. Washington, DC: U.S. Government Printing Office.

Roman, P., and T.C. Blum. 1987. "Notes on the New Epidemiology of Alcoholism in the USA." *Journal of Drug Issues* 17: 321–332.

Roman, P., and T.C. Blum. 1992. "Employee Assistance and Drug Screening Programs." Pp. 197–243 in *Treating Drug Problems*, Volume 2, edited by D.R. Gerstein and Henrik Harwood. Washington: National Academy Press.

Rorabaugh, W.J. 1979. *The Alcoholic Republic: An American Tradition.* New York: Oxford University Press.

Rumbarger, J. 1989. *Profits, Politics, and Prohibition.* Albany: State University of New York Press.

Sonnenstuhl, W.J. 1996. *Working Sober: The Transformation of an Occupational Drinking Culture.* Ithaca, NY: ILR Press of Cornell University Press.

Tolbert, C.M., P.M. Horan, and E.M. Beck. 1980. "The Structure of Economic Segmentation: A Dual Economy Approach." *American Journal of Sociology* 85: 1095–1116.

Vogel, E. 1963. "The Emotionally Disturbed Child as Family Scapegoat." Pp. 152–176 in *The Family*, edited by N. Bell and E. Vogel. Glencoe, IL: The Free Press of Glencoe.

Walsh, J.M., and R.L. Hawks. 1986. *Questions and Answers: Employee Drug Screening: Detection of Drug Use by Urinalysis*. Rockville, MD: National Institute on Drug Abuse.

Williams, R.M. 1970. *American Society*, 3rd edition. New York: A. A. Knopf.

Winfrey, J.C. 1998. *Social Issues: The Ethics and Economics of Taxes and Public Programs*. New York: Oxford University Press.

Zey, M. 1998. *Rational Choice Theory and Organizational Theory*. Thousand Oaks, CA: Sage Publications.

MEASURING EVERYTHING THAT MOVES
THE NEW SURVEILLANCE AT WORK

Gary T. Marx

ABSTRACT

This sensitizing and exploratory article considers recent changes in work monitoring. More intensive and extensive monitoring of both work and the worker are part of broader social changes in the nature of surveillance. The monitoring practices and rationales of an ideal-typical company are described. The implications of current surveillance trends for social control and deviance at work are discussed. Among issues covered are increased deviance (or at least greater official labeling of it); drowning in the data; difficulty in finding workers who measure up to the standards; a potential conflict between transparency and innovation and risk-taking; machines versus managers as interpreters of work monitoring data; and worker resistance and implications for equity. The often unintended and ironic outcomes of inappropriate monitoring must be understood if we are to have a society which is both productive and just, and in which the story of Dr. Frankenstein remains just a story.

Research in the Sociology of Work, Volume 8, pages 165-189.

ISBN: 0-7623-0608-4

A Bank of America vice president, commenting upon the 200 criteria used to assess workers in his credit card division proudly states, "I measure everything that moves." He also measures a lot that doesn't move. His observation captures a central feature of the new forms of surveillance—its omniscience.

Whether we consider video, phone, computer network, e-mail, fax, Internet, or location monitoring and recording; biometric means such as retinal identification patterns, drug tests, and DNA analysis; or elaborate computer matching and profiling, there has been an explosion in the ability to collect, store, retrieve, combine, share, and analyze personal information, including that related to work—whether involving background checks and tests for hiring or monitoring once hired—both on and off the job.

Elsewhere (Marx 1988) I have written about "the new surveillance" and "the maximum security society."[1] In its extreme form such a society is transparent and porous. Information leakage is rampant. Indeed it is hemorrhaging, as traditional boundaries weaken or disappear. Actions, as well as feelings, thoughts, pasts, and even futures are made visible, often independent of the individual's will or knowledge. Numerous "selves" or at least representations of individuals beyond their control and often awareness are created.

The line between the public and the private is weakened; we are under increased observation, ever more goes on a permanent record, and much of what we say, do, and even feel may be known and recorded by others we do not know—whether we will this or not. Data in many different forms, from widely separated geographical areas, organizations, and time periods can easily be merged and analyzed.

As the technology becomes ever more penetrating and intrusive, it becomes possible to gather information with laser-like specificity and with sponge-like absorbency. In Stan Cohen's (1985) imagery, if we draw a parallel between the information gathering net and a fishing net, then the mesh of the net has become finer and the net wider.

These developments are general—running across the society, if in varying degrees and ways. They touch us as citizens, consumers, patients, parents, children, and friends, and of course as workers. We are increasingly both watched and the watcher.

Of course work surveillance is hardly new. Every social situation has historical and cultural antecedents and involves at least some common human and social system elements and requirements. One can argue that what we are seeing in the present is not really new and shows continuity with the past.

Modern capitalism involving the pursuit of profit through efficient productivity involves the rationalization of activities. At the turn of the century, innovations in the collection and processing of information permitted better integration and control of complex systems of transportation, communication, and manufacturing (Beniger 1986). Measurement and analysis were central to this.

Recent developments in work monitoring are consistent with the notion of "scientific" management put forth by Frederick Taylor early in the twentieth century. "Taylorism" was based on precise measurements of the body and movements of the individual worker in a highly differentiated division of tasks. It became widespread in many sectors early in the century. Henry Ford built upon this.

An array of technologies for identifying employee behavior were developed—from time and motion studies, to counting individual output, to the bell that rang on a cash register when it was opened, to the police call boxes that required the walking patrolman to register his location by inserting a key in the box.

In industrial settings control was embedded in the technology (e.g., in the speed of an assembly line or safety guards on machines) and in creating formal bureaucratic expectations about work. Organizational hiring and training has always involved at least some assessment and screening (e.g., for factors such as motivation, strength, aptitude, experience, and preferred gender and ethnic characteristics).

With the development of the factory system, work and home were separated. Yet the border was often at least somewhat blurred. Reformers such as Robert Owen sought temperate workers. Henry Ford created a "Sociological Department" that concerned itself with the moral behavior of employees and their families. In a company town, behavior that was considered inappropriate by one's employer could cause one to lose both job and home.

Yet in spite of continuity, the contemporary developments described below represent a quantitative and in some ways qualitative change. They can take monitoring to new heights (or lows) depending on your point of view.

There are many ways to categorize work surveillance tools, but here let us note a distinction between means (1) directly measuring the quality and quantity of the work product (e.g., counting the number of pages and errors typed or parts assembled and rejected) (2) measuring conformity with workplace rules (e.g., dress codes, number of bathroom trips) (3) measuring aspects of a person's physiology and lifestyle not directly involved with the work product, or necessarily even at a workplace or time (e.g., drug testing, cholesterol monitoring), instead they are concerned with what a person "is" and may do away from work (4) a final aspect cutting across the above involves inventions designed to improve the work process by facilitating analysis and communication (beepers, cell phones, location devices), but which also lend themselves to surveillance (e.g., insuring that drivers follow preferred routes or that computers and telephones are not used for personal reasons).

The ability to monitor in all of these areas has been greatly strengthened in recent decades. Work monitoring is undergoing major changes.[2] Interest in monitoring the worker apart from the work has become increasingly important.

New electronic and chemical forms enhance and extend the traditional visual surveillance of the manager who had to rely on the senses, memory, and records which were often generated manually by those who were subject to the surveillance. In one important aspect, as Zuboff (1988) notes, there has been a radical break in the nature of the automation process. In contrast to prior automation tools, information technology now simultaneously reports on itself even as it carries out the production process. Microprocessors direct and also record data on what they have done.

One of the first persons to worry about deviance at work, as well as among convicts and paupers, was utilitarian philosopher Jeremey Bentham. In 1791 at the behest of the British government, he published *Panopticon or the Inspection House* in which he suggests a model for the ideal prison and factory. There was to be constant inspection of both prisoners and their keepers. This was aided by principles of architecture and uncertainty. His Panopticon was a polygonal structure with a central tower offering a full view of rows of glass-walled cells. Mirrors around the tower made it possible for the guards to look into each cell while staying invisible to inmates. Bentham used the term "universal transparency" (although this is a misnomer—"for authorities" should be added to it). Recent developments in telecommunications, along with other new means of collecting personal information give Bentham's image of the Panopticon contemporary significance. Foucault (1986) has applied this idea to the development of a variety of organizations concerned with managing persons.

Illustrating the new forms, a 1987 report by the Office of Technology Assessment identifies three common types of office monitoring:

computer or electronic monitoring systems which automatically record employee use of computers and telecommunications
service observation which involves listening (and sometimes watching and recording) an employee's conversation with a caller and interaction with other employees
telephone call accounting which involves computer-generated records of time, duration, and destination of phone calls and may involve recording all, or a sampling of calls.

Software products referred to as "Big Brotherware" for this and other types of monitoring are appearing constantly. Consider for example one called "Veranda Enterprise Messaging Reporter" which permits viewing all types of messaging: electronic mail, network, fax, and Internet. An advertizement promises "For individuals or departments, Veranda can track usage by volume, duration, destination, and time of day. Managers can quickly reveal the E-mail hogs, Internet loafers, and security risks, such as those who send resumes or files to competitors." (Dryden 1997) Another product is "Com.Policy" which tracks all computer activity and captures screen images at random to reveal exactly what a user is doing. An aptly named product—"CNTRl," permits managers to observe on their own screen all of a terminal operator's input and output. A similar product, "Peek and

Spy," gives managers the option of informing employees when they are being observed.[3]

Evidence of the rapid expansion of the new surveillance can be seen in surveys of corporate practice and in the sale of surveillance equipment. A 1987 OTA estimate suggested that several million workers each year were subject to electronic monitoring. Only six years later, a MacWorld (Bosses 1993) survey found that 20 million workers were subject to monitoring of their computer files, voice and electronic mail, and other networking communications. One-third of these companies did not notify employees of their practices. The larger the company, the more likely monitoring was. A study by the business-backed Labor Policy Association in a study of 102 Fortune 500 companies reports that video, telephone, and data entry monitoring was widespread (Ehrlich 1993). In 1993 the Communications Workers of America estimated that managers monitor and record 400 million telephone calls each year (Daily Labor Report 1993).

Drug testing has also expanded. The American Management Association began conducting an annual drug testing survey in 1987. In that year 22 percent of major companies reported that they applied drug tests. By 1996 this figure had increased to 81 percent (AMA 1996).

It is difficult to obtain information about the sale of surveillance technology, but the head of Sensormatic Electronics Corp. reports that "Security and surveillance are the wave of the future." In 1991, closed circuit television systems garnered $500 million in sales. Sensormatic's sales of CCTV and access control systems went from $35 million in 1995 to an expected $200 million in 1995 (Lewis 1995). One research firm estimated that employers would spend $2.1 billion dollars on CCTV equipment in 1996 (Frankel 1996).

A study by the International Labor Organization (Jankanish 1993a, 1993b) finds that surveillance technologies are used to a much greater extent in the United States than in other countries.

Another indicator of U.S. management's commitment to monitoring can be seen in the strong lobbying campaign of a broad coalition of businesses between 1987 and 1994. They successfully defeated rather mild Congressional legislation that sought to place some limits on the electronic monitoring of work (e.g., a notice requirement).

As part of a decade-long study of surveillance based on observation, interviews, documents, and the literature, I have created an "ideal-typical" brave new world workplace (ideal, that is, from a standpoint of the elements of the concept, not ethically). In a satirical statement (Marx 1990) I described an imaginary "omniscient organization"—a company called Dominion Swan—which engaged in continuous state-of-the art monitoring of the work product, the worker, and the work environment. The company was organized according to the following principles:

> Make the company a home to employees. Break down artificial and alienating barriers between work and home. Dissolve, through company initiative, feel-

ings of isolation. Great companies are made by great people; all employee behavior and self-development counts.

Hire people who will make a continuing contribution. Bring in people who are likely to stay healthy and successful, people who will be on the job without frequent absences. Candor about prospective employees' pasts is a key to the company's future. Prevention is better than cure.

Technical, hardware-based solutions are preferable to supervision and persuasion. We build the time-tested "command and control" model right into the machine. Machines are inexpensive and reliable and have advantages over managers. Employees want to do the right thing; the company wants nothing but this and will give employees the needed technical assistance. Employees accept performance evaluation from an impartial system more readily than from a superior, and appreciate technical solutions that channel behavior in a constructive direction.

Create accountability through visibility. Loyal employees enjoy the loyalty of others. They welcome audits, reasonable monitoring, and documentary proof of their activities—whether of location, business communications, weekly output, or lifestyles. Once identified, good behavior can be rewarded, inappropriate behavior can be improved. When the expectations are clear and easily measured, self-control, the best control is possible.

Such an organization aims to re-create elements of the company town and company store on an unprecedented scale—but without the traditional limitations of the geographical town-line border, the senses, or the clock. From the bathroom to the bedroom to the workplace to the field, a paternalistic bureaucracy seeks to manage its complex setting by relying on information technology. Its goal is the creation of a borderless environment with respect to space and time in which organizational omniscience enhances managerial omnipotence.

Virtual offices and telecommuting indicate how traditional work settings are no longer necessarily confined to a common workplace. Hakenk (1993) suggests using the term "worksites" or "workspaces" rather than work*places*. We lack an equivalent term for the change in the nature of company "on-duty time" to being "on duty all the time," or whenever called.

There is also increased colonization/illumination of work and workers who traditionally were relatively free of direct management supervision, being beyond the confines of an office, a factory, and a 9-to-5 schedule. Consider the modern techno-cowboy, with beeper and cellular phone that is subject to, and also using, advanced satellite technology to locate and identify cows—often from another kind of bronco than his predecessors.

The engineering tilt shifts the emphasis from humans to machines as data gatherers and interpreters. The size of middle management is reduced as machines lessen the need for supervisors. A scientific and rationalizing impulse results in engineering and monitoring the environment so that conformity with company expectations is built in. Many of the means designed to enhance control have low visibility for those subject to them (at least until they are implicated by them). Organizational outcomes however are likely to be transparent to those in positions of authority (the best analogy is to a floor that is a one-way mirror with visibility downward rather than through a window).

Engineering and monitoring can overlap, as with information clerks whose computers may be blocked from certain Web sites, even as a record is kept if there is an attempt to view a prohibited site. The situation is the same for access and location monitoring devices. One must have the right card, or code, or biolgy (that is possess or know something or "be" the entity suggested by a biometric measure, e.g., fingerprint, voice, hand geometry, retinal pattern, facial image) to enter a particular area, and a record is then kept of the time of entry and exit.

With some systems (one is called "birdog" and another "active badges") signals are constantly sent even indicating where the person is within the area and who else is present (or at least whose access card is present). Communications can be forwarded as the individual moves. The meaning of the term "never out of touch" has been extended by these distance eradicating technologies. A less complex technology simply uses chair sensors to determine the amount of time an employee stays seated.

DON'T CALL HIM "NUMBNUTS": MANAGEMENT JUSTIFICATIONS

Two Nissan employees who referred to their boss as "numbnuts" in personal e-mail (which they thought was password protected) claim they were fired because of this. They learned, to their detriment, that the Bill of Rights as it is currently interpreted stops at the company door, and that e-mail messages are more like postcards than first-class letters.

Many of the protections Americans have as citizens they lack as employees, e.g., freedom of speech or limitations on searches. Police for example can not access your phone or computer communications without a warrant. The 1986 Electronic Communications Privacy Act however gives employers considerable latitude in monitoring communications at work. What is more, electronic communication has an almost magical quality in which erasing it does not necessarily get rid of it, and passwords may not protect against insiders.[4]

The American doctrine of employment at will permits rejecting or firing employees for any reason that is not specifically forbidden by a contract or by law. Even with recent civil rights legislation, employers remain favored over employees. This separates the United States from Europe, where employers are more limited in their ability to unilaterally set the conditions of work and to fire employees without cause. Organizations representing workers are also stronger.

In Europe greater emphasis is given to measuring the productivity of the group with less emphasis put on the individual.

In job settings where workers have little power or few alternatives, managers do not worry much about justifying their behavior. Yet most workplaces resemble neither prisons nor slave systems, and workers have some rights and room.[5] If work conditions are too onerous, they may seek other employment or resist. Managers try to create legitimacy for surveillance practices with a variety of justifications.

Contemporary approaches to social control stress the importance of persuasion rather than coercion. In many job settings there is an effort to ease over the harsher edges of surveillance and the conflicts of interest that may be present by rationales such as the following:

> "this is for your own good—video and audio recordings, drug testing, and access controls are there to protect you from being an accident or crime victim or from false accusations. Surveillance enhances the safety of the workplace. For example in a unit where there has been a problem such as a theft or low productivity, without monitoring it might be necessary for us to fire all workers, whether they are guilty or not."
>
> "monitoring increases productivity and permits establishing objective quotas to assess performance. Surveillance helps our company stay competitive by permitting detailed analysis of work flows and costs. Without these efficiency-enhancing measures we might go out of business or have to reduce our size"[6]
>
> "monitoring is fair—it offers a way to reward workers according to the quantity and quality of their performance and to help others improve their performance through feedback. We are a profit-making organization, not a safe-haven for the guilty, nor a charity for the lazy. To be against monitoring is to protect those who shouldn't be working here and to hurt those who should."
>
> "monitoring not only means better business decisions but better service for our valued customers and better understanding of their needs. As our statement of goals indicates, we strive `to improve our customers' experience and to facilitate consumer empowerment.'"
>
> "monitoring helps us protect our corporate assets and image—whether we monitor telephone and computer time, tools, employee files, or company secrets. Theft and espionage cost American industry billions of dollars each year. Our increased reliance on information technology brings increased opportunities, but also new risks and threats. You would not like to have your personnel file available for all to see on our company Web site (and neither would we). Nor do we want employees on the job accessing pornographic or otherwise controversial Web sites, participating in discussion groups, or playing computer games when they should be doing the job they are paid for. Monitoring also helps us be sure that employees are not sending harassing e-mails or violating software copyrights for which the company could be held liable. We must also

guard against the introduction and use of unauthorized software downloaded from insecure Web sites with the risk of introducing viruses."

"monitoring helps us prove that we comply with laws and government regulations and reduces health and other insurance costs and the risk of costly litigation (e.g., careful screening of prospective employees helps us avoid negligent hiring suits). To receive government contracts and appropriate insurance we must engage in drug testing and meet minimum security standards. Much of our monitoring is required by government or our insurers.

"we must do our own extensive testing and investigations because privacy laws have made it very difficult for us to learn about a worker's past employment directly. Even if we could trust employee answers, current legislation prohibits the kinds of pre-employment screening we previously could do (e.g., applying polygraphs, asking directly about health, receiving full, candid assessments from previous employers or independent references)."[7]

"if you have done nothing wrong, you have nothing to fear from our surveillance.[8] Our monitoring combines two tried and true principles for insuring conformity. First is the `accountability principle' in which a permanent and objective record of behavior can be created for later review. Incidents and disputes can now be resolved by a documentary record, rather than by rival arguments. It is no longer true that management can not (at least in principle) be everywhere all the time. Of course that can get expensive, so we also rely on the 'uncertainty principle' in which persons can never be sure whether or not they are being watched. This requires us to inform workers of the great potential of our technology to know.[9] This also permits "self-control"—the most modern, humane, and efficient form."

"monitoring by machine is neutral, scientific, and accurate, and fairer than a manager could ever be."

"the system is voluntary. If you don't like it you are free to work somewhere else. One of the freedoms most prized by the modern citizen is the right to quit. Workers can vote with their feet unlike serfs or slaves."[10]

"yes this may involve some inconvenience or intrusion, but where possible, we offer rewards for participation."[11]

"we build surveillance into routine activities such that it is barely seen and comes to be taken for granted. You won't even notice it after awhile."

RHETORICS AND REALITIES

Amidst the chorus of self-serving entrepreneurs and ideologues who are not held to scientific standards of evidence, and journalists in search of instant answers, it is easy to confuse the rhetoric and reality of new technologies. While rhetorics can (and should) be analyzed on their own terms as a type of data, my purpose here is to urge caution and the need to disentangle: (1) the potential of a technology, (2) the form and degree of its implementation, and (3) popular beliefs about both of these. Beliefs about these often reflect superficial mass media depictions reflecting the claims of the concerned parties and examples whose typicality is not established.

There is much variation in the extent and form of monitoring, depending on the state of the economy, cultural traditions, type of work, and worker. Just where and when we find the various forms of surveillance, whether the surveillance is as effective and efficient, irrelevant, or as disastrous as varying public rhetorics claim, whether expert and popular beliefs are consistent with the known facts and what accounts for systematic differences in all of this, are research projects waiting to happen.

One of the intriguing aspects of this topic is that in spite of the ethos of rational and scientific measurement as applied to workers and the industrial process, monitoring itself has rarely been systematically evaluated. Those with the gold of course disproportionately effect the rules and it is rare for superiors to apply the same critical perspective to their preferred ways of behaving as it is to apply this to subordinates.

Some monitoring clearly has a fad-like quality. The symbolism monitoring may seek to convey about corporate omniscience and monumentality is a factor. From this perspective, whether it truly works or not is irrelevant—if employees believe it works and feel humbled and in awe of the power of the organization. That of course can be risky as Sir Walter Scott noted when he wrote "Oh, what a tangled web we weave, When first we practice to deceive!"

Given the vast expenditures on monitoring, it is striking that there has been so little analysis of whether its claimed benefits are real. Here we see the fallacy of intuitive appeal or surface plausibility (Corbett and Marx 1991). A policy may be adopoted because "it sure seems as if it would work." A study by the American Management Association which asked whether its members collected statistical evidence showing that testing reduced absenteeism, accidents, disability claims, theft, and violence in their companies found that only 10 percent reported such evidence (AMA 1996).

At present the evidence supportive of the pro-monitoring rhetoric is not strong. As we will note there are good reasons to expect unrestrained monitoring to be counterproductive. A possible negative impact on workers' physical and mental well-being may cancel out profits from supposed increased efficiency as a result of monitoring. A 1993 World Labor Report claims that "...stress costs American employers $200 billion a year through increased absenteeism, diminished productivity, higher compensation claims, rising health insurance fees and additional medical expenses" (U.S. Senate 1993, p. 19). Of course such estimates must be viewed cautiously, as must claims that employee crimes cost employers more than $40 billion a year (The Move 1993) or tht alcohol and drug abuse cost "...American industry $100 billion annually in lost productivity" (A Strategy 1990). Whatever the actual figures, we can however ask what causes what and not assume that monitoring is always a response, rather than also a cause, of some of these problems.

Ann Wood (1998) notes that if monitoring were as effective as proponents claim we would expect to see it widely adopted among industrial countries. Unlike mass production techniques which quickly spread worldwide, the kinds of work monitoring recently appearing in the United States have in general not spread (Jankanish 1993a, 1993b). Doubts about its effectiveness and concern over unintended consequences are factors here.

The remainder of the paper suggests some hypotheses about the location and nature of surveillance and notes a number of empirical outcomes whose frequency and correlates should be explored.

The extreme forms are likely to be more prevalent in non-unionized settings, disproportionately employing unskilled workers, females, minorities, and immigrants in repetitive, nonjudgmental tasks that can be easily measured and in contexts where labor organizations are weak or absent.[12] Monitoring in the private sector is far less restrained than in the public sector where the Bill of Rights and other federal legislation applies.

We also find a large proportion of employees in telecommunications, data processing, insurance, and banking subject to some forms of electronic monitoring. In such settings information technology is a central feature of the work and at the same time reports on itself, not unlike the automated machines studied by Zuboff (1988). More extensive and intensive monitoring is also found where the risks of failure can be catastrophic (e.g., nuclear power plants, airlines).

Yet the new forms of monitoring are not restricted to specialized groups or sectors whose work directly involves the use of information technology, powerless workers, or grave risks. There is a move toward electronic and other monitoring of groups such as drivers,[13] waiters, and hotel maids (whose handheld computers remotely transmit information on their activities) as well as white collar groups such as lawyers, stockbrokers, nurses, doctors, architects, and even professors.

The food service industry, a work setting where information technology is not central, offers an interesting example.[14] A product called Hygiene Guard makes use of "smart badges" for the monitoring of restaurant workers in bathrooms. A badge worn by the employee communicates with sensors in the washroom to determine if the employee uses the soap dispenser and stands for the required time in front of a sink with running water—presumed to offer evidence of hand washing. If this isn't the case, the infraction is recorded by computer. To be sure this is better than video cameras in the washroom, but still...[15]

In what follows I reflect on the implications of current surveillance trends and potentials for social control and deviance in the workplace. I emphasize the latter rather than many other related issues such as the effect of information technology and related means on the organization of work, education and job skills, the economy, stratification, law, or technological diffusion.

IRONIES OF SOCIAL CONTROL?

According to their advocates, engineering solutions and increased transparency should decrease rule breaking and increase conformity with management's expectations, as well as identify areas for amelioration.

What are the impacts? Given the newness of many of the techniques and the absence of research we can not say with much certainty what the impacts are, or better under what conditions different impacts are likely. However, from social theory and anecdotes it is possible to speculate on a variety of unintended consequences.

As a result of varying work contexts and different personalities, needs, expectations, and perceptions of workers, no sweeping generalizations can be made about impacts. There are differences by type of work and organizational culture. There are also individual differences within a setting. Some workers favor a well-ordered, tightly run, standardized, hierarchical, transparent workplace with clearly defined, comprehensive expectations. A supervisor's presence may make them nervous. The veiled, depersonalized authority of the machine may lessen feelings of inequality at work. They may prefer receiving directions from a machine rather than a manager who has the potential to behave inappropriately. In an interesting reversal, the presence of the machine rather than a person may increase feelings of privacy.[16] Some workers value compensation based on a highly detailed analysis of their individual productivity. They may believe that sacrifices at work are required to keep the company competitive in a global economy. The employer may be viewed as a concerned parent who has their best interest at heart. Such attitudes are supportive of the relatively low level of class consciousness in the United States.

But there are also many reasons for expecting other workers to respond in an opposite fashion. The creation of a vast system of one-way mirrors into the work, private life, and even the bodies of employees is unlikely to be passively accepted. They may act back and respond in kind. In a free society humans are neither morally nor practically frail vessels to be automatically controlled at will by those with greater power. Machines channel and record behavior, but humans are hardly indifferent nor inert, unlike the raw materials of production. They are both used by and will use the machine.

The technologies come with some ironic vulnerabilities. Every new form of control introduces new possibilities for failure, resistance, and deviation. Omniscient organizations invite the challenge of beating or retaliating against the system and may offer workers new ways of advancing their own interests.

Unless done with the cooperation of workers (although this raises other issues as we note) and in a restrained fashion, the new surveillance can easily backfire, increasing rule breaking, or at least its identification, and offering new opportunities for deviance, as well as resulting in other unintended and unwanted outcomes. Time spent beating the system is also time spent not working.

NEW STANDARDS

The availability of vast amounts of personal information may tilt toward standardization, or in the term Foucault (1986) used, "normalization." He identifies a principle of "indefinite discipline" where "never-ending judgments, examinations, and observation" emerge as a new mode of control. New areas become subject to measurement and old areas are measured in greater detail. Precise formal standards are created against which individuals are judged. These may involve behavioral rules at work (with or without a strong moral underpinning, for example, contrast the traditional "don't steal" with "more than four trips to the bathroom require explanation to your supervisor"). But many have nothing to do with behavior. They involve expectations about being a certain kind of person, only indirectly (if at all) related to the work tasks and the product, or even what happens at work, for example, restrictions on weight and prohibitions (on and off the job) regarding smoking and drugs.[17]

Beyond new standards for judging the individual, powerful discovery techniques may reveal more traditional infractions as well. The breaking of borders and the merging of previously distinct data can result in the discovery of departures from expectations that in the past would have been unseen or ignored.

It is difficult to say where the job stops and private life begins when (as in some companies) employees' cars are equipped with onboard computers using satellite transponders that permit tracking and in addition to locator and paging devices, all employees above a certain level are given fax machines and computers for their homes which must be turned on at all times. When away from home or the office (if for example going on a hike) employees may be expected to carry cell phones the company provides (regardless of weekends or time of day). The company may also know more about family and health matters than in the past if it provides day care, recreation, and health maintenance plans.

DROWNING IN DATA?

The vast expansion of the supervisory gaze can mean an overabundance of data. Managers may find that they are drowning in the data and may be unable to separate the meaningful from the meaningless. This raises issues planners may not have anticipated.

> With so much data available on failings, those workers who are sanctioned may ask why they were singled out when there is evidence that infractions are widespread.
>
> Or to avoid that problem managers may take no action, sending the message that violations are tolerated. Violations may then increase. When the economy

is strong and competition for workers is intense—there may be pressure to dilute or ignore the system.

The abundance of information on violations may lead unscrupulous managers to misuse their discretion—singling out workers they wish to sanction for personal reasons but lack official grounds to do so. They may save up the data, like squirrels hoarding nuts. Unless there are criteria for relative importance and limits on the retention and use of such data, it may be applied discriminatorily and long after the fact. Since much monitoring may occur secretly, workers may not know or recall the incident for which they are being sanctioned. This raises due process concerns.

IS THERE ANYONE LEFT TO HIRE?

The extension of management's supervisory gaze to ever more areas expands the realms in which the potential or actual worker may be found to be lacking. The vast quantities of minute data will likely reveal some infractions, or potential failings (given a predictive profile against which the individual is compared) on almost everyone. With performance and personal conduct standards raised and expanded to new areas on and off the job, fewer employees may be able to meet ideal standards. This may lead to a failure to feel appreciated and a decline in morale.

It may also make it difficult to find workers. There may be fewer persons left to hire or retain. Eventually the work force (and social participation more generally) may become more clearly divided between people who are thought to be good risks and others. Rigid pre-employment screening and testing may have the consequence of creating a larger and more permanent class of unemployables who are denied a second chance. In the past, when traditional records systems were less efficient, it was often possible for persons to start over. But now one's past may become an indelible mark. This would be an enormous waste of human resources. If persons are denied chances for legitimate employment, it is not surprising if they turn to illegitimate means, or need to be publicly supported.

Intensive screening of new employees and the proliferation of inspections can lead to a narrow, even intolerant, timid, blindly conforming work force lacking imagination and flexibility. Will creative persons outside the norms be excluded or choose to avoid certain jobs because they don't fit conventional selection profiles? Will workers in general take fewer risks once on the job?

IF SOME IS GOOD, IS MORE NECESSARILY BETTER?

The "neutral" data-generating technology seems to imply that all information is good. But things are more complex than that. The desirability of full rule conformity and complete openness regarding rule departures are myths which, if they are taken too literally, may have negative social consequences. Organizations may be unable to function if they are held to 100 percent enforcement of their own rules. There is a sense in which there is "bad" and "good" rule breaking (or in the case of the latter at least creative and innovative rule bending and stretching) which serves organizational and societal goals beyond crass self-interest or incompetence. Unrestricted transparency may undercut that.

Increased transparency at work can interfere with the flexibility and discretion that is helpful in interpreting and applying rules in complex, ever-changing organizational contexts. The common refrain in some work settings "you don't want to know" or "look the other way" captures elements of this, as does Merton's (1956) concept of "institutionalized evasion."

An enduring paradox is that group life is impossible without rules, and yet too rigid conformity to rules may undermine the group. Pioneers, inventors, and innovators are often persons who use discretion creatively, pushing limits and extending grey areas, even venturing into forbidden zones to solve problems. This can get them in trouble, but it can also make them heroes and lead to the rules being changed or seen in a new light. Transparency in an environment of rigid rules makes this less likely. The enhanced order and security of the omniscient organization may undermine its competitiveness relative to other more flexible organizations.

MACHINES VERSUS MANAGERS

Mechanical surveillance and engineered solutions are often introduced without adequate causal analysis. Mechanical solutions may be seen as quick and inexpensive, just purchase and plug in. "Have electricity, will control." But if managers have lost their authority, surveillance is unlikely to get it back, and may even erode it further. In addition, many human situations are exquisitely complex and are (as yet) beyond the capacity of machines to evaluate effectively.[18] The utopian quest for full conformity for all rules all of the time for all persons is unwise.

Analysis may sometimes suggest that it is better to live with a "problem" (even if there is no legal or moral question that it is a problem), than to try to fix it. The latter may be impossible, or fixing it may be too costly and bring other undesirable consequences, including disruption of informal systems, which on balance can be functional for the organization, even if they would be questionable for public relations if they were widely known.

Consider for example the minor rule violations found in most job settings (such as using paper and pens and e-mail for personal use or making phone calls on company time on a company phone). Such "perks" have traditionally been accepted as part of the job and even though they can now, in principle, be more easily controlled via technology, it is generally unwise to do so absent flagrant abuse. The situation is even more striking in efforts at prison reform which interrupt the informal delegations of authority to selected inmates in return for their cooperation in controlling others (Sykes 1971).

Relying on technology for control and automatic judgements to the exclusion of sensitive managers who can analyze problems, interpret the data, and work at building trust and reciprocal relationships with workers is questionable policy. Traditionally, a major means of creating commitment and loyalty to organizations has been a shared history and some sense of common destiny between managers and workers (and more recently among workers). But with some new systems, the supervisor's role is more constricted involving review of a printout highlighting deviations from general standards.

Productivity and loyalty are more likely to come out of the employee's commitment to others in the workplace than to be induced via technology (whether from remote electronic monitoring; embedding property and people with sensors; or manipulation via music, scents, subliminal messages, and diet).

In our culture, computer-generated results, with their aura of scientific infallibility, are sometimes granted an unwarranted legitimacy as "fact." That machines do fail is rarely acknowledged (Perrow 1984; Vaughan 1996: Neuman 1995). Certainly machines can be more accurate and objective than an incompetent or biased supervisor. But do they know from fairness or compassion? And what of a good supervisor?

In the film "Hard Times," Charlie Chaplin plays a hapless worker at the mercy of machines in an automated factory. The film's humor (as with most cases of jokes involving humans and machines) involves the automatic and repetitive quality of the technology and its literalness.

Machines can do both more and less than humans. They may fail to take account of atypical and extenuating circumstances because they have not been programmed to consider the richness of a dynamic reality. They are acontextual, abstracting out of the situation only a limited number of factors.

Consider, for example, an employee who was fired when he was caught taking an expensive tool home (the tool had an embedded chip that caused an alarm to go off when he exited). The employee had used (and returned) the tool many times previously on weekend jobs before the new monitoring system was in place. Or consider a telephone operator who was criticized because her average time spent on calls was a few seconds over the average—a fact she explained by noting that she took additional time with the large number of calls she received from the elderly and foreign born in her district.

Evaluations may be weighted toward what can be measured best by the technology instead of toward what it is most important to measure. In a form of goal displacement, the means may come to determine the end. Workers may seek to maximize satisfying the measurement goal at the expense of what the goal is intended to measure. A conflict between quality and quantity may favor the latter.

SURPRISE: YOU'RE ON CANDID CAMERA

Draconian surveillance, particularly when it is suddenly introduced in a top-down fashion, may lead to resistance and challenges. The process of introducing the surveillance may itself become an issue. Employee indignation is likely to be expressed at the surprise discovery that e-mail is monitored or that a hidden video camera is in place, when there has been no prior consultation or even warning. When the surveillance itself is a form of deviance, violating reasonable expectations (as with cameras hidden in bathrooms or locker rooms, or an employee posing as a friend who has infiltrated the workplace during a unionization drive) anger may be intensified.

This can lead to attitudes such as "if you don't play fair with us, we won't play fair with you" and "turnabout is fair play." To the extent that workers feel they are being treated like children (needing permission to go to the bathroom) and engineered workplaces are interpreted to symbolically say, "we don't trust you to be honest or to make reasoned choices. We expect you to behave irresponsibly, to take advantage, and to screw up unless we remove all temptation and prevent, trick, or force you to do otherwise." Some workers will adopt the attitude "you've got the name, play the game." In other words, if you are thought to be untrustworthy then behave that way. This can bring new meaning to the self-fulfilling prophecy.

A certain human contrariness, particularly in a conflictual work setting, may impel some workers to find ways to beat new control systems. Management's actions, particularly if they are perceived to be done in a highhanded fashion may be taken as a challenge. Beyond game elements and self-interest, this may be accentuated by feelings of stress and alienation.[19]

To the extent that the technologies create feelings of powerlessness (over inability to have a say in or control the pace and conditions of work, see the watchers, know when one is being monitored, or confront one's accuser), unreasonable stress, dehumanization, invasion, estrangement, disrespect, demoralization, anger, and rule violations may increase. There may be a decline in the quality and quantity of productivity, absenteeism, illness, errors, "time theft" (a term used by those selling monitoring devices to refer to loafing or socializing on the job) and an increase in more traditional forms such as sabotage and theft—whether of material property or the selling of company secrets.

Typists, for example, may hold one key down to increase the number of key strokes recorded, deleting the file later. Telephone agents may avoid calls that add to their average case time—by either disconnecting the call or giving out information that discourages the caller. In addition, monitoring may generate a market for means of getting around controls (for example, once drug testing became an issue, books advising how to beat it and companies offering to deliver drug-free urine appeared).

The coordinated and interdependent nature of production means that slowing down or obstructing one part of the system may spread to other parts, even if workers there are motivated to cooperate. The vulnerability of complex systems is the worker's silent ally and can serve as a brake, along with values, laws, and concern over negative publicity, limiting the full potential of monitoring.

EQUITY CONCERNS

Another possible source of employee discontent and resistance to many of the new forms of monitoring involves equity concerns. Are the techniques available to workers as well as the company? Some, such as miniature audio and video recorders, are. When workers can record managers, as well as the reverse, the situation is more balanced. But one must ask what kind of a work environment is it if the level of trust is so low, and suspiciousness or possible abuse so high, that people must be constantly on guard, taking protective actions.

An interesting characteristic of the new surveillance is its sweeping and categorical character. Video and audio systems can be indiscriminate, catching all within their purview (whether it is work-related or not and regardless of status in the organization). In principle, monitoring can extend up as well as down the organizational hierarchy. Card key systems required to enter a room or computer access codes make demands on all who encounter them and drug testing can be mandatory for all, including the CEO. Systems for analyzing computer network usage can look at everyone (although they may be programmed not to look at what managers do).

If the advantages claimed for omniscient environments are real, then the same methods should be applied to managers and higher-level executives as to workers. In fact, the case for monitoring the former is much stronger than that for monitoring those lower in the hierarchy, because if the managers are performing inadequately or illegally, much greater damage can be done. We might even adopt a principle that the more central a position and the higher the costs from poor performance, the greater the degree of monitoring should be.

Deviance at work involves white-collar crimes as well as others. If management is sometimes incapable of watching itself (as white-collar crime—whether in banking, insurance, medicine, defense contracting, or environmental protection—suggests), we might consider having monitoring units made up of workers, stockholders, and consumers watch the managers.

Imagine what could be uncovered if a full audio and visual record of all the job-related behavior of senior executives and managers was available, or if their files were subject to the same oversight as those of data entry clerks—for example, tobacco industry executives' discussions of health, smoking, and marketing.

Equity and efficiency would seem to require that invasive tactics used against less powerful members of an organization also be used against the most powerful—particularly if these methods are as effective as advocates claim. The credibility of those in management who advocate monitoring increases to the extent that they are willing to apply the same technologies to themselves. Of course this suggestion is unrealistic. But its very unrealism helps to illustrate stratification at work and how higher status carries rewards and also the power to protect itself.

HIERARCHY AND WORK

A related aspect of equity and democracy is the extent to which workers participate directly in setting the conditions of work—factors which are hardly considered by traditional approaches.

The scientific management approach of Taylor, for example, subjected the isolated worker to rigid control by the mechanical and social organization of the factory under the guise of a presumed rationality as applied to efficiency and profit-maximization.

The bureaucratic model, as analyzed by Max Weber, located authority within a system of rules and offices. While this was hierarchical and the rules were rarely arrived at democratically, authority in principle rested in the office, not in the person of the manager. As such, it offered some protection to subordinates who knew what the rules were, and also that the rules applied within a delimited boundary.[20] The boundary smashing implications of the new surveillance technologies raise interesting challenges to this model (Marx 1997), as do recent participatory approaches to work.

In the contemporary period, the electronic monitoring of work has appeared as an important control element. In this paper, we have contrasted control by surveillance technology versus direct control by a manager, and argued for the increased prevalence of the former. While it is hardly dominant across all work settings, the trend in some sectors is clear.

In principle, the results of such monitoring are available to all employees to better engage them in production. In practice, the transparency is often restricted, and it follows traditional lines of organizational stratification.

Yet we can also note the development of a participatory approach to work in which information and authority are shared, and there is less reliance on bureaucracy and centralized authority. New information technology may enhance this.[21] This is part of a broader shift in management styles from coercion to consensus (Buraway 1979).

The communal and team aspects of interdependent work settings can permit a bottom-up approach which involves the users of the technology. In this peer group approach, workers watch each other and are granted considerable discretion to determine how work is carried out. The traditional surveillance hierarchy becomes flatter, and informal expectations grow at the expense of formal rules. Creating a consensual workplace and sharing power are viewed as the best ways (both economically and morally) to generate commitment, trust, inclusion, and community.

The new information technologies make it possible to join electronic and team monitoring. Consider, for example, a work group given a monthly production quota. The group can decide how best to meet it (both in terms of the pace of the work and the form of its production). Team members' video-display terminals can show how productive the individual or team has been for the last hour, day, week, or month relative to other units or compared to their own previous performance.[22]

Sewell (forthcoming) suggests that in some industrial settings where teamwork is important, we are seeing a hybrid, "chimerical" form which brings together the vertical control of the panopticon with the horizontal (and seemingly more egalitarian and democratic) control of the peer group. This is not easy to classify as either coercive or consensual.

This approach, of course, comes with particular costs and benefits. Closer to the complexities, fluidity, and meanings of work production, peer surveillance may be more fine-grained and fairer than that of a manager or a machine. Legitimacy may be enhanced because self-control and democratic decision-making are valued in our culture. There is evidence (particularly from social psychological lab experiments) that on the average, team approaches and worker involvement are more effective. Yet devoid of bureaucratic protections or adequate oversight, they may become tyrannical and counterproductive.

Just how autonomous and independent these work groups are; to what extent power is truly shared and bureaucracy is cut back; and the impact on productivity, safety, job satisfaction, and so on are empirical questions (which are also affected by how the concepts are defined and measured).

Inequality in power and reward will not disappear, although they may be reduced. No matter how democratic the organization is, workers are unlikely to be able increase their salaries at the expense of executives or stockholders, or fire their managers.

The rational pursuit of goals remains. Participatory approaches are still engineering approaches, but the basic technology involves group dynamics. Building control into organizational culture, the taken for granted way of doing things, and collegial relations may be even more subtle, invisible, and harder to resist than building it into the design of a machine.

In spite of our efforts to impose conceptual order, human situations are usually messy and fluid, and often show contradictory elements. There also may be cycles with the relative emphasis on the coercive and consensual, hard and soft, direct and indirect, rigid and flexible, closed and open forms of engineered control varying as the limits of each is reached. The type of task also affects the balance, as does an organization's history, culture, and general economic conditions.

The recent greater emphasis in the United States on teamwork, participatory design, and computer-supported cooperative forms of work also nicely illustrates the role of social and cultural factors with respect to technological applications. In writing about technologies in place, it is easy forget that choices have been made, and to slip into the belief that because something *can* be done it will be done. In the United States we tend to overemphasize the deterministic quality of a technology. Technology is not a given, nor are its most severe applications predetermined. It grows out of and is applied in a social context, even as it reciprocally shapes that context.

Note that monitoring technology can be either a window or a one-way mirror. Contrasting the initial approach to information technology in the United States and Scandinavia illustrates this. In Scandinavia, greater emphasis was given to collaborating with workers to determine how to use the technology.[23] For example, one important question asked was: "How can the technology be used to make work better for the worker?" In contrast, in the United States that question was (until recently) rarely asked. Instead, information technology tended to be viewed in terms of economics and efficiency. Employee participation, job satisfaction, and growth were hardly considered. The extent to which peer approaches to industrial production will modify this is an important question for research.

This is a sensitizing and exploratory article. I have considered some issues that theory, research, and public policy need to consider if we are to have a society that is both productive and just, and in which the story of Dr. Frankenstein remains just a story.

ACKNOWLEDGMENT

I am grateful to the Woodrow Wilson International Center for Scholars, Washington D.C. for providing a monitor-free environment where work on this paper was done and to Ann Wood for research assistance.

NOTES

1. The maximum-security society is made up of five interrelated sub-societies: (1) a dossier society; (2) an actuarial or predictive society; (3) an engineered society; (4) a transparent or porous society; and (5) a self-monitored society (Marx 1988, p. 221). Related materials can be found at the following Web site: m.i.t.edu/gtmarx/www/garyhome.html. See also the discussions in Rule (1973); Laudon (1986); Clarke (1988); Webster and Robbins (1992); Gandy (1993); Lyon (1994); and Lyon and Zureik (1996).

2. See for example Howard (1985); Shaiken (1985); U.S. Congress (1987); Garson (1988); Zuboff (1988); Grant (1990); Hakenk (1993); Kling (1996); and Rosenberg (1998).

3. According to an ad, "The PEEK program allows a watcher to make a software connection between his terminal and another 'target' user's terminal. Thereafter whatever the target user's program outputs is sent to both terminals.... The PEEK program may be used only with the target user's explicit permission." Failure to offer permission would no doubt be noted. This is in contrast to the SPY program, with which "the user is not warned that he is being watched." Managers are told they can "...look in on Sue's computer screen.... In fact, Sue doesn't even know you're there!.... All from the comfort of your chair."

4. Passwords may offer protection against outsiders, but these can be overridden by those with higher-level access inside the system. One issue is whether employees can take defensive measures such as encrypting their communications and hence prevent management from accessing them.

5. It would be interesting to compare practices in the emerging privatized "prison-factory" movement and the occasional cases of (usually immigrant) employees held in bondage with the work done in public prisons and conventional work environments. My concern here is with relative differences and with historical trends. Keeping the above extremes in mind can serve to temper the too loose use of contemporary metaphors in comparing work and prison settings.

6. As one security expert put it: "Competitive advantage—that's how you sell security to the Roseanne crowd. You tell them that if they want to have a job down the road, they'd better be prepared to accept workplace security measures, including monitoring." (As cited in Whalen 1995).

7. Bland assessments with only factual information (dates of employment, salary) are the rule because of fear of suits for defamation of character. The Americans With Disabilities Act limits the kinds of questions that can be asked about health status absent direct relevance to the task before any offer of employment has been made. The increased pressure to know, combined with restrictions on some forms of knowing, fuels an intensified search for new surveillance tools.

8. This is a common refrain which misses the points that (a) the reason for the ideal of some grounds for suspicion before undertaking a search (as in the Fourth Amendment) is not out of an interest in protecting the *guilty* but out of an interest in protecting the *innocent* from abuses of authority; (b) the record may be in error or dated or the indicator may be unreliable; (c) respect for the dignity of the person may involve not crossing certain personal barriers that are important for self-presentations and self-respect; and (d) non-incriminating bits of information can be aggregated and used for discrimination and manipulation against the person's interests.

9. A management attorney stressed this as both a value and a strategy when he stated, "you do not want them to have a reasonable expectation of privacy. Employees should realize that if they come to the place of work, the employer is going to be opening up anything, anytime, anyplace." *Los Angeles Times,* December 20, 1987. Here informing people is also viewed as offering legal protection.

10. This may generate a feeling of free choice. A key question is whether those who choose not to participate are disadvantaged as a result and not seen as team players, and whether equivalent work settings are available without the monitoring.

11. For example General Mills offers workers reduced premiums if they wear seat belts, don't smoke, drink moderately, and control weight and blood pressure (Smith 1993). An Oregon company permits employees enrolled in its health program to "...win up to $350 and an extra week of vacation if they meet standards that can include swearing off coffee or limiting fast food to no more than once a week" (Sipress 1991).

12. See, for example, the data entry firm described in "Mr. Edens Profits from Watching His Workers' Every Move," *The Wall Street Journal,* December 1, 1994, p. A11.

13. Remote monitoring technology—whether it is used for measuring location, speed, and other engine characteristics; or physiological characteristics such as pulse, body temperature, or drug and alcohol presence—helps solve a traditional management problem of knowing just where employees are and what they are doing. While truck drivers were expected to keep log books recording where and when they traveled, and there were sometimes meters on the vehicle, these yielded much less data and could be more easily faked than can remote sensing satellite or electronic tachtograph records (Jacobs 1989). In specifying routes and speeds, the discretion of the driver is greatly reduced.

14. At least it has not traditionally been central. Yet this may change. In what a June 16, 1998 press release hailed as "a sizable technological step toward realizing optimized business processes," Microsoft, in conjunction with Tricon Global Restaurants, the largest owner of restaurants in the world (with 30,000 Kentucky Fried Chickens, Pizza Huts, and Taco Bells) announced plans for "ActiveStore," an in-store information system aimed at integrating most activities within an establishment and across retail chains. Information technology may at last come to labor-intensive retail service industries. Beyond their relatively low pay, such jobs appear to be headed toward more intense electronic

monitoring and perhaps robotics and "smart machine" technology which will further reduce the need for unskilled workers.

15. This also is far less invasive (if also less powerful and "useful") than a "smart toilet"—popular in Japan. After entering a unique identifier, the toilet can capture things such as temperature, pulse, blood pressure and weight and can automatically analyze urine for pregnancy, diabetes etc. each time it is used. The data is saved for trend analysis. The Japanese company has not been successful in introducing this into the United States. A satirical version of such a toilet as part of an imaginary Restroom Trip Policy (RTP), written before I learned one actually existed can be found in Marx (1987).

16. Here we need to differentiate privacy as being unobserved in a physical and immediate sense from the long-term observation that may be associated with a documentary record. Permanent records which can migrate far beyond the work site and time can also involve the invasion of privacy.

17. Drug testing raises many issues that are beyond the scope of this paper, not the least of which involve: (1) the reliability and validity of the test; and (2) the direct relevance of the test to work performance. The research supporting the claims of advocates is underwhelming—a factor apart from the often latent moral concerns that seem to be important in driving the testing. See for example Macdonald and Wells (1994). Effectiveness apart, the cost needs to be weighed against other means or uses of the resources required for testing. Jankanish (1993b) for example notes that out of almost 30,000 federal employees given drug tests in 1991, 152 tested positive. The cost of drug testing was $11.7 million. It thus cost $77,000 to identify each employee who tested positive.

18. This effort to engineer social control at work (whether in hardware, software, or "humanware") is part of the broader phenomena of the engineering of social control. Types and limitations are treated in Marx (1995).

19. Smith, Carayon, Sanders, Lim, and LeGrande (1992) finds that electronically monitored workers on the average experience greater stress and dissatisfaction than those not so monitored. There is variation within each group as well. But in comparing monitored with non-monitored workers in the communications industry, what is striking in the Smith study is the high level of stress reported by both groups of workers (thus eight out of 10 of the former reported high tension on the job, but so too did almost seven out of 10 of the latter). Aiello and Shao (1993) report that workers subject to individual monitoring report greater stress than those subject to team monitoring. After a study of monitored telephone workers revealed that 67 percent experienced high or very high pressure, Bell Canada restricted monitoring for training purposes only (DiTecco et al. 1992).

20. An element of equity as a universalistic process is present here in two ways. Workers can expect that in principle the rules will be applied equally to all persons in a given status and that all supervisors will apply the same rules. Whether or not these are viewed as good rules by those in different social locations is a different question.

21. Some of the debate about the impact of computers on work involves different images of the phenomena. Large mainframe computers in a central location with limited access contrast with inexpensive personal computers that can be used almost anywhere and can remotely tie into sophisticated data networks. Indeed one of the developers of the Apple Computer saw it as a democratizing tool that could free workers from traditional hierarchical centralized control (Siegel 1986).

22. More ominously there is also the potential for the computer to communicate subliminally with messages such as "you are not working as fast as the person next to you," "work faster," and "concentrate" (Harmon 1995).

23. The proceedings of a conference at the Centre for Technology and Culture of the University of Oslo expand on this. In particular volumes edited by Hakken and Haukelid (1997) and Haukelid (1997).

REFERENCES

"A Strategy to Stop Substance Abuse." 1990. Security Management 9(September).

Aiello, J., and Y. Shao. 1993. "Electronic Performance Monitoring and Stress: The Role of Feedback and Goal Setting." Pp. 1011–1016 in *Human-Computer Interaction: Applications and Case Studies*, edited by M.J. Smith and G. Salvendy. The Netherlands: Elsevier.

American Management Association. 1996. *1996 AMA Workplace Survey: Workplace Drug Testing and Drug Abuse Policy*. New York: AMA Publications.

Beniger, J. 1986. *The Control Revolution: Technological and Economic Origins of the Information Society*. Cambridge, MA: Harvard University Press.

"Bosses With X-Ray Eyes: Your Employer May be Using Computers to Keep Tabs on You." 1993. *MacWorld* 7(July).

Burawoy, M. 1979. *Manufacturing Consent*. Chicago: University of Chicago Press.

Clarke, R. 1988. "Information Technology and Dataveillance." *Communications of the ACM* 31: 29–45.

Cohen, S. 1985. *Visions of Social Control*. Cambridge: Polity Press.

Corbett, R., and G. Marx. 1991. "Critique: No Soul in the New Machine: Technofallacies in the Electronic Monitoring Movement." *Justice Quarterly* 8(3) (September): 399–414.

Daily Labor Report. 1993. "Full Text Section: Testimony Before Senate Subcommittee on Employment and Productivity on S 984." 119(June 23).

DiTecco, D. et al. 1992. "Operator Stress and Monitoring Practice." *Applied Ergonomics* 23(1).

Dryden, P. 1997. "Monitoring Tools Help IS Be Users' Big Brother." *Computerworld* (March 31): 12.

Ehrlich, S. 1993. *Electronic Technology in the Workplace: Policy Paper*. Washington, DC: Employment Policy Foundation.

Foucault, M. 1986. *Discipline and Punish: The Birth of the Prison*. New York: Vintage Books.

Frankel, M. 1996. "Candid Camera: Corporate Snooping 101, Workplace Surveillance." *The New Republic* 214(21) (May 20).

Garson, B. 1988. *Electronic Sweatshop*. New York: Simon and Schuster.

Gandy, O. 1993. *The Panoptic Sort*. Boulder, CO: Westview Press.

Grant, R. 1990. *Silicon Supervisors: Computerized Monitoring in the Service Sector*. Washington DC International Center for Information Technology.

Howard, R. 1985. *Brave New Workplace*. New York: Viking.

Hakenk, D. 1993. "Computing and Social Change: New Technology and Workplace Transformation, 1980–1990." *Ann. Rev. Anthropology* 22: 107–132.

Hakenk, D., and K. Haukelid. 1997. *Technology and Democracy: User Involvement in Information Technology*. Oslo: Centre for Technology and Culture.

Harmon, A. 1995. "High-Tech Hidden Persuaders." *Los Angeles Times*. (Oct. 1)

Haukelid, K. 1997. *Technology and Democracy: Worker Participation*. Oslo: Centre for Technology and Culture.

Jacobs, I. 1989. "Technology Applications: Finally Getting the Message." *Communications*. 26(7): 34–41.

Jankanish, M., et al. 1993a. *Conditions of Work Digest: Workers' Privacy Part II: Monitoring and Surveillance in the Workplace*. Geneva: International Labor Organization Publications.

Jankanish, M., et al. 1993b. *Conditions of Work Digest: Workers' Privacy Part III: Testing in the Workplace*. Geneva: International Labor Organization Publications.

Kling, R. 1996. *Computerization and Controversy*. New York: Academic Press.

Laudon, K. 1986. *The Dossier Society: Value Choices in the Design of National Information Systems*. New York: Columbia University Press.

Lewis, K. 1995. "To Catch a Thief: Sensormatic Electronics Corp." *Forbes Annual Report on American Industry*. (January 2).

Lyon, D. 1994. *The Electronic Eye: The Rise of the Surveillance Society*. Cambridge, England: Polity Press.

Lyon, D., and E. Zureik. 1996. *Computers, Surveillance, and Privacy*. Minneapolis: University of Minnesota Press.

Macdonald, S., and S. Wells. 1994. "The Impact and Effectiveness of Drug Testing Programs in the Workplace." Pp. 121–142 in *Drug Testing in the Workplace*: Vol. II, edited by S. Macdonald and P. Roman. New York: Plenum Publishing.

Marx, G. 1987. "Raising Your Hand Just Won't Do." *Los Angeles Times* (April 1).

Marx, G. 1988. *Undercover: Police Surveillance in America.* Berkeley, CA: University of California Press.

Marx, G. 1990. "The Omniscient Organization." *Harvard Business Review* 90(2): 12–16.

Marx, G. 1995. "The Engineering of Social Control: The Search for the Silver Bullet." Pp. 235–246 in *Crime and Inequality*, edited by J. Hagan and R. Peterson. Stanford, CA: Stanford University Press.

Marx, G. 1997. "The Declining Significance of Traditional Borders (and the Appearance of New Borders) in an Age of High Technology" Pp. 484–494 in P. Droege, *Intelligent Environments.* Amsterdam: Elsevier.

Merton, R. 1956. *Social Theory and Social Structure.* Glencoe, IL: Free Press.

Neuman, R. 1995. *Computer-Related Risks.* Reading, MA: Addison-Wesley.

Perrow, C. 1984. *Normal Accidents: Living With High-Risk Technologies.* New York: Basic Books.

Rosenberg, R. 1998. "The Workplace on the Verge of the 21st Century." Paper presented at Ethicomp '98, Rotterdam.

Rule, J. 1973. *Private Lives, Public Surveillance.* London: Allen-Lane.

Seigel, L. 1986. "Microcomputers: From Movement to Industry. *Monthly Review* 38(3).

Sewell, G. 1998. "The Discipline of Teams: The Control of Team-Based Industrial Work Through Electronic Surveillance," *Administrative Science Quarterly* 43: 397–428.

Shaiken, H. 1985. *Work Transformed: Automation and Labor in the Computer Age.* New York: Rinehart and Winston.

Sipress, A. 1991. "Private Lives Becoming Employers' Business." *Philadelphia Inquirer* (March 31).

Smith, L. 1993. "What the Boss Knows About You." *Fortune* (August).

Smith, M.J., P. Carayon, K.J. Sanders, S.Y. Lim, and D. LeGrande. 1992. "Electronic Performance Monitoring, Job Design, and Worker Stress." *Applied Ergonomics* 23: 17–27.

Sykes, G. 1971. *Society of Captives.* Princeton, NJ: Princeton University Press.

"The Move to Curb Worker Worker Monitoring: Congress Wants to Clamp Down on an Employer Tool for Ensuring Quality and Productivity." 1993. *Nation's Business* 12(December).

United States Congress, Office of Technology Assessment. 1987. *The Electronic Supervisor: New Technology, New Tensions.* Washington, DC: U.S. Government Printing Office.

United States Senate. 1993. *The Privacy for Consumers and Workers Act, Senate Bill 984: Hearing Before the Subcommittee on Employment and Productivity of the Committee on Labor and Human Resources United States Senate.* Washington, DC: U.S. Government Printing Office.

Vaughan, D. 1996. *The Challenger Launch Decision.* Chicago: University of Chicago Press.

Webster, F., and K. Robins. 1993. "I'll Be Watching You: Comment on Sewell and Wilkinson." *Sociology* 27(2) (May).

Whalen, J. 1995. "You're Not Paranoid: They Really Are Watching You". *Wired* 5(3): pp. 76–85.

Wood, A. 1998. "Omniscient Organizations and Bodily Observations: Electronic Surveillance in the Workplace." *International Journal of Sociology and Social Policy* 18 (5/6): 136–174.

Zuboff, S. 1988. *In the Age of the Smart Machine.* New York: Basic Books.

CONTROLLING WORKPLACE DEVIANCE

STATE REGULATION OF OCCUPATIONAL HEALTH AND SAFETY

Bridget M. Hutter

ABSTRACT

This chapter considers violations against state occupational health and safety (OSH) laws as a form of workplace deviance. Regulatory offending is an ill-understood area of deviance and one that is not always regarded as deviant or criminal. This is despite the very serious consequences that may result from noncompliance. Compliance with and deviations from OSH laws are considered from the perspectives of regulatory officials and those subject to regulation. In particular this paper draws upon research into the enforcement and impact of OSH regulation in England and Wales.

This chapter is concerned with workplace laws which are widespread and far reaching in terms of their objectives and scope but about which there is a great

Research in the Sociology of Work, Volume 8, pages 191-209.

ISBN: 0-7623-0608-4

deal of ignorance, namely the regulation of occupational health and safety (OSH). Controversy surrounds the deviant or criminal status of noncompliance with OSH laws, yet since the nineteenth century regulation has become a core feature of advanced industrial societies. Occupational health and safety laws now affect the vast majority of workplaces and the vast majority of workers in advanced industrial societies.[1]

REGULATION

There are many definitions of regulation (Mitnick 1980). It is now recognized that the concept of regulation embraces a broad range of activities, many of which go beyond the legal activities of the state (Grabosky 1995). But for the purposes of this chapter I will use the classic formulation of regulation as the use of the law to constrain and organize economic activity (Kagan 1978). This definition has become known as "command and control" regulation. It involves the "command" of the law and the legal authority of the state.

The use of the law as a regulator of economic life first came to prominence in nineteenth-century industrial society. In the 1970s this form of regulation experienced a surge of popularity. Advanced industrial societies witnessed a proliferation of laws designed to regulate economic activities across a broad economic spectrum (Rose-Ackerman 1992; Sigler and Murphy 1988; Sunstein 1990). The popularity of command and control regulation waned in the late 1980s/early 1990s when some countries (notably the United States and Great Britain) witnessed attempts to "roll back" the state and deregulate. It is debatable that regulation was much reduced since there is evidence of re-regulation and also the employment of alternative forms of regulation (Majone 1989).

Command and control regulation has proved controversial, partly because it is central to debates about the extent to which governments should attempt to influence economic life, and also because of the use of the criminal law and criminal sanctions as regulatory tools. Some authors negate the criminal status of regulatory offenses and refer to them as "quasi-criminal," so workplace deviance involving OSH violations would be distinguished from "real crime." The argument is that regulatory offenses are administratively and morally distinct from traditional crimes (Baucus and Dworkin 1991). For others, new categories of criminal law and criminal behavior have been created and the important question is why these may be seen as qualitatively different from other criminal offenses.

The extension of the criminal law has created "criminals" who are not readily identifiable with those who are the subjects of orthodox criminology. This is partly a matter of class and status, because directors and managers of business and industry do not fit the conventional stereotypes of working-class criminality (Chapman 1968). It also raises the subject of corporate offending, which may be regarded differently from individual wrongdoing (Wells 1992). Another reason for the differential handling and perception of much regulatory law is that it seeks to control activities proactively.[2] It typically regulates situations and activities that are potentially harmful; in other words actual harm need not have been caused for an offense to have been committed. Even when harm has been caused, the source of an offense may be difficult to detect because of the complex technical nature of the activities subject to control (Hawkins 1984). Another factor that may affect perceptions of regulatory legislation is that much of it (in Britain for instance) has abandoned the concept of *mens rea* and accepted the principle of strict liability. Notions of individual guilt and moral culpability are firmly embedded in the criminal legislation, so their abandonment may be seen as a dramatic change which may have diluted the moral force of the law (Hutter 1988; Richardson, Ogus, and Burrows 1983).

This chapter will examine how the regulatory agencies responsible for implementing occupational health and safety regulations approach their work and how those the regulations aim to control, view, and respond to regulation. It will consider regulatory objectives and how this form of workplace deviance is regarded by those involved in its regulation. I will draw upon the broad regulation literature and focus in particular upon two research projects I have undertaken into the regulation of occupational health and safety in England and Wales. The first is an in-depth examination of the breadth and variety of meaning encompassed by the concept of compliance—a concept identified by many previous studies as central to regulatory enforcement. The findings are derived from extensive fieldwork with three Inspectorates, namely the Factory, Industrial Air Pollution, and Railway Inspectorates for England and Wales.[3] The second is an examination of the impact of regulatory law upon the railway industry. This involved a detailed study of the regulatory responses of industry in Britain to health and safety legislation, paying attention to the views of the regulators, the regulated, and the protected. Data were collected about how the regulated view the controls upon their activities. The study aimed to develop an "in-the-round" account of the regulation of health and safety at differing levels of responsibility within British Railways (from Joint Managing Director, Railways, to the lowest grade manual worker).[4] The research has also involved discussions and interviews with senior trade union officials and safety representatives.

OCCUPATIONAL HEALTH AND SAFETY REGULATION

Regulatory Objectives

There are difficulties in considering regulatory objectives. For example, they are not always articulated or clear. There are likely to be a variety of objectives that may or may not conflict with each other. Moreover, they may change in many different ways and participants in the regulatory process may have varying interpretations of objectives.

In many senses, the use of the criminal law to regulate economic life has caused some confusion about the role of regulatory law. Not only is there debate about whether or not regulatory offenders are criminals or not, there is also debate about whether or not regulatory law is effective in controlling economic crime. Ayres and Braithwaite (1992, p. 20) refer to a history of "barren dispute" over these issues, barren in part because those involved are working from very different bases that are in many senses irreconcilable. Indeed, regulatory law may present enforcement officials with objectives that are fundamentally irreconcilable and involve approaches to deviance which depart from those normally associated with the criminal law (Hutter 1988; Stenning, Shearing, Addario, and Condon 1990).

Legal Mandate

Occupational health and safety legislation emerged in Britain during the nineteenth century. Originally, it was limited in scope, but over time the ranges of the law and the powers it accorded to inspectors were greatly extended. In England and Wales this was a piecemeal process until the enactment of the Health and Safety at Work etc. Act, 1974 (HSW Act) which represented a watershed in thinking about the legal regulation of health and safety in the workplace. OSH laws aimed to *regulate* the workplace in a *protective* capacity. Deviance was therefore defined as a failure to protect the workforce according to law.

Initially, the responsibility for compliance lay with employers, but the Robens Report into *Safety and Health at Work* (1972), upon which the HSW Act is based, recommended radical changes. The emphasis here is not upon rights, as it is in the United States (Sunstein 1990), but upon welfare and a *corporatist* philosophy that regarded health and safety as the everyday concern of everyone at work. The HSW Act thus holds a broad range of participants in the workplace responsible for their own compliance and deviance. It also empowers a wide range of participants in maintaining order and controlling deviance in the workplace. Crucially, it does this within a self-regulating ethos. The role of inspectors should be to consider the broader aspects of health and safety at the workplaces they visit, to educate and advise and to use sanctions if necessary, while the main responsibility for OSH lies with employers.

The HSW Act remains the main piece of occupational health and safety legislation in Britain.[5] Its objectives are both constitutive and controlling. It regulates market entry through prior approval procedures and, more importantly for this paper, it contains a number of provisions for controlling deviance in the workplace. It sets broad standards and provides for surveillance of the workplace by both those in industry and outside regulatory inspectors. It also contains provisions for dealing with noncompliance, for example, legal notices and prosecution. Importantly, it is an "enabling Act" which comprises, among other things, a statement of general principles, general duties, and broad statutory standards. These are supplemented by supporting instruments that are much more precise and tightly framed. But essentially deviance is broadly conceived and its precise interpretation is very much reliant upon the meanings and understandings attributed by those implementing the law (Hutter 1997).

Implementation

Historically there were numerous agencies created to enforce OSH regulation in Britain, and the HSW Act brought them together into one institutional framework (Wilson 1980). The regulatory objectives of officials are emergent through their policy making and through their action. Much attention has been directed to the enforcement approach of front-line regulatory officials, and it is to this that I want to turn to gain some idea of how these officials interpret their mandate, approach their work, and in turn regard workplace deviance.

Enforcement Approaches

Consideration of regulatory enforcement led socio-legal scholars to develop a series of models to enhance our understanding of law enforcement. These models are ideal types which take account of the methods and techniques used by enforcement officials and the objectives towards which they work. The enforcement style most often associated with regulatory officials is variously referred to as the accommodative (Richardson, Ogus, and Burrows 1983; Hutter 1988) or compliance (Hawkins 1984; Reiss 1984) strategy of enforcement. Securing compliance through both the remedy of existing problems and, above all, the prevention of others is the main objective of this strategy. The preferred methods to achieve these ends are cooperative and conciliatory. Persuasion, negotiation, and education are the primary enforcement techniques and the use of formal methods, especially prosecution, are regarded as a last resort.

This model of enforcement is contrasted with another termed the sanctioning strategy by Hawkins (1984) and the deterrent model by Reiss (1984). This is a penal style of enforcement which accords prosecution an important role. The methods preferred in such a model are penal and adversarial. Reiss regards both deterrence and compliance systems as preventive, whereas Hawkins regards the sanctioning model as punitive. In the important and empirically significant middle ground between the sanctioning and compliance models lie less extreme models, characterized by differences in rule interpretation and varying propensities to use legal coercion (Bardach and Kagan 1982; Braithwaite, Grabosky, and Walker 1987; Hutter 1988).

So here we have two broad models. One is concerned with "states of affairs" and the other with rules, one achieved by a broad array of enforcement techniques and the other that are more narrowly focused on the legal sanction. Whereas order in the first model refers to a state of affairs and the maintenance of order involves a continual process of surveillance, order in the second model is related to rule compliance (Stenning et al. 1990). The nature of rules varies between the two models. The compliance/accommodative model regards rules as guidelines whereas the sanctioning/deterrence model accord rules a much more central role as rule adherence is the primary regulatory objective. So the regulatory objectives attaching to different enforcement models appear to vary. Essentially, the compliance/accommodative model, so typically preferred by OSH inspectors in Britain, appears to be selected where the form of deviance subject to control is "amenable to strategies of correction or control" (Hawkins 1984, p. 6); where technically complex situations are encountered; and where enforcement officials are in long-term, repeated relationships with the regulated.[6]

Views of Deviance

Implicit in the enforcement approaches taken by enforcement officials are their views of workplace deviance. The regulated population comprises industries; individual companies and businesses; and employers, managers, and employees. Some of these groupings are complex, well organized, and multi-national; whereas others are simple, small-scale, and local. Compliance may vary between different sectors of an industry and even between different parts of one site. Moreover, compliance may change over time. At an organizational level, the focus of inspectors was upon safe systems of work, and at the micro level it was upon categories of people, for instance, employers and employees; specialists and generalists; skilled and unskilled; and the experienced and inexperienced.

OSH inspectors are therefore dealing with the deviance of companies and a complexity of individuals within them. Workplace deviance can therefore be analyzed at a variety of levels and from a complexity of perspectives. For the purposes of limitation we will concentrate on companies and draw on the data from my research on OSH inspectors in England and Wales.

Companies

Inspectors characterize the companies they encounter in a variety of ways referring, for example, to "poor," "reasonable," "fairly good," "responsible," "very good," and "exemplary" companies (Bardach and Kagan 1982). These characterizations may be applied to companies and to different areas of the same site. They are constructed, and may change, according to a range of factors. Six main criteria arose from my research as significant, each of which had implications for the way deviance was perceived. First were inspectors' perceptions of the company's commitment to health and safety or the environment. This had many facets including consideration of the time, energy, and finances the company devoted to health and safety or the environment. Also important in deciding a company's commitment was the attitude its staff had towards compliance. Where staff were safety-conscious and cooperative, then a company was described positively, but where inspectors detected obstinacy to their suggestions and sloppiness among managers and employees, the characterization would be negative.

Closely related to this was the third criterion identified, namely the company's record of compliance. This included not only the extent to which they had complied with inspectors' recommendations, but also the speed with which they had complied, their accident rate, and the level of complaint against them. A fourth criterion was the quality of management on-site, including the management's record in responding to inspectors' demands and their record in imposing discipline about health and safety or environmental requirements among the workforce. Fifth, inspectors considered a company's ability to comply. This included both its financial position and the degree of technical knowledge it possessed. A sixth criterion centered upon a company's treatment of its workforce.

Inspectors would typically characterize a company based on several of the above criteria. These characterizations were pragmatically generated moral typifications which had important implications for the way in which inspectors regarded deviance and the action they would initiate in the case of noncompliance. For example, inspectors' assessments of an employer's attitude to health and safety were significant in their decision about whether or not to initiate legal action and, if so, whether to opt for a notice or prosecution. If an employer was regarded by inspectors to have a generally good attitude towards health and safety, and there were only one or two problems, the inspector was concerned to remedy, then it was likely that a notice would be selected as the most appropriate enforcement tool. In contrast, prosecution was more likely with an employer who was generally or persistently not complying with health and safety demands.

The *size* of a company could be significant in deciding how inspectors view corporate deviance. Differential enforcement according to size of organization is a persistent feature of regulatory enforcement. Researchers in the United States, Australia, and the UK (Grabosky and Braithwaite 1986; Snider 1987; Yeager 1991) have all noted a tendency for formal legal enforcement action to figure less prominently in regulatory officials' dealings with larger and more powerful organizations than in their dealings with small organizations. Inspectors held mixed views about small companies. On the one hand they understood that the self-employed and small businesses were the least likely to know about the law and how to comply, so inspectors could spend large portions of their time educating and advising them. On the other hand, there is a well-researched tendency for regulatory officials to believe that big business is more law-abiding than small business (Grabosky and Braithwaite 1986, p. 215ff). Snider (1987, p. 49) similarly argues that "regulators tend to believe that only "fly by night" organizations typically stoop to crime."

Dawson, Willman, Bamford, and Clinton (1988, p. 261) found that the gap between standards of health and safety in large and small firms was considerable.

This is partly related to the capacity of organizations to comply (Grabosky and Braithwaite 1986; Yeager 1991) and their greater capacity to challenge how deviance is defined (Snider 1987; Yeager 1991). Large companies could, however, pose problems for inspectors partly because their potential for deviance was much greater. As Di Mento points out "Size correlates with differentiation in a firm and the greater the differentiation the greater the possibility of noncompliance" (1986, p.156; see also Vaughan 1982). All of this again underlines the fact that corporate deviance was interpreted in the context of inspectors' more general experience of a company.

Differentiating within Companies

Inspectors did not treat companies as homogeneous. They were sensitive to differences between areas, across areas, and within sites. It was the intention of the Robens Committee that "Reform should be aimed at creating the conditions for more effective self-regulation by employers and work people jointly" (1972, paragraph 452), by making those involved understand that health and safety are their concern and not just the remit of external agencies. Inspectors were therefore directed to consider different levels with an organization.

In practice the Inspectorates I researched varied in their communications with management and workforce. Inspectors' emphasis is in practice upon management (Hutter 1993). Indeed, their characterizations of sites often included reference to *management*, because how "good" managers were perceived to be was considered to influence things greatly. Determining how "good" or "bad" managers were depended on a variety of criteria. In many respects these mirror the criteria used for judging how a company was rated, namely acceptance of inspectors' recommendations; an assessment of managers' ability to detect and remedy problems on their own; the state of a site; and consistency was the final major criterion considered by inspectors. They also considered the performance of managers. This would include, for example, their behavior towards inspectors, other managers, safety representatives, and the workforce; their ability to identify risks and remedy any deficiencies; and their ability and willingness to act upon inspectors' requests. Erratic performance would concern inspectors as would a consistently negative performance. Only if managers were persistently rude or obstructive would inspectors take note and act upon this. In such cases, of course, inspectors may consider that their authority and credibility is being threatened, and this typically has serious implications for the moral typification of the deviant.

Where managers were regarded as especially incompetent inspectors manipulated the situation, perhaps writing directly to the managing director of a company to let them know of legal action being instituted against one of their works when inspectors had experienced problems with the local manager. In extreme cases, inspectors might simply refuse to deal with managers they had no faith in.

The interaction between Factory and Railway Inspectors and the *workforce* and their representatives were variable. Inspectors typically interacted with members of the workforce when they saw evidence of noncompliance. Their role in such cases was usually educational, and the inspectors I witnessed sometimes went to great lengths to explain to the noncompliant the reasons for the law. Inspectors tended to regard worker noncompliance as a company's disciplinary matter.

The influence of the company upon the behavior of the workforce was taken into account in several different ways. Company rules and policies were important. They were also watchful of the provision of safety equipment and clothing for the workforce. Inspectors were also very sensitive to workforce morale, in particular because of the effects it could have upon health and safety. Situations that were often seen to lead to poor standards were those where staff were poorly paid, occupations where there was a high turnover of staff, and firms where there had been staff cutbacks.

Inspectors characterized occupations according to broad stereotypes. Hence scrap metal merchants, secondhand salespeople, and scaffolders were attributed negative images; whereas those engaged in more precision work, such as certain types of engineering, chemists, and craftsmen were regarded as adhering to higher standards. The implication is that people with steady, professional jobs were more likely to be law-abiding and compliant than those in manual work, especially those without secure long-term employment. Another category of worker which concerned inspectors was contractors. Contract staff are not always familiar with the industrial settings within which they are sent to work, so inspectors considered them to be at greater risk of injury than regular staff.

Reasons for Compliance and Noncompliance

The range of violations encountered by regulatory inspectors is considerable, and the reasons for compliance and noncompliance are various (Di Mento 1986, p. 2ff). Different theoretical traditions have identified different reasons for compliance (Olsen 1992). There are a number of common explanations that emerge from the rudimentary literature that exists on this topic. Self-interest is regarded as a major reason for compliance, especially corporate compliance. The most striking example of this involves sites where strict compliance is necessary to the viability of the works (Genn 1993). But self-interest could take other, less dramatic, forms. Another variant on the self-interest theme was compliance motivated by a concern to protect corporate reputation (Miller and Sturdivant 1977; Olsen 1992). Large companies were seen as particularly concerned with protecting their image, and so were those whose relationships with the public were already or were potentially strained. Business was clearly perceived as susceptible to external pressures from a variety of sources, ranging from consumers to peer group pressure (Di Mento 1986, p. 86).

The OSH inspectors I researched also believed that some companies complied because of genuine concern for the environment or the health and safety of the workforce, which we might refer to as a moral reason for compliance. It is more than compliance out of an obligation to comply with the law; it is a commitment to the spirit and the letter of the law. Where this commitment was absent, enforcement of the regulations could itself be a motivation to comply (Gunningham 1984).

Other authors, notably Bardach and Kagan (1982, p. 60ff), have detailed a range of reasons for compliance besides those we have already mentioned. These include the threat of private lawsuits, increased insurance premiums, and worry about compensation payments and claims. These were not mentioned by any of the inspectors in this research, possibly because they were less pertinent in the British context than they were in the American context discussed by Bardach and Kagan. Other reasons mentioned by these authors, such as intra-organizational pressures to comply and avoiding the indirect costs of accidents, including "downtime" and labor's dissatisfaction, were discussed in inspector–company interactions, but never as a reason for compliance.

Cost is a much cited reason for noncompliance (Chelius and Smith 1987). Few authors, however, would simply relate compliance and noncompliance to cost. Wilson (1980, p. 359) notes that profit maximization is "an incomplete statement of corporate goals." Likewise, Di Mento (1986, p. 137) emphasizes that financial resources alone are an insufficient explanation of compliance—and one might add, noncompliance. Low worker morale was a major reason for noncompliance identified by inspectors in my research. Low morale could result for a variety of reasons. For instance, it could be a consequence of low pay or industrial action such as a work to rule or strike. Often, of course, these factors were related. A frequently cited reason for noncompliance among the workforce is that safety clothing and equipment hinder them in their work. I came across no inspectors who would accept that safety equipment hindered work, although some did accept that safety clothing could be more comfortable.

Underlying these explanations of compliance and noncompliance were assumptions about the type of people who were subject to regulation. Regulatory inspectors do not generally regard those they regulate to be blatant offenders. Ignorance and incompetence are more likely to be perceived as explanations of deviance than intent (see also Hawkins 1984; Hutter 1988). In part, this explains why many regulatory inspectors adopt an accommodative approach to achieving compliance, although there were variations between Inspectorates. All inspectors are responsible for what Bardach and Kagan (1982) refer to as "bad apples." But it should be emphasized that such companies were considered by all inspectors I have studied to be a small minority of those they regulated. If one considers the characteristics shared by those falling into this category, they tended to be short-term temporary sites and small, opportunistic firms. Moreover, they were regarded as culpable, blatant offenders who were morally deserving of the most serious sanctions being invoked against them. Of course there could be substantial economic advantage to be gained by not complying with the law, and this was something that inspectors considered in their perceptions of intent. Another factor that indicated a lack of commitment to health and safety was persistent or repeated noncompliance.

We should, however, be cautious about simplifying inspectors' views about and reactions to workplace deviance. Regulatory officials are case driven and make case-by-case judgements rather than adhering to abstract principles to guide their work. The only thing we know for certain is that there is no simple explanation of workplace deviance. Businesses vary in their ability and motivation to comply, and they also differ over time and across issues.

THE REGULATED'S UNDERSTANDINGS OF WORKPLACE DEVIANCE

A number of themes emerge from the limited literature on the subject of workplace understandings of and responses to OSH regulation. The first is that there is great variation between workplaces with respect to their knowledge of OSH regulation and their motivation to comply. In her study of "Business Responses to the Regulation of Health and Safety in England" Genn (1993) draws a distinction between companies that are "highly motivated" to comply with OSH regulation and those that have "low motivation." The well-motivated companies were proactive in their attitudes towards promoting compliance and controlling deviance. They shared several characteristics such as having a detailed safety policy; setting internal standards that may exceed regulatory standards; and setting up an internal OSH system involving safety officers, the workforce, and inspection and review procedures (Genn 1993, p. 227). They also tended to be the larger companies—a finding that reflects those of previous studies. Dawson et al. (1988), for instance, found that the size of a firm and the size of the site were the key variables in indicating how responsive a site may be to OSH regulation, with the large sites and those belonging to larger firms being the most responsive to OSH regulation. A union report into OSH regulation in Britain (GMB 1986) similarly notes that small companies find compliance problematic and often do not comply, as do studies of regulatory impact in other regulatory areas (Brittan 1984) and in other countries (Gricar 1983).

According to these criteria, British Railways was clearly a highly motivated company. It had a highly developed internal system of health and safety involving lengthy rulebooks, training, disciplinary procedures for noncompliance, safety officers, and a review system for accidents. In other words, its organizational responses to OSH regulation were sophisticated. The research question which remains, and which was the subject of my research, was the extent to which the different groups within the organization knew about OSH regulation and how they approached workplace deviance.

Knowledge of the Law

The literature suggests that knowledge of the law may affect compliance in a variety of ways. Ignorance of OSH regulation emerges as an important explanation of patterns of compliance. Genn (1993, p. 230), for instance, found that ignorance of the law was widespread among managers where there was low motivation to comply, but that in highly motivated firms there were likely to be both specialized OSH personnel and many sources of information about OSH. Dawson and colleagues (1988) found that even in larger firms there was often ignorance of the law at the lower levels of line management. This is, of course, important because it offers us vital information about the extent to which there may have been even the most rudimentary knowledge of what constituted workplace deviance or, more legalistically, criminality.

Respondents in my railway study did generally know about the HSW Act; 30 percent (36/121) spontaneously referred to the HSW Act[7] and, when prompted, an additional 54 percent (65/121) said that they had heard of this Act. More specific questions were directed to finding out how much was known about health and safety legislation beyond a simple naming of specific laws. The question "What do these laws require you to do?" elicited many responses with the majority in all categories perceiving the law as placing responsibilities upon themselves. This said, a notable proportion of respondents were unable to give very detailed or substantive replies. For instance, half of the workers interviewed had no clear idea of what their duties were in law. Half of the supervisors interviewed had no idea of what the law required of managers, which is perhaps a surprisingly high proportion given that supervisors do themselves occupy junior managerial positions within the industry. Managers and supervisors were most inclined to refer to the workers' responsibilities towards others as well as themselves. The only person to refer to managers' responsibilities for their own safety was a member of the workforce. Moreover there was only one manager who mentioned the responsibilities they have towards the public. This reflects Brittan's finding that water dischargers had a vague knowledge of their legal responsibilities (1984, p. 75).

Given that company policies and OSH systems are organized responses to the legislation, it is possible that employees know the law indirectly through the medium of company policies. Most of those interviewed did know that there were company OSH policies, and most knew where to find the relevant documentation should they need it.[8] The overwhelming majority of respondents in all categories were aware that there was information about health and safety available to them. Written sources were most commonly identified, in contrast to a relatively high proportion (47.5 percent) who claimed that they had not received OSH training as policy suggested they should have. A variety of documentary sources were cited, but while the existence and location of the policies were known about, there was great variation in understanding of these policies. For example, 62 percent of managers, 45 percent of safety representatives, 29 percent of supervisors, and only 14 percent of the workforce could offer any details about what the policies said. There was a general undercurrent of feeling that OSH training and information were not a high priority within the industry.

The aims and the content of the policies were generally praised, but there was a widespread view that the reason for the detailed documentation was to remove responsibility for health and safety from the Board to the staff:

> I often feel that there is an element of buck passing. I have received the document therefore I am lily-white and if you have not read it...and you have missed something then that is your fault because you are responsible for it now (Manager).

> ...basically it's the railways' insurance if anything goes wrong, to claim that we have got it (the rule book), that if we haven't abided by that rule-book then we haven't got a leg to stand on (Worker).

This perception is important because management commitment is one factor necessary to secure compliance. Sigler and Murphy (1988), for example, argue that there must be serious and vocal dedication to compliance at the top of a company, because suggestions that there is less than full commitment may lead to deviance.

Some railway respondents found the policy documents inaccessible. The problem was identified by one manager who explained that the policies are "...well intentioned but not aimed at the right level for the majority of people that work on the railways." Again this is important because effective communication of regulations is identified in the literature as one of the factors in influencing patterns of compliance. Indeed clarity of the law and regulations has been found to be crucial to compliance. Clay (1984), for instance, cites the complexity of OSH rules as a reason for noncompliance with OSHA regulations (see also Di Mento 1986; Hasseldine 1993). What is clear from my railway research is that neither the law nor company interpretations of the law were clear for many staff, and the implications of these findings are that many staff had only a vague understanding of the rules and definitions of deviance.

Enforcement

The effective enforcement of regulation emerges as centrally important from a range of regulatory studies (Barrile 1995; Di Mento 1986; Hasseldine 1993; Sigler and Murphy 1988). The basic argument here is that the threat of the law and formal sanctions must be credible for legal regulation to be effective and compliance to be achieved (Snider 1987).[9]

Studies focusing on the regulated have found that the existence of regulatory inspectors is generally known about at the company level and that those in managerial positions have views about the way in which the law is enforced (Brittan 1984; Dawson et al. 1988; Genn 1993). My study found that institutional arrangements for OSH were most fully understood by managers across a wide range of subjects. They were very likely to know that there were governmental checks on health and safety; to cite the Railway Inspectorate (RI) by name; to know the name and appearance of their local inspector; and to know where the local agency offices were. The workforce were the least likely to know about these matters, while supervisors and safety representatives had about the same levels of knowledge. To probe respondents' knowledge of the Inspectorate and its enforcement of health and safety legislation in greater detail, interviewees were questioned about the latest visit to their area by an inspector. Awareness of visits was again positively related to the respondents' place in the hierarchy, although the majority of those interviewed did not know how frequently their premises, area, or activities were inspected. This was the case with all grades of staff.[10] Staff were asked whether they took notice of inspectors' comments. The overwhelming majority did take notice for a variety of reasons. Prominent among these was that they had no choice, this being the most frequently mentioned reason between managers and supervisors. They also considered that inspectors gave sensible and authoritative advice.

The enforcement and implementation of the policies within British Railways were perceived to be lacking. This is perhaps reflected in the fact that knowledge of the systems in place to enforce the policies was patchy among the workforce, but common knowledge among managers, supervisors, and safety representatives. The perceived lack of enforcement was interpreted by some as symbolic of disinterest among the higher echelons of the organization.

Deviance and Compliance

Respondents were asked about their own compliance with OSH regulations. Most managers and supervisors tried to comply, but acknowledged that they did not always succeed. Of the workforce, 76 percent admitted that they had ignored either the law or company rules. All grades of staff cited similar examples of noncompliance. These included failing to wear safety clothing and not complying with rules about working on or about the track (the area where most fatalities occur). Studies of the regulated suggest several explanations of workplace deviance which are reflected in my railways research. The most common explanation of workplace deviance is ignorance or a lack of awareness of the law (Brittan 1984; Clay 1984; Dawson et al. 1988; Genn 1993). This did not emerge as an explanation offered by the railways respondents, although their levels of understanding of the law and company policies suggest that it might be an area that has explanatory value. What does emerge as significant is a lack of awareness of the risks involved in not complying. This emerged as a central managerial explanation of workplace deviance. It is in part reflected in a common explanation of noncompliance, namely "laziness," which is taking the easiest and most convenient option:

> I: Do you think that the workforce comply willingly with health and safety regulations?
>
> R: In general they do, where it is easy to do so, but they don't where it's an encumbrance, there's no doubt about that. I mean if you've got to put a helmet, ear defenders and a mask and everything on...it is an encumbrance and the natural human tendency is to take it off and get on with the job (Manager).

There is some suggestion in the medical literature on risk taking that individuals engage in cost–benefit analysis in deciding whether to comply with treatment. Notions of "cost" and "benefit" are socially constructed on the basis of previous experience, their understanding of the risks of noncompliance, information from a variety of sources including professional advice and colleagues, as well as their own beliefs (Donovan and Blake 1992; Emcke 1992). Similar explanations emerge from my data:

> I think sometimes they [workforce] think it [compliance] is unnecessary. The reason they don't do it [comply] is because they don't see the risk as high enough to make the effort necessary and worthwhile (Manager).

A director makes a similar argument when explaining workplace deviance:

> ...it really is just too much effort. They are either thinkingly or unthinkingly, probably the latter, making some sort of personal assessment about the value of the precaution against the risk involved.

The discomfort of safety clothing or impracticality of rules was offered as an explanation of workplace deviance. For instance, 59 percent of the workforce believed that safety equipment and OSH regulations made a difference to the way they work, with 31 percent regarding them as a hindrance. These explanations also figure in other studies. Genn (1993, p. 230) concluded that employees do not play a major role in promoting better safety standards partly because they do not understand OSH regulation and partly because of workforce resistance to protective clothing, guards, and safety procedures.

A related explanation of workplace deviance is that not complying is partly a consequence of a broader pressure to complete the job (Dawson et al. 1988). One might ask, for example, whether this contributed to so much ignorance about workplace deviance. Moreover, why should compliance feature in the everyday life of workers when they have so many other competing demands on their time and attention? There was a perception among railway staff that OSH considerations slow up the work. When railway staff were asked about the priority they give to health and safety, especially in relation to other responsibilities, the majority claimed that OSH had prime or fairly high priority. But its relative importance was not so clear-cut. The workforce accorded OSH slightly greater importance in relation to their other responsibilities than managers and supervisors, who tended to regard OSH as equal in importance to their other concerns. Two main factors were thought to encourage compliance in the industry, namely that the working environment is intrinsically dangerous and a moral duty to promote OSH. The majority felt that nothing weighed against OSH, the minority who disagreed with this regarded the cost and the time involved in OSH as weighing against compliance.

Workplace deviance is also related to a lack of enforcement, in particular poor management:

> I: Do your workforce comply willingly with health and safety regulations?
>
> R: When we enforce them, yes...if we enforced rigidly we would get acceptance, we haven't and we don't.

Disciplinary procedures were argued by my sample not to follow very frequently from noncompliance. The threat of disciplinary action did not seem to have a positive influence upon staff because it was not seen as credible. This said, there was no suggestion of ideological resistance to compliance (cf. Whitehurst 1977) or of a normative culture which encouraged deviance (cf. Massey 1979).

Clearly, explanations of workplace deviance involve a complex of factors (Di Mento 1986; Massey 1979; Sigler and Murphy 1988) as do explanations of compliance which in many respects mirror explanations of deviance. The workforce most frequently cited an awareness of the risks involved in explaining their compliance, whereas management referred to the need for them to "set an example" to staff. It was also felt that compliance was most likely when the rules were seen to be enforced. There was a belief that compliance did sometimes result from a moral duty to promote health and safety.[11]

SUMMARY

Deviance from workplace regulations is still an under-researched and ill-understood area of academic study. Traditional legal structures have been invoked to control deviance that is not universally regarded as problematic despite the very real and high costs which may be associated with this form of workplace deviance. This is complicated by the fact that criminal law is being used to regulate rather than prohibit. Moreover, it is being used to regulate sometimes complex and technical activities in a preventive, rather than reactive, capacity. This form of workplace deviance is committed by organizations and by those within them.

This influences the work of regulatory officials and can complicate attempts to regulate deviance within the organization. This is especially so where the risks associated with deviance are not adequately understood and communicated. The issues raised are undoubtedly important for our understanding of the role and limits of the law and also perceptions of the risks associated with the workplace.

ACKNOWLEDGMENTS

Some of the research in this paper was carried out with the support of the Health and Safety Executive and the British Academy. I am grateful to them and to the former British Railways and the railway unions, all of whom cooperated freely with the research. I would like to thank Clive Briault and Paul Rock for their helpful comments on an earlier draft, and Martin Innes for bibliographic assistance. The views expressed are those of the author.

NOTES

1. There are of course exceptions, such as those working either illegally or for organizations which are not covered by occupational health and safety laws.

2. Proactive enforcement is law enforcement through agency initiative, so it involves officials seeking out offences. This is in contrast to reactive enforcement where the agency response is prompted by an outside person or event, typically a complaint or accident. See Reiss (1971).

3. This chapter will draw upon the work of the Factory and Railways Inspectorates because they are responsible for the implementation of OSH law; the Industrial Air Pollution Inspectorate was not concerned with OSH laws, but with environmental controls. It should be noted however that their approach to regulation is very similar to that of OSH inspectors in Britain. This research is fully reported in Hutter (1997).

4. At the time of my research, British Railways was a nationalized industry and was responsible for most of the railway network in Great Britain. In 1994 British Railways was privatized and replaced by a highly complicated structure of independent companies.

5. European legislation, such as the so-called "six-pack" of health and safety regulations has also gained in importance.

6. See Kagan (1994) for an excellent summary. See also Aalders (1993); Grabosky and Braithwaite (1986); Hutter (1997); and Shover, Clelland, and Lynxwiler (1982).

7. There was a heavy bias in this answer towards managerial staff. Of those who spontaneously cited the HSW Act, 56.6 percent were managers; 42 percent were supervisors; 29 percent were safety representatives; and 4.5 percent were members of the workforce ($n = 36$).

8. All managers, 89 percent of safety representatives, and 80 percent of the workforce knew that the policies existed.

9. These arguments refer to those who do not view it as desirable to comply irrespective of the threat contained in law. Authors vary in their views of how much of the population this refers to; some think all businesses need threats, others differentiate between companies.

10. Of those interviewed on this subject, 55 percent of managers, 67 percent of supervisors, 50 percent of safety representatives, and 65 percent of workers did not know how frequently inspectors inspected their areas.

11. Brittan's (1984) study of the impact of water pollution control on industry found that a "moral obligation" to compliance was the major explanation of compliance. In contrast, legal obligation played little role in compliance.

REFERENCES

Aalders, M. 1993. "Regulation and In-Company Environmental Management in the Netherlands." *Law and Policy* 15: 75–94.

Ayres, I., and J. Braithwaite. 1992. *Responsive Regulation.* New York: Oxford University Press.

Bardach, E., and R. Kagan. 1982. *Going by the Book: The Problem of Regulatory Unreasonableness.* Philadelphia: Temple University Press.

Barrile, L. 1995. "Why Not Lock 'Em Up?: A Humanist Strategy for Combatting Corporate Violence." *Quarterly Journal of Ideology* 18: 67–106.

Baucus, M., and T.M. Dworkin. 1991. "What is Corporate Crime? It Is Not Illegal Corporate Behavior." *Law and Policy* 13: 231–244.

Braithwaite, J., P. Grabosky, and J. Walker. 1987. "An Enforcement Taxonomy of Regulatory Agencies." *Law & Policy* 9: 323–351.

Brittan, Y. 1984. *The Impact of Water Pollution Control on Industry.* Oxford: Centre for Socio-Legal Studies.

Chapman, D. 1968. *Sociology and the Stereotype of the Criminal.* London: Tavistock.

Chelius, J., and R. Smith 1987. "Firm Size and Regulatory Costs: The Case of Worker's Compensation Insurance." *Journal of Policy Analysis and Management* 6: 193–206.

Clay, T.R. 1984. *Combatting Cancer in the Workplace.* Unpublished. Ph.D. Dissertation, University of California.

Dawson, S., P. Willman, M. Bamford, and A. Clinton. 1988. *Safety at Work: The Limits of Self-Regulation.* Cambridge: Cambridge University Press.

Di Mento, J.F. 1986. *Environmental Law and American Business: Dilemmas of Compliance.* New York: Plenum Press.

Donovan, J., and D. Blake (1992) "Patient Noncompliance: Deviance or Reasoned Decision-Making?" *Social Science and Medicine* 34: 507–513.

Emcke, I. 1992. "Medical Authority and its Discontents: A Case of Organized Noncompliance." *Critical Sociology* 19: 57–80.

General, Municipal, Boilermakers, and Allied Trade Union. 1986. *The Freedom to Kill?* Esher: GMB.

Genn, H. 1993. "Business Responses to the Regulation of Health and Safety in England." *Law and Policy* 15: 219–234.

Grabosky, P. 1995. "Using Non-Governmental Resources to Foster Regulatory Compliance." *Governance* 8: 527–550.

Grabosky, P., and J. Braithwaite 1986. *Of Manners Gentle.* Melbourne: Oxford University Press.

Gricar, B.G. 1983. "A Preliminary Theory of Compliance with OSHA Regulation." *Research in Corporate Social Performance and Policy* 5: 121–141.

Gunningham, N. 1984. *Safeguarding The Worker.* Sydney: The Law Book Company.

Hasseldine, J. 1993. "How Do Revenue Audits Affect Taxpayer Compliance?" *Bulletin for International Fiscal Documentation* 47: 424–435.

Hawkins, K. 1984. *Environment and Enforcement: Regulation and Social Definition of Pollution.* Oxford: Clarendon Press.

Hutter, B.M. 1988. *The Reasonable Arm of the Law?: The Law Enforcement Procedures of Environmental Health Officers.* Oxford: Clarendon Press.

Hutter, B.M. 1993. "Regulating Employers and Employees: Health and Safety in the Workplace." *Journal of Law and Society* 20: 452–470.

Hutter, B.M. 1997. *Compliance: Regulation and Environment.* Oxford: Clarendon Press.

Kagan, R.A. 1978. *Regulatory Justice.* New York: Russell Sage Foundation.

Kagan, R.A. 1994. "Regulatory Enforcement" In *Handbook of Regulation and Administrative Law,* edited by D.H. Rosenbloom and R.D. Schwartz. New York: Marcel Dekker.

Majone, G., ed. 1989. *Deregulation or Reregulation?* London: Pinter.

Massey, J. 1979. "Deterrence: A Social Learning Approach." Paper given at the *Midwest Sociological Society Meeting.*
Miller, K., and F. Sturdivant. 1977. "Consumer Responses to Socially Corporate Behavior." *Journal of Consumer Research* 4: 1–7.
Mitnick, B. 1980. *The Political Economy of Regulation.* New York: Columbia University Press.
Olsen, P. 1992. *Six Cultures of Regulation.* Copenhagen: Handelshøjskolen 1 København
Reiss, A.J., Jr. 1971. *The Police and the Public.* New Haven, CT: Yale University Press.
Reiss, A.J., Jr. 1984. "Selecting Strategies of Social Control Over Organizational Life." In *Enforcing Regulation,* edited by K. Hawkins and J. Thomas. Boston, MA: Kluwer-Nijhoff.
Richardson, G.M., with A. Ogus and P. Burrows. 1983. *Policing Pollution: A Study of Regulation and Enforcement.* Oxford: Oxford University Press.
Robens Report. 1972. *Safety and Health at Work: Report of the Committee.* London: HMSO.
Rose-Ackerman, S. 1992. *Rethinking the Progressive Agenda: The Reform of the American Regulatory State.* New York: Free Press.
Shover, N., D. Clelland, and J. Lynxwiler. 1982. *Constructing a Regulatory Bureaucracy: The Office of Surface Mining Reclamation and Enforcement.* Washington, DC: D.J. National Institute of Justice.
Sigler, J., and J. Murphy. 1988. *Interactive Corporate Compliance.* Westport, CT: Quorum Books.
Snider, L. 1987. "Towards a Political Economy of Reform, Regulation, and Corporate Crime." *Law and Policy* 9: 37–68.
Stenning, P.C., C.D. Shearing, S.M. Addario, and M.G. Condon. 1990. "Controlling Interests: Two Conceptions of Order in Regulating Financial Markets." Pp. 88–119 in *Securing Compliance: Seven Case Studies,* edited by M.L. Friedland. Toronto: University of Toronto Press.
Sunstein, C.R. 1990. *After the Rights Revolution: Reconceiving the Regulatory State.* Cambridge, MA: Harvard University Press.
Vaughan, D. 1982. "Transaction Systems and Unlawful Organizational Behavior." *Social Problems* 29: 373–379.
Wells, C. 1992. *Corporations and Criminal Responsibility.* Oxford: Clarendon Press.
Whitehurst, W. 1977. "Suffocation by Regulation." *Journal of Social and Political Studies* 2: 17–24.
Wilson, J.Q. 1980. *The Politics of Regulation.* New York: Basic Books.
Yeager, P.C. 1991. *The Limits of the Law: The Public Regulation of Private Pollution.* Cambridge: Cambridge University Press.

DISCLOSING MISCONDUCT IN WORK ORGANIZATIONS

AN EMPIRICAL ANALYSIS OF THE SITUATIONAL FACTORS THAT FOSTER WHISTLEBLOWING

Joyce Rothschild and Terance D. Miethe

ABSTRACT

Certain assumptions seem often to be made about the type of person who would be inclined to blow the whistle on his or her employer, exposing workplace misconduct of various types. Having collected data from employees in a variety of work settings, the current study is positioned to examine the relevance of numerous personal and organizational characteristics in distinguishing between (1) non-observers of misconduct; (2) observers of misconduct who choose to remain silent; (3) individuals who blow the whistle to supervisors inside their work organizations; and (4) individuals who blow the whistle to external authorities. We conclude that, contrary to popular images of whistleblowers, the objective requirements of the specific roles or jobs that employees find themselves in, coupled with employee's perceptions of the ethics, openness, and democracy of their employing organization, have much more influence over the propensity to blow the whistle than do psychological or dispositional characteristics.

Research in the Sociology of Work, Volume 8, pages 211-227.

ISBN: 0-7623-0608-4

Early investigations in this century into the nature of crime and deviance led by Sutherland noted that the essential prerequisites of such acts may be dispositional or situational (1947). Of the two, Sutherland suggested, the situational may prove the more important in the last analysis. Nevertheless, a comprehensive review of the cumulative research on this topic finds that in the ensuing five decades, sociologists have tended to focus on dispositional explanations to the near exclusion of situational ones (Birkbeck and LaFree 1993). The authors conclude their review of the extant research by urging future researchers to turn their attention to aspects of the situational context, both objectively and subjectively understood, as key to a deeper understanding of criminal or deviant acts. The research reported on in this paper answers this call, and its analysis supports Sutherland's general contention that situational variables may prove more weighty than dispositional ones in understanding deviant behavior.

The subjects of our study are employees, or former employees, popularly called "whistleblowers," because they willingly challenge and expose organizational practices that they have come to observe in the context of their jobs, and which they believe are wasteful, illegal, abusive to employees, or harmful to the public. We are not the first researchers to study whistleblowers as "conscientious dissenters" (Glazer and Glazer 1989; Perrucci, Anderson, Schendel, and Tractman 1980). However, the extensive data we have collected during the past few years sheds important new light on this phenomenon, allowing us to identify organizational or situational conditions that propel or inhibit different forms of whistleblowing and to dispel the media-inspired image that there is a "whistleblowing personality" that explains this action.

WHISTLEBLOWING: REVIEW OF THE LITERATURE

By all indications, whistleblowing is a widespread phenomenon in American society. National surveys reveal that a large minority, if not slight majority, of U.S. employees have observed misconduct at work and have reported it to someone within or outside the company (Miethe and Rothschild 1994; U.S. Merit Systems Protection Board 1993). Federal agencies in the U.S. have set up "hotlines" over the last decade to receive calls from employees concerning waste, fraud, and abuse they have witnessed in their agencies, and these calls are formally investigated by a system of special counsels. Many states in the U.S. have set up a parallel system of hotlines to investigate possible waste in state agencies, and many corporations have followed suit as well.

Virtually every week the American media covers stories of whistleblowers standing up, against all odds, to eliminate misconduct in their employing organizations, and the public seems fascinated with these David-and-Goliath accounts of whistleblowers facing off against the powers that be in large organizations. Management and the business community, on the other hand, tend to depict whistleblowers as less than balanced persons with some sort of ax to grind. Interestingly, *both* sides tend to assume that whistleblowers must be an unusual breed of person, who by dint of personality, are moved to take this exceptional action of speaking out, usually to their own detriment. Social scientists who have studied this phenomenon have tended to make the same assumption and, accordingly, have searched for the characteristics that would define this "whistleblower personality" (Miceli and Near 1992; Jos, Tompkins, and Hays 1989).

One psychological image of whistleblowers evident in the literature is that they are principled individuals with strong moral convictions (Miceli and Near 1990; Jos, Tompkins, and Hays 1989; Graham 1986; Dozier and Miceli 1985). This image is echoed in the description of whistleblowers as "ethical resisters" (Glazer and Glazer 1989) and "difficult people" (Jos, Tompkins, and Hays 1989), and whistleblowing as "principled organizational dissent" (Graham 1986). Among the psychological attributes thought to characterize whistleblowers are higher levels of moral development, universal standards of conduct, self-esteem, and personal efficacy.

Several researchers (Glazer and Glazer 1989; Jos, Tompkins, and Hays 1989) have argued that belief in universal standards of conduct seems to be an underlying personality attribute of whistleblowers. Compromise and situationally-specific actions are rarely used to explain whistleblowers' behavior. In fact, clinicians have described their whistleblower clients as "principled individuals, nearly to a fault" (Jos, Tompkins, and Hays 1989). Aside from several case studies and anecdotal accounts, however, little is known about whether different types of whistleblowers (e.g., internal reporters versus external reporters) are more likely to hold absolute standards and whether either of these groups are different from other employees. Although strong religious beliefs may also characterize whistleblowers (especially those beliefs related to helping others), scant attention has been given to the salience of religious beliefs in accounting for differences in whistleblowing behavior (Glazer and Glazer 1989; Miceli and Near 1990).

Personal efficacy is another personality factor that may distinguish whistleblowers from other employees. Specifically, employees with high levels of personal efficacy have higher self-esteem and view themselves as in control of their actions. Having an internal locus of control (Rotter 1966), individuals with high levels of personal efficacy should feel greater responsibility for reporting misconduct and may be more willing to believe that their actions will be effective. Miceli and Near (1990, 1992) provide several reasons why whistleblowing should be more common among employees with an "action orientation." While empirical data on this factor are limited, much of the literature assumes that whistleblowers possess a high level of efficacy and a sense of social responsibility.

Differences in whistleblowing by the employee's gender, age, educational level, and marital status have also been discussed in previous studies. However, the empirical evidence for particular demographic differences is ambiguous, and conflicting theoretical reasons can be offered for why some social groups should have higher reporting rates than others. For example, men may have higher rates of whistleblowing than women because they are less susceptible to majority opinion, they are more likely to be members of professional groups with codes of ethics that encourage whistleblowing, and they are more likely to have higher self-esteem and feelings of personal efficacy (Miceli and Near 1990). Alternatively, women may exhibit higher rates of whistleblowing than men because they are more likely to occupy focal positions (e.g., tellers, secretaries, administrative assistance) that observe misconduct and may feel a greater responsibility to try to prevent harm from coming to others (Gilligan 1990). Similarly, older employees and those with higher levels of educational attainment may be in occupational positions more likely to witness wrongdoing, but such employees may also be more vested in the company and less willing to report misconduct because of fear of "rocking the boat" within the organization. Married workers may be more likely to report misconduct because they can rely on the social support of their families, but it can be equally argued that they will be less prone to report misconduct because fear of losing their jobs is intensified by family obligations and needs. Previous research tends to reveal somewhat higher levels of whistleblowing among employees who are male, older, higher educated, and married. The overall magnitude and direction of the differences by social group, however, varies widely across studies.

While the literature on whistleblowers has tended to concentrate on the above stated demographic and personality characteristics, we would contend that such a focus has only obscured the more important contextual factors that inhibit or give rise to whistleblowing. This greater salience of organizational factors over psychological attributes in understanding organizational behavior is put directly by Elliott Jacques:

> It is badly organized social systems that arouse psychotic anxieties and lead to their disturbing acting out and expression in working relationships. The reason we have bad or dysfunctional organizations is not a reflection of pathological psychological forces to be understood and resolved.... Far from it. The reason is that there has never been an adequate foundation of understanding of organizations *per se* [and]...in our failure to clarify and specify the requirements of the *roles* in our major organizations (1995, pp. 343–344).

When applied to the study of whistleblowing, Jacques' (1995) view suggests that the organizational dynamics of whistleblowing and the behavior of whistleblowers themselves are not illuminated by psychological constructs, and are much better understood as the outcome of requirements and accountabilities pertaining to specific work roles and situations. Our research findings in large measure support this perspective.

Previous researchers have embarked on what we believe is a mistaken search for individual-level variables that could be said to predispose individuals to become whistleblowers. This research is understandable in light of management's practical interest in identifying and avoiding such employees. However, as we seek to show in this paper, this search is futile because it is certain features of the organizational system and of the situation that account for whistleblowing (and, we suspect, the organizational misconduct that underlies it), not individual idiosyncrasies. Furthermore, previous research (Rothschild and Miethe 1994) has demonstrated that it is the organizational response (i.e., retaliation) in the face of whistleblowing that destroys employee's trust in "higher-ups" and transforms their self-concept in such a way that they now see themselves as persons of exceptional integrity and moral principle. Given that different organizational experiences are likely to shape individuals' perceptions of the appropriateness of whistleblowing, it seems especially germane to investigate the organizational factors that directly influence the propensity for whistleblowing and that modify the importance of demographic (e.g., age, sex, marital status) and psychological attributes (e.g., self-esteem, belief in universal standards). These organizational factors include the observer's position and role accountabilities within the company, and the organization's structure and culture.

The overall values of the organization, especially those held by the CEO, may be important determinants of the likelihood and prevalence of whistleblowing inasmuch as upper management is often seen as setting the ethical tone for the corporation (Clinard 1983). For example, we found that when upper management is seen as unethical or inert toward evidence of organizational wrongdoing, internal whistleblowing may remain unlikely even among persons who are in the best position to see the wrongdoing or who are under some ethical standard to report misconduct. In these cases, whistleblowing may be suppressed altogether or pushed outside the organization.

There is also debate about whether whistleblowers are core or fringe members of the organization. On the one hand, core members of the organization have greater access to pivotal positions for observing misconduct, greater credibility in issuing reports of misconduct, and may have greater commitment to changing practices that reflect poorly on their organization, thereby increasing their likelihood of whistleblowing. Fringe members and novice employees, in contrast, may be less influenced by organizational constraints or have less stake in organizational conformity, thereby also increasing their likelihood of whistleblowing. Data on this relationship is limited, but previous research suggests that whistleblowers are core members and more highly paid members of the organization (Ling 1991; Miceli and Near 1984, 1988, 1990). Whistleblowing also tends to be more common among persons who are high performers and get satisfactory evaluations of their work performance (Miethe and Rothschild 1994; Glazer and Glazer 1989; Jos et al. 1989).

The role of professional ethics has also been examined. The presumption is that individuals who are members of professional associations with codes of ethics promoting public disclosure of misconduct should be more likely to consider whistleblowing. Nonetheless, persons in such associations may view the immediate risks of whistleblowing (e.g., losing one's job, being shunned by co-workers) as far greater than the remote chance of professional sanction. Similar to the sociodemographic profile, insufficient data hampers previous empirical studies of this organizational characteristic of whistleblowers.

Finally, both the nature and prevalence of whistleblowing may be influenced by other characteristics of the organization. For example, internal whistleblowing may be normative behavior that is engaged in equally by all employees within organizations that are more democratic in their organizational structure and offer employees opportunities to participate in decision making. However, in less democratic organizations and those less receptive to criticism, both internal and external reporting may require exceptionally strong-willed and principled individuals who can overcome organizational resistance. Under these conditions, basic structural characteristics of the organization and its receptivity to employee input may strongly influence both the type of whistleblowing and the socio-demographic characteristics of whistleblowers.

In this paper we present a unique and large data set that we have collected from whistleblowers from all walks of life. In our analysis, we try to shed light on the organizational factors that foster or inhibit the reporting of observed organizational wrongdoing and that modify the effect of the demographic and psychological characteristics that were previously emphasized in the literature.

RESEARCH DESIGN AND METHOD

Sample Description

Survey instruments, containing both open and closed-ended questions, were given to five different groups of employees to examine the factors that distinguish whistleblowers from other workers. Self-administered surveys were provided at the entrance and exits of a high-security manufacturing firm, a large petro-chemical plant, an administrative unit within a major university, and a bookstore. In all, 284 surveys were returned using this procedure. The surveys we constructed were also completed and returned from 86 of a possible 300 whistleblowers across the country who asked for more information following an article on whistleblowing that appeared in *Parade Magazine*.[1]

Although there is no direct way in the current study to assess how many people picked up our survey and failed to return it, we can nonetheless speculate that our sample design would tend to yield respondents across all samples with greater personal interest or more direct experiences with whistleblowing than non-respondents. We recognize that the sampling of more concerned employees could inflate our overall estimates of the prevalence of observing misconduct and whistleblowing. However, such population estimates are not a central focus in this paper. We are primarily interested in comparing the attributes of different

Table 1. Measures of Variables and Descriptive Statistics for Samples of Non-Observers (NONOBS), Silent Observers (SILOBS), Internal Whistleblowers (INTWBER) and External Whistleblowers (EXTWBER)

Independent Variables	*Coding*	*Mean Ratings on the Independent Variables for each Group*				
		NONOBS	*SILOBS*	*INTWBER*	*EXTWBER*	*eta*^{2}
Demographic Characteristics:						
Gender	0=Male; 1=Female	.37	.40	.52	.34	.012
Age	0=> 40; 1=<40	.33	.46	.37	.23	.032
Marital Status	0=unmarried; 1=married	.76	.72	.73	.73	.002
Education Level	1=< hs grad to 6=grad school	4.28	4.35	4.18	4.92	.048
Cognitive Beliefs/Values:						
Decisions should be made on Universal Standards	1=strongly agree to 4=strongly disagree	2.98	2.94	2.75	2.60	.034
Make Sacrifices for Greater good	1=strongly agree to 4=strongly disagree	2.09	2.13	1.92	1.87	.025
Responsible for Prevent Harm to Others	1=strongly agree to 4=strongly disagree	1.38	1.46	1.35	1.23	.025
I'm a Person of Worth	1=strongly agree to 4=strongly disagree	1.44	1.61	1.33	1.42	.034
What Happends to me is a Matter of Luck	1=strongly agree to 4=strongly disagree	3.08	3.26	3.22	3.20	.012
Religious Beliefs	1=not religious to 3=very religious	2.25	2.13	2.15	2.20	.008
Organizational Position/Attributes:						
Freq. of Misconduct Seen	0 to 8 types of offenses	0.00	.67	1.12	2.71	.330
Years Worked at Company	1 to 5 or more	8.06	7.18	7.90	5.14	.092
Number of Promotions	0 to 5 or more	1.81	1.66	1.77	1.42	.014
Supervisor Position	0=no; 1=yes	.48	.39	.39	.47	.007
Code of Ethics for Work	0=no; 1=yes	.82	.77	.86	.83	.006
Employer has strong Moral Values	0=no; 1=yes	.78	.59	.51	.11	.204
Decisions are Democratic	0=no; 1=yes	.53	.31	.39	.11	.093
Workers Participate in Decision-making	0=no; 1=yes	.63	.50	.42	.13	.119

types of whistleblowers and other employees, and there is no reason to expect any specific bias in this respect.

When compared to other studies of whistleblowers, the specific sampling frame used in the current study tends to provide a wider array of whistleblowers. For example, the analyses by Miceli and Near (1990, 1992) are based on samples that include only federal employees or directors of internal auditors. The sample by Jos, Tompkins, and Hays (1989) of 161 whistleblowers involves mostly federal employees and mostly persons who have contacted national support organizations for whistleblowing. The 64 whistleblowers in the study by Glazer and Glazer (1989) include mainly high-profile cases in the U.S. that were covered by the mass media. In contrast, the whistleblowers in the current study are ordinary employees from many different industries and occupations, they report on many types of organizational misconduct, and cover situations that vary widely in their level of public visibility. Under these conditions, the whistleblowers examined here may be a better representation of the "typical" whistleblower in the general public.

Measures of Variables

Four groups of employees are identified in the current study: (1) internal whistleblowers (i.e., those who report wrongdoing only to persons within the company); (2) external whistleblowers (i.e., those who report misconduct to persons outside the company); (3) silent observers (i.e., those who observe misconduct but do not report it); and (4) non-observers of misconduct. The proportion of sample respondents in each group are 14 percent, 19 percent, 37 percent, and 30 percent, respectively.

The primary independent variables involve socio-demographic attributes of employees, their organizational position, and the characteristics of the organization. Socio-demographic characteristics include measures of cognitive elements (for example, their values, moral beliefs, feelings of personal efficacy) and basic demographic attributes (for example, age, gender, education, marital status). Measures of all independent variables and their mean ratings by the type of whistleblowing experience are summarized in Table 1.

Our measure of absolute or universal standards involves the extent to which respondents agree that decisions should be made according to universal rules rather than on a case-by-case basis. High levels of social responsibility are indicated by the extent of agreement with the statements that "people should make sacrifices for the greater good" and "people have a responsibility to prevent harm from being done to others if they can." High self-esteem is measured by the level of agreement with the item "I feel that I'm a person of worth," whereas high self-efficacy is indicated by the level of disagreement with the statement "what happens to me is largely a matter of luck." Individuals' self-ratings of the intensity of their religious beliefs range from "1" (not at all religious) to "3" (very religious).

Previous research suggests that whistleblowers will be more likely than other employees to endorse universal rules, have higher social responsibility, report higher levels of self-esteem and self-efficacy, and have stronger religious beliefs.

The demographic attributes of the employees include their gender, age, educational level, and marital status. Age is dichotomized to compare persons aged 40 and older with younger employees. The level of formal educational training ranges on an ordinal scale from "1" (some high school) to "6" (advanced college degree). Marital status is coded in such a way to compare persons who are currently married with other persons.

Measures of the individual's organizational position and characteristics of the organization include the frequency of observing misconduct in the organization, the number of employees at the local company, the number of years of employment in the company, the number of promotions, supervisor status, the presence of a code of ethics for this type of work, perceptions of the moral values of management, views about whether decisions are made in a democratic fashion, and the opportunity for workers to participate in decision making. The coding of each of these variables is shown in Table 1.

RESEARCH RESULTS

Two separate analyses are undertaken to examine the socio-demographic and organizational characteristics that distinguish between different types of whistleblowers, observers of misconduct who remain silent, and non-observers of occupational misconduct. First, bivariate comparisons of means and correlations are performed to examine differences in the dependent variable (i.e., type of whistleblowing experience) by the demographic attributes of employees and their organizational characteristics. Second, logistic regression models are estimated to identify those socio-demographic and organizational characteristics that significantly differentiate between and within categories of whistleblowers. Measures of the `whistleblowing personality" are first entered into the regression models, followed by organizational characteristics. An estimation of these successive models allows us to assess whether and to what extent organizational factors condition and mediate the impact of socio-demographic variables on the likelihood and type of whistleblowing. The results of these analyses are summarized below.

Bivariate Relationships

As shown in Table 1, organizational characteristics and employee's perceptions of organizational practices are far more highly correlated with whistleblowing experiences than an individuals' demographic profile and general beliefs and values. None of the demographic and cognitive belief characteristics shared at least five percent of common variance with the type of whistleblowing experience, but six separate organizational attributes explained more than five percent of the variation in whistleblowing. The strongest bivariate correlates of whistleblowing are the frequency of observing misconduct, organizational size, the perceived moral values of the company, years employed in the organization, and worker's beliefs about democratic practices and participatory decision making in their company. External whistleblowers (and, to a lesser extent, internal whistleblowers) observe misconduct much more frequently than other employees and are more likely to view their employer as immoral, non-democratic, and to feel that they had little opportunity to participate in decisions. External whistleblowers also are less likely to be employed in large companies (that is, companies with more than 1,000 employees) and they have shorter employment histories within the company than other employees. In terms of job performance ratings, there are no significant differences between groups in the number of promotions, even though external whistleblowers tend to have fewer promotions prior to their disclosures.

Table 2. Logistic Regression Models of Type of Whistleblower Experience

Predictor Variable	*Model 1* *Wber/non-Wber*	*Model 2* *Internal/External*
Gender	.597	-.296
Age	-.857**	-2.185**
Marital Status	.103	1.257
Educational Level	.357**	.976***
Universal Standards	-.253	.189
Make Sacrifices	-.822***	-.678
Preventing Harm	-.153	-.892
Person of Worth	-.414	.481
Matter of Luck	.025	.599
Religious Intensity	-.115	-.400
No. of Offenses	.728***	.637***
Years at Company	-.117*	-.285**
No. of Promotions	.162	-.328
Supervisor Position	.779**	.625
Code of Ethics	.630	-.680
Employer's Morals	-.996**	-1.244
Democratic	.260	-.904
Worker Participate	-.667	.157
Sample Size	294	92
Model X^2	121.85	47.50
df	18	18
probability	.00001	.0002

Notes: Model 1 contrasts whistleblowers (both internals and externals) with non-whistleblowers (both silent observers and non-observers). Model 2 contrasts internal whistleblowers and external whistleblowers.
$^*p < .10$; $^{**}p < .05$; $^{***}p < .01$.

There are no major differences between groups in regards to whether there is a code of ethics for the employee's particular type of work.

Concerning the presumed "whistleblowing personality," both types of whistleblowers (i.e., internal and external) are only slightly more likely than other employees to subscribe to universal rules for decision-making (rather than on a case-by-case basis) and tend to have slightly higher levels of social responsibility (for example, to believe that people should make sacrifices for the greater good, and to believe that people have a responsibility to prevent harm from being done to others). In terms of self-esteem, self-efficacy, and religious beliefs, there are also no substantial differences across groups. Non-observers and silent observers are just as likely as whistleblowers to believe that they are people of worth and that what happens to them is largely a matter of luck. The typical survey respondent is "somewhat religious" regardless of their whistleblowing experience. Furthermore, for each of these measures of the psychological profile, there are no substantial differences between internal and external whistleblowers.

Models of Types of Whistleblowers

Two logistic regression models were estimated to assess the magnitude of particular socio-demographic and organizational differences between whistleblowers and other employees. The first regression model contrasts whistleblowers with non-whistleblowers. The second model is based on the sample of whistleblowers only, and examines the net impact of various socio-demographic factors thought to comprise of the "whistleblowing personality" (called model 1 in Table 2) and then adds to this baseline the set of organizational characteristics (called Model 2). The logit coefficients and measures of fit of these models are summarized in Table 2.

As shown in Table 2, several socio-demographic and general attitudinal characteristics significantly differentiated whistleblowers from other employees, but most of these differences become insignificant once controls are introduced for organizational factors. Specifically, employees with higher education, higher endorsement of universal rules of conduct, and those who have stronger beliefs about making sacrifices for the greater good have higher chances of being whistleblowers than other employees, but only differences by education remain after controlling for various organizational characteristics and perceptions of the organization. However, with respect to situational or organizational factors, several made a significant difference in the chance of becoming a whistleblower (versus being a non-whistleblower): (1) Employees who observe wrongdoing more frequently in their company were more likely to become whistleblowers; (2) employees in professions with a written code of ethics were more likely; (3) employees in smaller organizations were more likely; and (4) employees who view their employer as more immoral were more likely to blow the whistle.

The logistic regression analysis revealed few significant net differences between external and internal whistleblowers on personal and organizational attributes (see Table 2). Education (with external whistleblowers having higher educational attainment) was the only personal attribute that distinguished between types of whistleblowers, but differences based on this variable became insignificant once controls were included for organizational factors. The size of the organization was the only characteristic that significantly differentiated external from internal whistleblowers. Contrary to the conventional wisdom that larger, more bureaucratic organizations constitute the type of work environment that fosters external reporting of misconduct, employees in the larger companies in the current study had significantly *lower* likelihood of external whistleblowing than employees in smaller organizations.

DISCUSSION AND CONCLUSIONS

There has been much speculation, but little empirical data, on whether a "whistleblowing personality" or disposition exists. Media accounts and previous studies using small samples, case accounts, and anecdotal reports suggest that whistleblowers are strong-willed, opinionated individuals with high levels of self-esteem and self-efficacy (Miceli and Near 1992; Glazer and Glazer 1989; Jos et al. 1989). However, concerning their organizational position, previous research is inconclusive or silent about whether whistleblowers are core or fringe members of the organization, what their relative job performance is, and the extent to which they may be moved by their explicit job duties to report the infraction.

The empirical question of whether a certain personality predisposes one toward whistleblowing is important for a number of theoretical and practical reasons. From the perspective of management, for example, the identification of a "whistleblowing personality" could serve as a basis for avoiding particular types of employees, especially if they were seen as prone to external whistleblowing. From a social control perspective, whistleblowing by employees is one of the few methods for the early detection and possible control of occupational and organizational misconduct (Miethe and Rothschild 1994). If there exists a whistleblowing personality that holds across organizational contexts, external enticements for reporting misconduct (e.g., protective legislation, court awards, organizational rewards) would be unable to alter the relative frequency of whistleblowing behavior. Under these conditions, only through the recruitment of particular types of employees (i.e., those who fit the "profile") could whistleblowing become a viable strategy for the detection and control of occupational crime.

The results of the current study, however, provide no support for the "whistleblowing personality" hypothesis put forth by others. Neither socio-demographic characteristics nor general attitudes toward universalism and social responsibility significantly differentiate between whistleblowers and other workers after taking into account organizational characteristics.

While our results reveal that several organizational factors (especially the size of the company) are strong predictors of the likelihood and type of whistleblowing, supplemental analysis suggests that external whistleblowing is often generated out of certain situations. Specifically, we found that particular types of observed wrongdoing such as financial fraud, health and safety violations, and poor production activities were more likely to generate external reporting, whereas internal whistleblowing was more likely where employees observed counterproductive work activity (for example, coming to work late, taking unauthorized work breaks). As shown in Table 1, persons who became external whistleblowers had observed more than twice as much misconduct as those who stuck to internal whistleblowing and more than four times more misconduct than the silent observers in our study. The importance of one's occupational role and situational factors in understanding whistleblowing is perhaps best illustrated with our qualitative interview material.

Consider the case of Robert (not his real name), an intelligent and able "reliability engineer" with more than 20 years of experience with a research division of the U.S. military. Robert's explicit job responsibility was to make sure that extremely complex weapon system designs would actually function as specified once they were built. A system can not be built until a reliability engineer like Robert signs off on the design, testifying that if it is constructed as designed, it will function as required. Unfortunately for Robert, a multi-billion dollar weapons system to which he was assigned, and to which his supervisors were very much committed, turned out to be a dud. Because he refused to sign off on its design, Robert was subjected to intense pressure from his superiors, culminating in their efforts to remove him from his job responsibilities and to have him declared a "paranoid security risk" by a pentagon-appointed psychiatrist. Unanticipated by his supervisors, the psychiatrist found Robert to be sound as a bell, and a review board, after extensive and lengthy review, found his report on the weapons system to be accurate in all respects.

This experience as a "whistleblower" changed Robert's life, his sense of himself, and his job conditions forever. Robert clearly understood the corruption that laid behind this particular weapons system. He had seen it before in the "rubber-stamps" that other engineers had been pressured to give other malfunctioning projects:

> I loved my job and somehow I thought I could do it in spite of the corruption. It was as if they were saying to me if you want to keep your job, you better cover up our criminal activity. I couldn't do it. I knew I would lose either way. If I covered up for them and let them build their thing, I would lose my integrity. I believed that the truth would have power in itself, and that is what gave me the confidence to do my job.... But I miscalculated. I didn't realize the lengths they would go to torment me..."

As Jacques (1995) would suggest, it is the responsibilities and accountabilities inherent in Robert's *role* that explain far more than reference to any personality trait how he was brought to his whistleblowing behavior. We found that a similar pattern emerged in the comments from many other external whistleblowers in this study.

In our analysis of the data, we found that the strongest correlates and predictors of whistleblowing are not psychological attributes or attitudes (e.g., belief in universal standards, self esteem, personal efficacy, sense of social responsibility). Instead, the major predictors, even after controlling for personality factors, are the organization's size, the presence of a code of ethics for the employee's work role, and the perception of management as being "immoral." The fatal flaw of previous arguments for a whistleblowing personality (Miceli and Near 1990) is that they can not adequately explain this variation across different occupational and organizational contexts.

Further, our secondary analysis of a recent federal survey (U.S. MSPB 1993) further reveals variation in rates of whistleblowing by occupational category. Among workers who observed misconduct at work, the percent of employees who are internal whistleblowers ranges from 27 and 30 percent (for technicians and legal professionals) to 42 and 46 percent (for engineers and scientists). The percent of external whistleblowers ranges from eight percent and nine percent (for scientists and manual/craftworkers) to 31 percent (for legal professionals). The only way that a psychological approach could explain these occupational differences would be to argue that there are different proportions of workers in each of these types of occupations who hold universal standards and have high self-esteem, high personal efficacy, and high levels of social responsibility. Instead, we maintain that these differences by occupation are best explained by differences in the role responsibilities and accountabilities for each type of occupation.

The importance of the organizational context in understanding whistleblowing is most evident in the impact of organizational size. Organizational size is the single best predictor of both the likelihood of whistleblowing and its form. The unexpected finding that larger organizations have lower rates of whistleblowing is explained by the wider economic conditions in which the large companies in the current study are operating. That is, the large companies (with more than 1,000 workers) in our study were the largest employers in their respective counties, and jobs in these companies were highly valued because of their relatively high wages. In terms of a climate for whistleblowing, the downsizing that was occurring at the time in these companies contributed to greater feelings of job insecurity and a decreased willingness to speak out about possible organizational abuses. In this context, the low rates of internal and external whistleblowing that we found within these large bureaucratic organizations is understandable. These findings further emphasize the importance of the wider context (rather than personal attributes) in understanding whistleblowing.

Finally, the results of this study have important implications for future research and social policy regarding whistleblowing. Specifically, as society becomes more complex and organizations become more information-rich and information-driven, it becomes less and less realistic to expect outside regulatory agencies (such as government agencies) to be able to effectively monitor the internal workings of the organizations they are assigned to monitor. Often the only people who are in position to observe and expose organizational misconduct are specific employees who hold positions that allow them to see and professional roles that may compel them to reveal misconduct. Thus, we should not be surprised to see more and more workplace misconduct revealed by employees on the inside, i.e., whistleblowers. This is how the truth of the tobacco industries manipulation of nicotine levels was brought out in the open. This was how the truth of the Challenger disaster was revealed, and thousands of other cases. We notice that one of the leading books on white-collar crime fails even to mention the potential role of whistleblowers in detecting and exposing it (Coleman 1998). Yet, we expect that without the aid of conscientious employees who are willing to speak up when they observe repeated instances of waste, fraud, or abuse in their employing organization, the public will not learn of said wrongdoing, even when it most affects them, as with, for example, product flaws or environmental damage. Our society is looking increasingly to whistleblowers to break the cloak of organizational secrecy and to expose organizational wrongdoing.

Given our finding that a clear whistleblower personality probably does not exist, future efforts to understand whistleblowing should focus on the organizational context that fosters criminality in the workplace in the first place, and then on the role responsibilities and situational factors that encourage or dissuade whistleblowing of the observed misconduct. The absence of a whistleblowing personality also suggests that organizations could be quite successful in providing various rewards or punishments (e.g., pay raises, promotions, awards versus demotions, firings) and using other types of social influence strategies (e.g., shunning the whistleblower, retaliative authority versus open communication channels, hotlines, leadership by moral example) to either encourage or discourage different types of whistleblowing. Such efforts by organizational hierarchies to either encourage or suppress the exposure of organizational misconduct would be futile if all potential whistleblowers were steadfast and uncompromising in their proclivity to report misconduct. But since, as we have shown, employees are moved by their role responsibilities and by their perceptions of the organization's purposes and qualities, whistleblowing behavior is conditioned: It can be encouraged by giving someone the job to monitor and by opening up a specific internal channel for such communications; it can be suppressed or moved outside by sending the message that the hierarchy will discredit and retaliate against suspects. Contrary to the popular media image of whistleblowers as heroes or weasels, we find that whistleblowing behavior can be little explained by reference to sociodemographic characteristics, or the personality or attitudes of the observer. In the final analysis, whistleblowing is best understood as a complex social phenomena that occurs in an organizational context, and it is attributes of the organization or situation that act to encourage or inhibit such expression.

ACKNOWLEDGMENT

The authors gratefully acknowledge the support received from the Aspen Institute for the conduct of this research.

NOTE

1. The authors appreciate the assistance of Donald Soeken for providing access to this sample of whistleblowers. The article in *Parade Magazine* described his organization, Integrity International, and a retreat for whistleblowers called "Whistle Stop."

REFERENCES

Birkbeck, C., and G. LaFree. 1993. "The Situational Analysis of Crime and Deviance." *Annual Review of Sociology* 19: 113–137.

Clinard, M. 1983. *Corporate Ethics and Crime*. Beverly Hills, CA: Sage.

Coleman, J.W. 1998. *The Criminal Elite: Understanding White-Collar Crime*. New York: St. Martin.

Dozier, J.B., and M.P. Miceli. 1985. "Potential Predictors of Whistleblowing: A Prosocial Behavior Perspective." *Academy of Management Review* 10(October): 823–836.

Gerth, H., and C.W. Mills (translators). 1946. From Max Weber: Essays in Sociology. New York: Oxford University Press.

Glazer, M., and P. Glazer. 1989. The Whistleblowers: Exposing Corruption in Government and Industry. New York: Basic Books.

Graham, J.W. 1986. "Principled Organizational Dissent: A Theoretical Essay." Pp. 1–52 in *Research in Organizational Behavior*, Volume 8, edited by L.L. Cummings and B.M. Staff. Greenwich, CT: JAI Press Inc.

Jacques, E. 1995. "Why the Psychoanalytic Approach to Understanding Organizations is Dysfunctional." *Human Relations* 48: 343–349.

Jos, P., M.E. Tompkins, and S.W. Hays. 1989. "In Praise of Difficult People: A Portrait of the Committed Whistleblower." *Public Administration Review* (November/December): 552–561.

Ling, E. 1991. "Whistleblowing: Toward a Sociological Understanding." Paper presented at the Annual Meetings of the American Society of Criminology, San Francisco, CA. November.

Miceli, M.P., and J.P. Near. 1984. "The Relationships among Beliefs, Organizational Position, and Whistle-Blowing Status: A Discriminant Analysis." *Academy of Management Journal* 27: 687–705.

Miceli, M.P., and J.P. Near. 1988. "Individual and Situational Correlates of Whistleblowing." *Personnel Psychology* 41: 267–282.

Miceli, M.P., and J.P. Near. 1990. "Is There a Whistleblowing Personality? Personal Variables that May Be Associated with Whistleblowing." Working Paper Series (WPS 90-19), College of Business, Ohio State University, March 1990.

Miceli, M.P., and J.P. Near. 1992. *Blowing the Whistle*. New York: Lexington Books.

Miethe, T.D., and J. Rothschild. 1994. "Whistleblowing and the Control of Organizational Misconduct." *Sociological Inquiry* 64(3): 322–347.

Perrucci, R.M., R.M. Anderson, D.E. Schendel, and L.E. Tractman. 1980. "Whistleblowing: Professionals' Resistance to Organizational Authority." *Social Problems* 28: 149–164.

Rothschild, J., and T.D. Miethe. 1994. "Whistleblowing as Resistance in Modern Work Organizations: The Politics of Revealing Organizational Deception and Abuse." Pp. 252–273 in *Resistance and Power in Organizations*, edited by J. Jermier, D. Knight, and W. Nord. New York: Routledge.

Rotter, J. 1966. "Generalized Expectancies for Internal versus External Control of Reinforcement." *Psychological Monographs* 80: 1–28.

Sutherland, E. 1947. *Principles of Criminology*, 4th edition. Philadelphia: J.B. Lippincott.

U.S. Merit Systems Protection Board. 1993. "Whistleblowing in the Federal Government: An Update. A Report to the President and Congress of the United States by the U.S. Merit Systems Protection Board." U.S. Government Printing Office: Washington, DC.

Printed and bound by CPI Group (UK) Ltd, Croydon, CR0 4YY
16/09/2026
14963401-0002